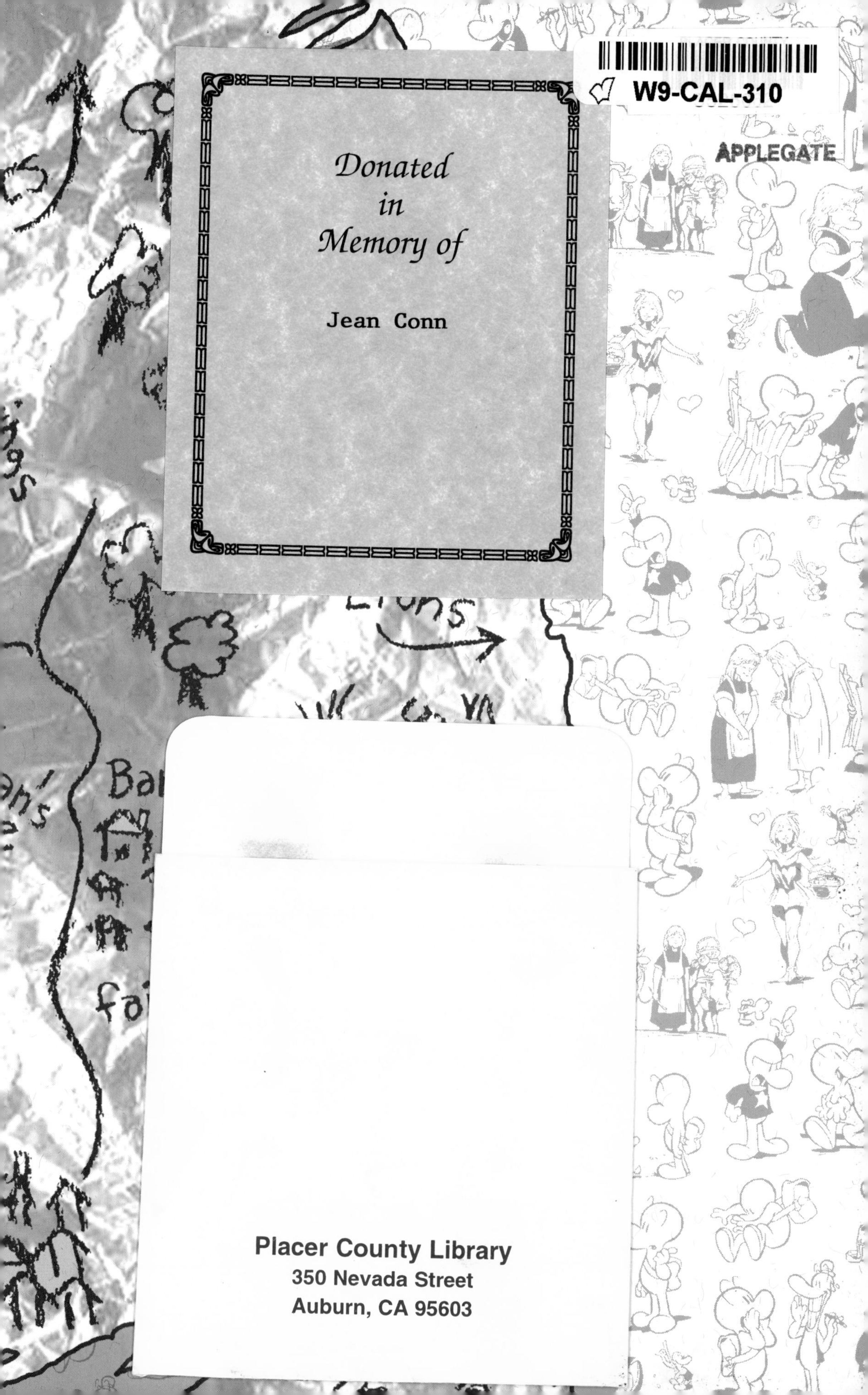
APPLEGATE

Part Three

(Harvest)

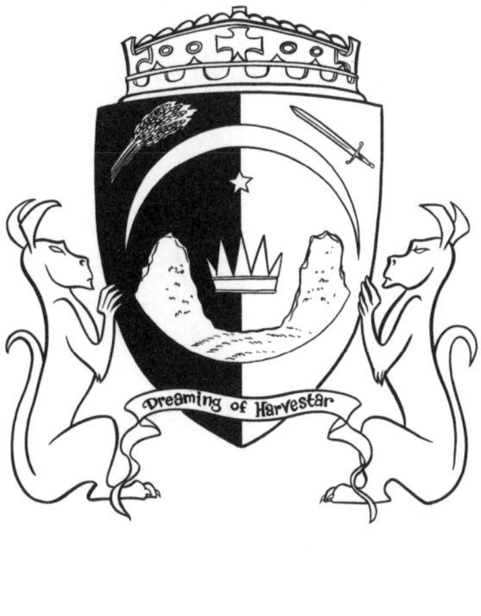
Dreaming of Harvestar

OTHER BOOKS BY JEFF SMITH

THE FIRST TRILOGY

BONE VOLUME ONE: OUT FROM BONEVILLE

BONE VOLUME TWO: THE GREAT COW RACE

BONE VOLUME THREE: EYES OF THE STORM

THE SECOND TRILOGY

BONE VOLUME FOUR: THE DRAGONSLAYER

BONE VOLUME FIVE: ROCKJAW, MASTER OF THE EASTERN BORDER

BONE VOLUME SIX: OLD MAN'S CAVE

THE THIRD TRILOGY

BONE VOLUME SEVEN: GHOST CIRCLES

PREQUELS

STUPID, STUPID RAT TAILS: THE ADVENTURES OF BIG JOHNSON BONE,
FRONTIER HERO
(WRITTEN BY TOM SNIEGOSKI, DRAWN BY JEFF SMITH)

COMING SOON:
ROSE
(WRITTEN BY JEFF SMITH, PAINTED BY CHARLES VESS)

GHOST CIRCLES

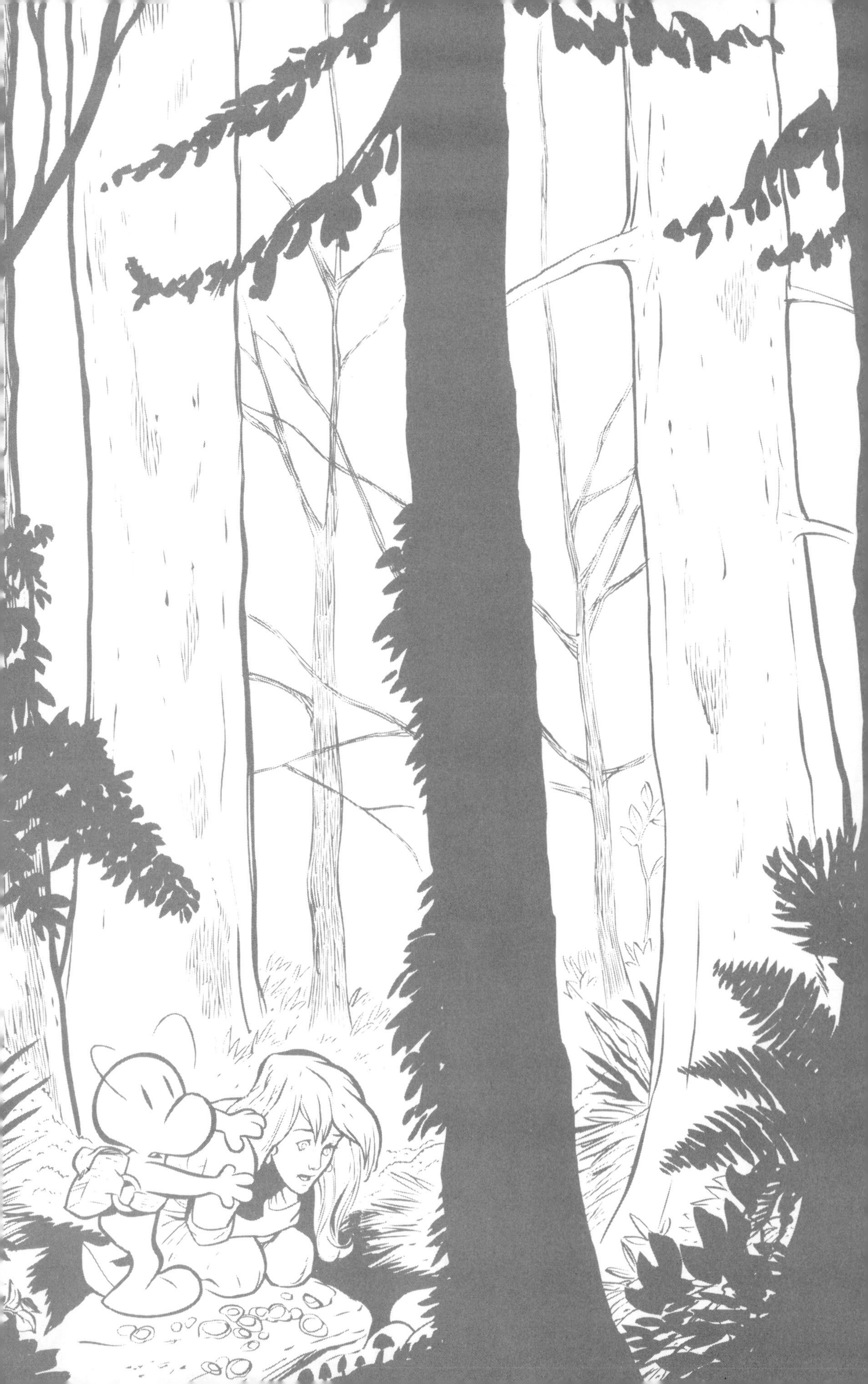

Volume Seven:
Ghost Circles

Jeff Smith

Cartoon Books
Columbus, Ohio

THIS BOOK IS
FOR
CHARLES VESS

BONE Volume Seven: Ghost Circles copyright ® 2001 by Jeff Smith
All rights reserved. No part of this book may be reproduced or utilized in any form or by any means, electronic or mechanical, including photocopying, recording, or by any information storage or retrieval system, without written permission except in the case of reprints in the context of reviews. The chapters in this book were originally published in the comic book BONE and are copyright © 2000 and 2001 by Jeff Smith. BONE® is © 2001 Jeff Smith. Acknowledgements: The Harvestar Family Crest designed by Charles Vess.
Color by: Elizabeth Lewis.
For information write:
Cartoon Books
P.O. Box 16973
Columbus, OH 43216

Hardcover ISBN: 1-888963-08-5
Softcover ISBN: 1-888963-09-3
Library of Congress Catalog Card Number: 95-68403

10 9 8 7 6 5 4 3 2 1

Printed in Canada

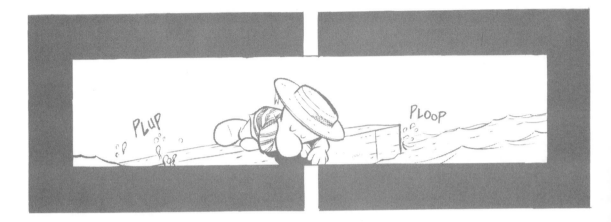

 FTER BEING RUN OUT OF BONEVILLE, THE THREE
BONE COUSINS, FONE BONE, PHONEY BONE, AND
SMILEY BONE, ARE SEPARATED AND LOST IN A
VAST UNCHARTED DESERT.

ONE BY ONE, THEY FIND THEIR WAY INTO A DEEP,
FORESTED VALLEY FILLED WITH WONDERFUL AND
TERRIFYING CREATURES . . .

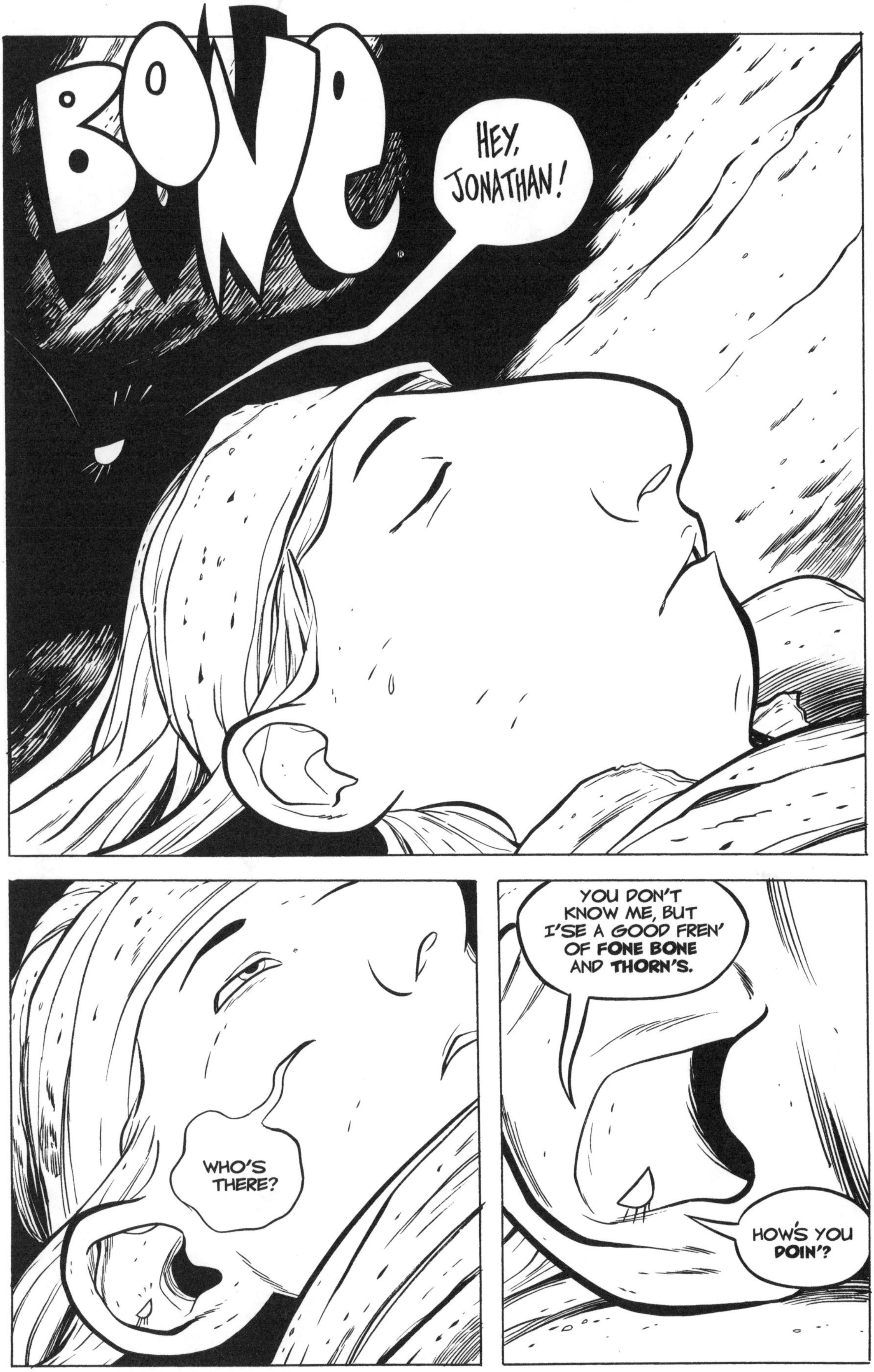
BONE®
HEY, JONATHAN!
WHO'S THERE?
YOU DON'T KNOW ME, BUT I'SE A GOOD FREN' OF **FONE BONE** AND **THORN'S.**
HOW'S YOU **DOIN'**?

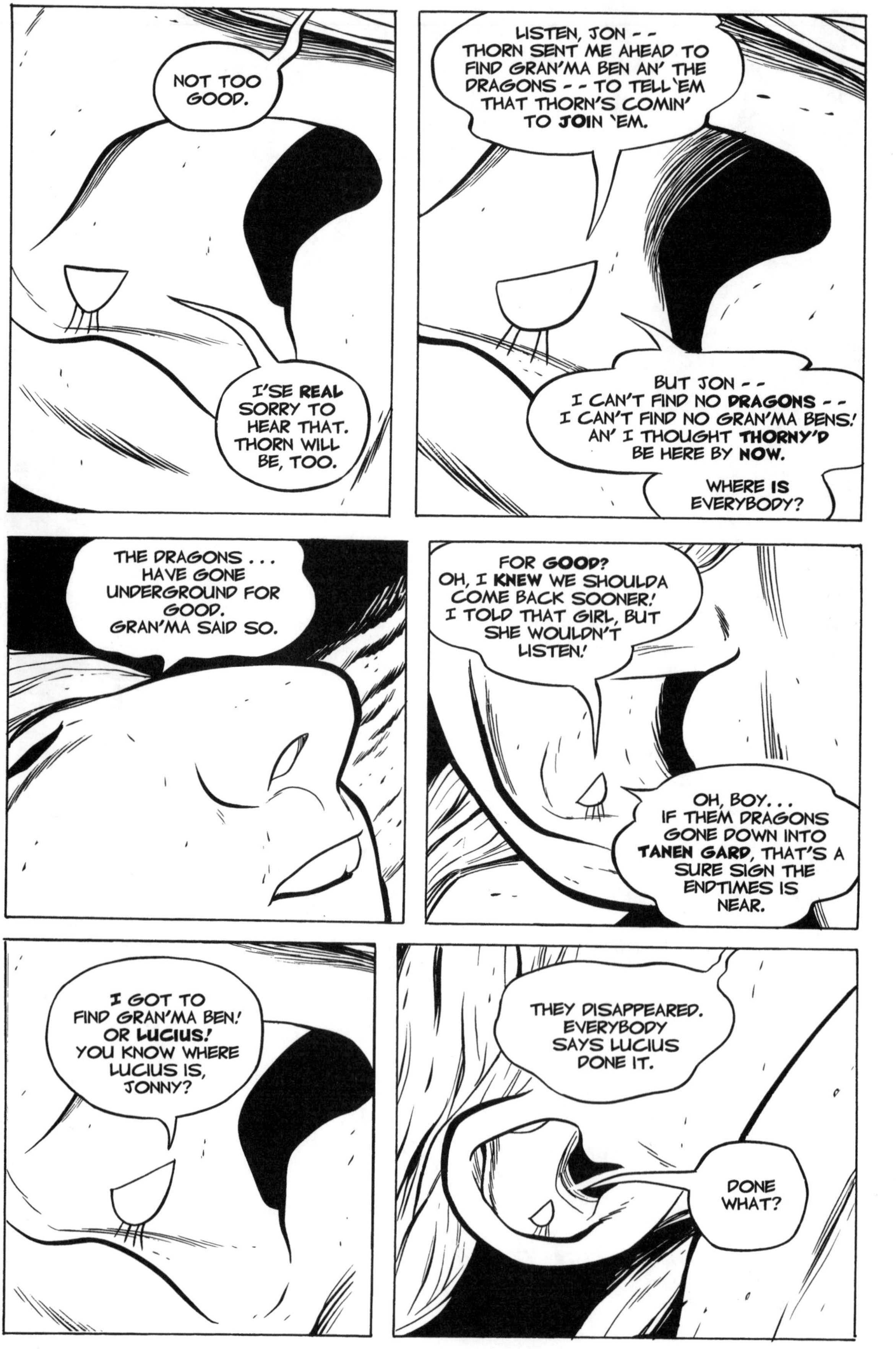

NOT TOO GOOD.
I'SE REAL SORRY TO HEAR THAT. THORN WILL BE, TOO.
LISTEN, JON - - THORN SENT ME AHEAD TO FIND GRAN'MA BEN AN' THE DRAGONS - - TO TELL 'EM THAT THORN'S COMIN' TO JOIN 'EM.
BUT JON - - I CAN'T FIND NO DRAGONS - - I CAN'T FIND NO GRAN'MA BENS! AN' I THOUGHT THORNY'D BE HERE BY NOW.
WHERE IS EVERYBODY?
THE DRAGONS . . . HAVE GONE UNDERGROUND FOR GOOD. GRAN'MA SAID SO.
FOR GOOD? OH, I KNEW WE SHOULDA COME BACK SOONER! I TOLD THAT GIRL, BUT SHE WOULDN'T LISTEN!
OH, BOY. . . IF THEM DRAGONS GONE DOWN INTO TANEN GARD, THAT'S A SURE SIGN THE ENDTIMES IS NEAR.
I GOT TO FIND GRAN'MA BEN! OR LUCIUS! YOU KNOW WHERE LUCIUS IS, JONNY?
THEY DISAPPEARED. EVERYBODY SAYS LUCIUS DONE IT.
DONE WHAT?

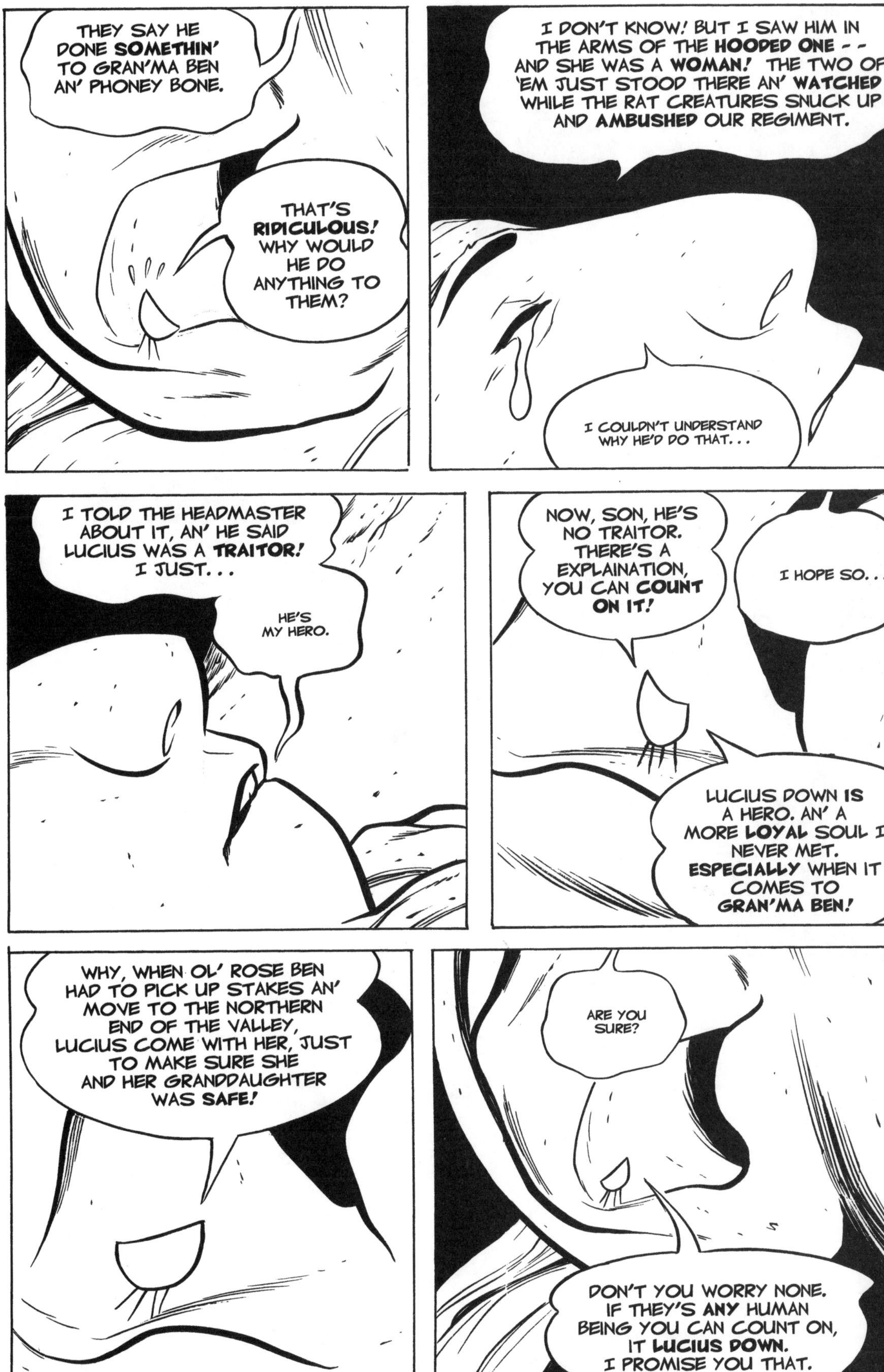
THEY SAY HE DONE SOMETHIN' TO GRAN'MA BEN AN' PHONEY BONE.
THAT'S RIDICULOUS! WHY WOULD HE DO ANYTHING TO THEM?
I DON'T KNOW! BUT I SAW HIM IN THE ARMS OF THE HOODED ONE - - AND SHE WAS A WOMAN! THE TWO OF 'EM JUST STOOD THERE AN' WATCHED WHILE THE RAT CREATURES SNUCK UP AND AMBUSHED OUR REGIMENT.
I COULDN'T UNDERSTAND WHY HE'D DO THAT. . .
I TOLD THE HEADMASTER ABOUT IT, AN' HE SAID LUCIUS WAS A TRAITOR! I JUST. . .
HE'S MY HERO.
NOW, SON, HE'S NO TRAITOR. THERE'S A EXPLAINATION, YOU CAN COUNT ON IT!
I HOPE SO. . .
LUCIUS DOWN IS A HERO. AN' A MORE LOYAL SOUL I NEVER MET. ESPECIALLY WHEN IT COMES TO GRAN'MA BEN!
WHY, WHEN OL' ROSE BEN HAD TO PICK UP STAKES AN' MOVE TO THE NORTHERN END OF THE VALLEY, LUCIUS COME WITH HER, JUST TO MAKE SURE SHE AND HER GRANDDAUGHTER WAS SAFE!
ARE YOU SURE?
DON'T YOU WORRY NONE. IF THEY'S ANY HUMAN BEING YOU CAN COUNT ON, IT LUCIUS DOWN. I PROMISE YOU THAT.

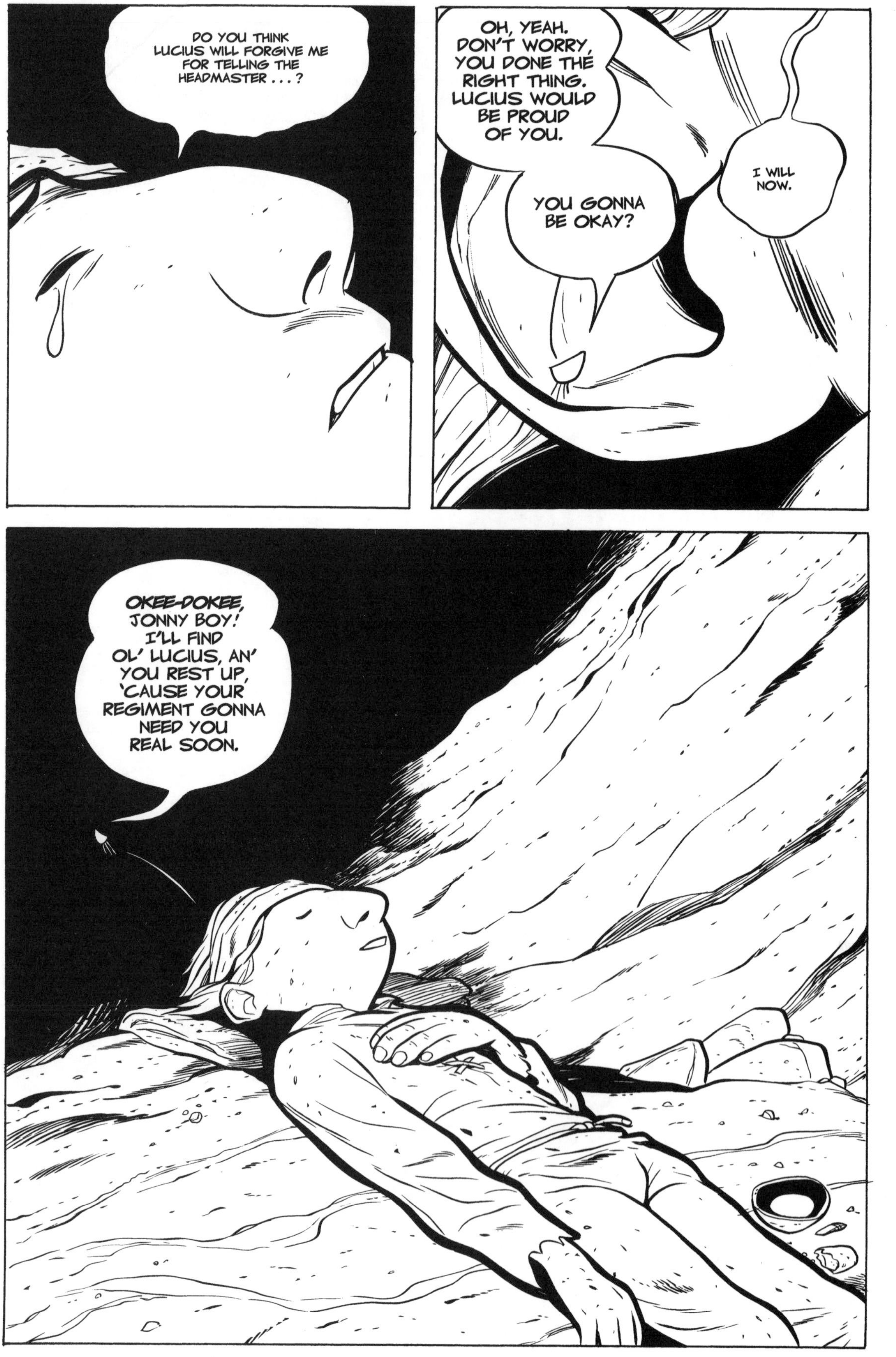
DO YOU THINK LUCIUS WILL FORGIVE ME FOR TELLING THE HEADMASTER . . . ?
OH, YEAH. DON'T WORRY, YOU DONE THE RIGHT THING. LUCIUS WOULD BE PROUD OF YOU.
YOU GONNA BE OKAY?
I WILL NOW.
OKEE-DOKEE, JONNY BOY! I'LL FIND OL' LUCIUS, AN' YOU REST UP, 'CAUSE YOUR REGIMENT GONNA NEED YOU REAL SOON.

GHOST CIRCLES

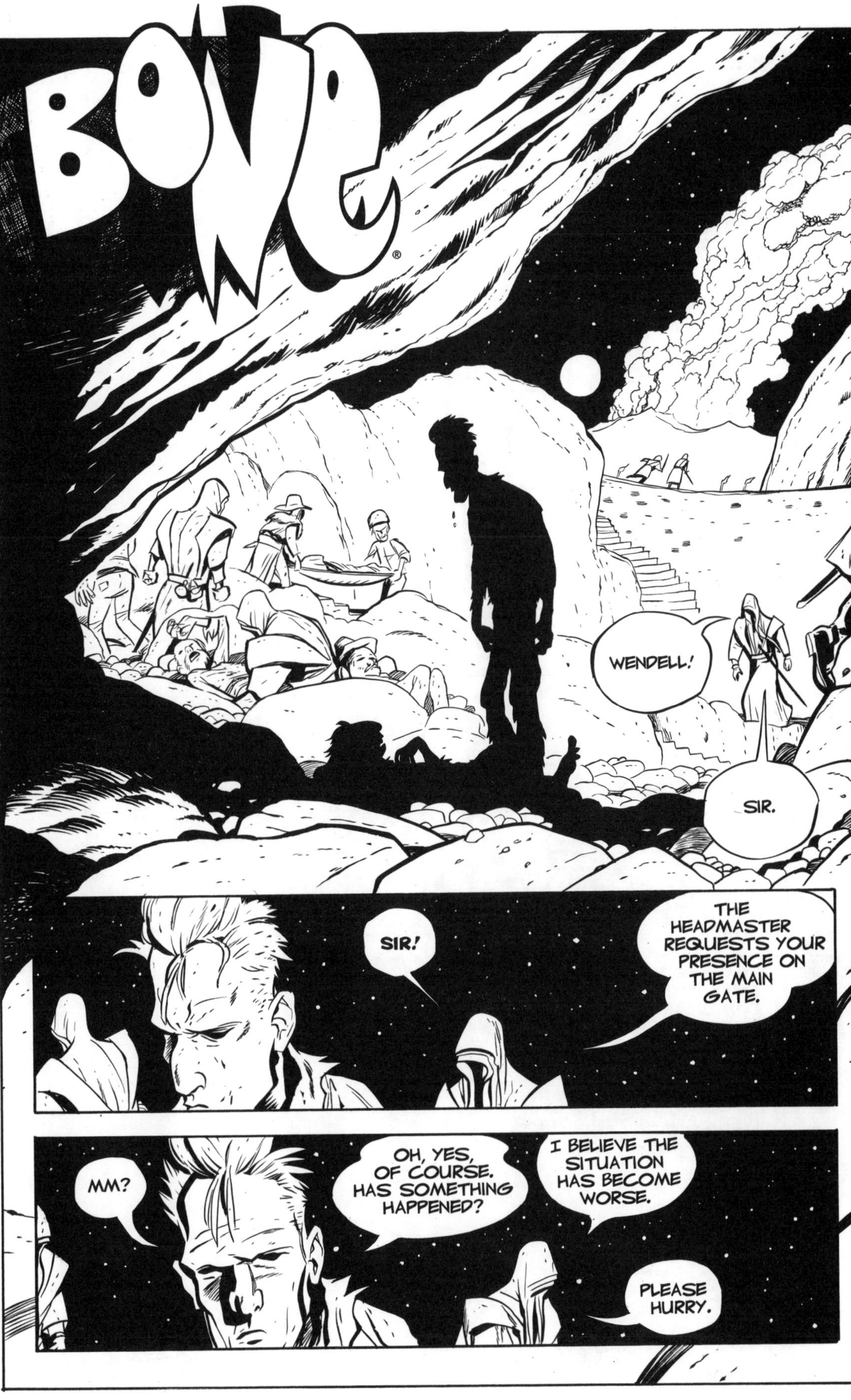
BONE®
WENDELL!
SIR.
SIR!
THE HEADMASTER REQUESTS YOUR PRESENCE ON THE MAIN GATE.
MM?
OH, YES, OF COURSE. HAS SOMETHING HAPPENED?
I BELIEVE THE SITUATION HAS BECOME WORSE.
PLEASE HURRY.

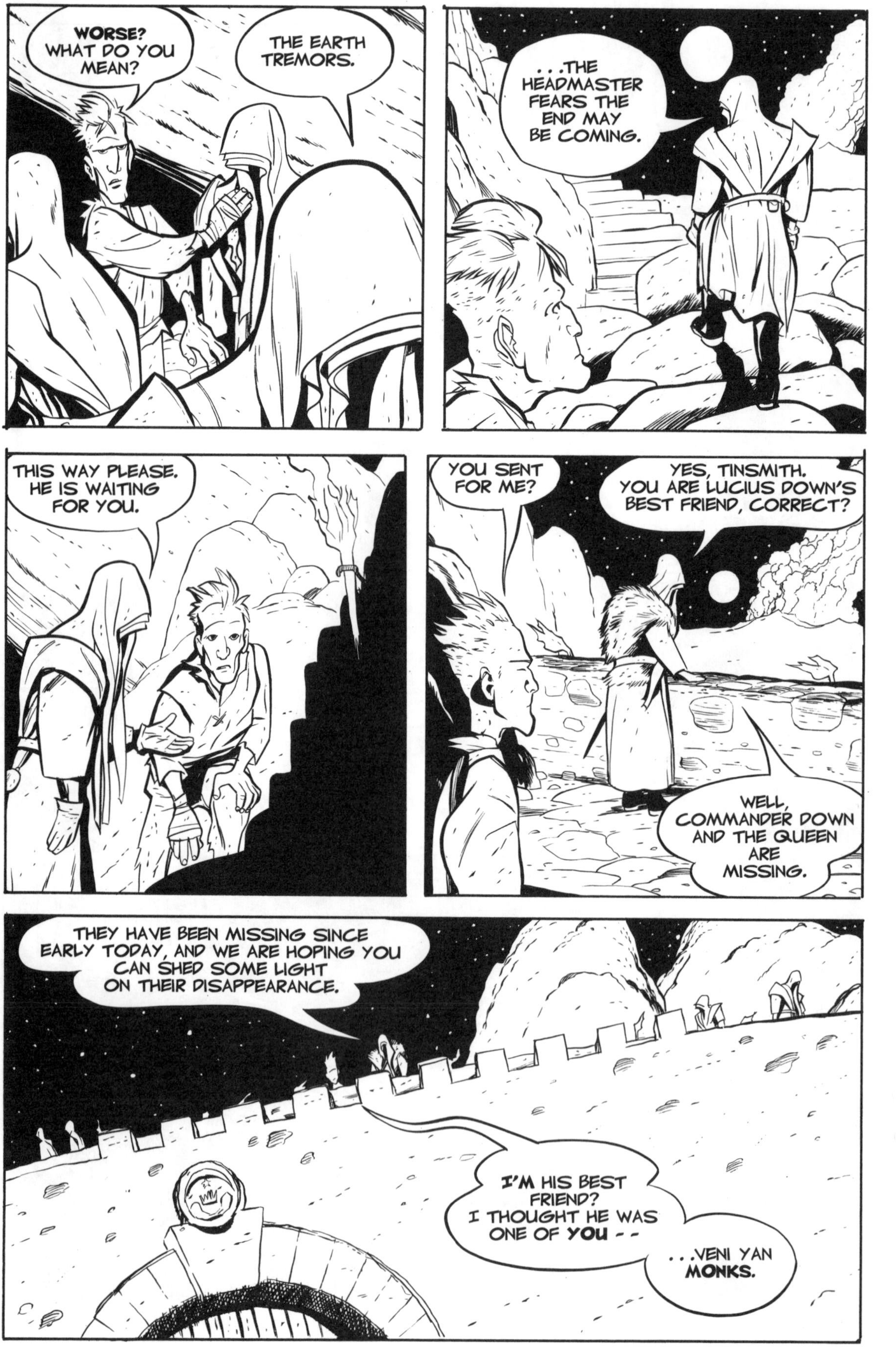

WORSE? WHAT DO YOU MEAN?
THE EARTH TREMORS.
. . .THE HEADMASTER FEARS THE END MAY BE COMING.
THIS WAY PLEASE. HE IS WAITING FOR YOU.
YOU SENT FOR ME?
YES, TINSMITH. YOU ARE LUCIUS DOWN'S BEST FRIEND, CORRECT?
WELL, COMMANDER DOWN AND THE QUEEN ARE MISSING.
THEY HAVE BEEN MISSING SINCE EARLY TODAY, AND WE ARE HOPING YOU CAN SHED SOME LIGHT ON THEIR DISAPPEARANCE.
I'M HIS BEST FRIEND? I THOUGHT HE WAS ONE OF YOU - -
. . .VENI YAN MONKS.

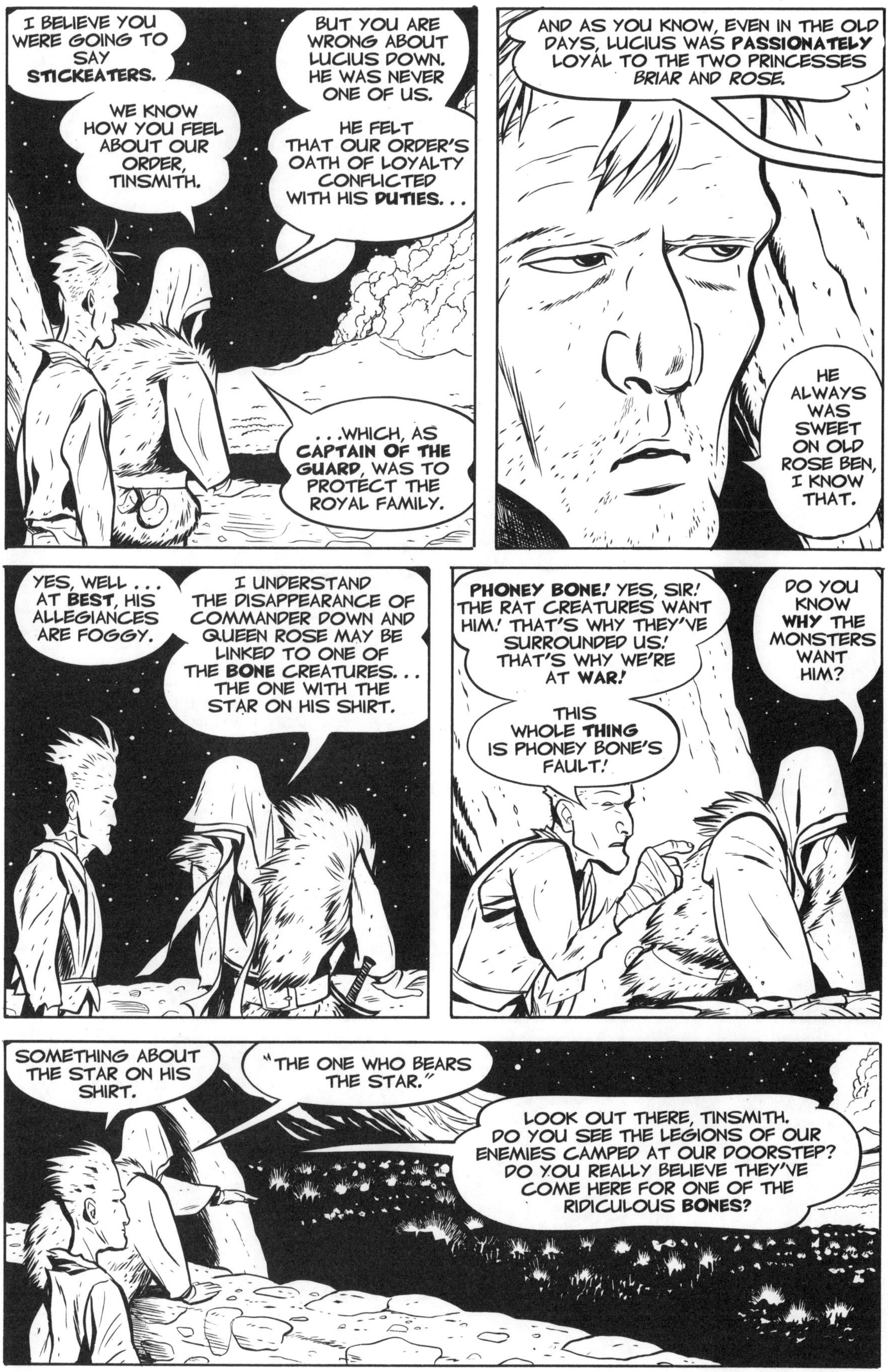
I BELIEVE YOU WERE GOING TO SAY **STICKEATERS.**
WE KNOW HOW YOU FEEL ABOUT OUR ORDER, TINSMITH.
BUT YOU ARE WRONG ABOUT LUCIUS DOWN. HE WAS NEVER ONE OF US.
HE FELT THAT OUR ORDER'S OATH OF LOYALTY CONFLICTED WITH HIS **DUTIES**. . .
. . .WHICH, AS **CAPTAIN OF THE GUARD**, WAS TO PROTECT THE ROYAL FAMILY.
AND AS YOU KNOW, EVEN IN THE OLD DAYS, LUCIUS WAS **PASSIONATELY** LOYAL TO THE TWO PRINCESSES *BRIAR* AND *ROSE*.
HE ALWAYS WAS SWEET ON OLD ROSE BEN, I KNOW THAT.
YES, WELL . . . AT **BEST**, HIS ALLEGIANCES ARE FOGGY.
I UNDERSTAND THE DISAPPEARANCE OF COMMANDER DOWN AND QUEEN ROSE MAY BE LINKED TO ONE OF THE **BONE** CREATURES. . . THE ONE WITH THE STAR ON HIS SHIRT.
PHONEY BONE! YES, SIR! THE RAT CREATURES WANT HIM! THAT'S WHY THEY'VE SURROUNDED US! THAT'S WHY WE'RE AT **WAR!**
THIS WHOLE **THING** IS PHONEY BONE'S FAULT!
DO YOU KNOW **WHY** THE MONSTERS WANT HIM?
SOMETHING ABOUT THE STAR ON HIS SHIRT.
"THE ONE WHO BEARS THE STAR."
LOOK OUT THERE, TINSMITH. DO YOU SEE THE LEGIONS OF OUR ENEMIES CAMPED AT OUR DOORSTEP? DO YOU REALLY BELIEVE THEY'VE COME HERE FOR ONE OF THE RIDICULOUS **BONES**?

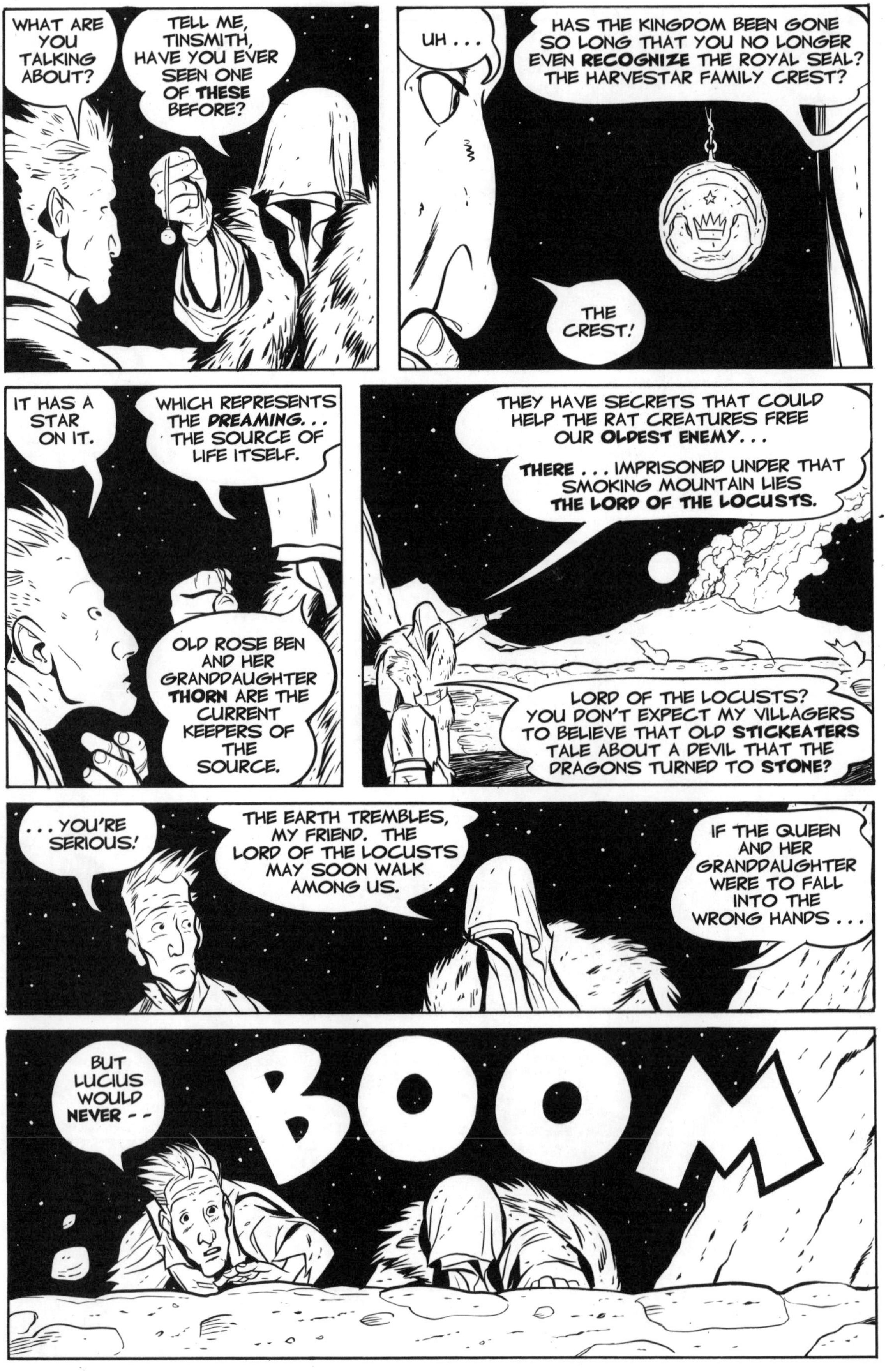
WHAT ARE YOU TALKING ABOUT?
TELL ME, TINSMITH, HAVE YOU EVER SEEN ONE OF **THESE** BEFORE?
UH . . .
HAS THE KINGDOM BEEN GONE SO LONG THAT YOU NO LONGER EVEN **RECOGNIZE** THE ROYAL SEAL? THE HARVESTAR FAMILY CREST?
THE CREST!
IT HAS A STAR ON IT.
WHICH REPRESENTS THE **DREAMING**. . . THE SOURCE OF LIFE ITSELF.
OLD ROSE BEN AND HER GRANDDAUGHTER **THORN** ARE THE CURRENT KEEPERS OF THE SOURCE.
THEY HAVE SECRETS THAT COULD HELP THE RAT CREATURES FREE OUR **OLDEST ENEMY**. . .
THERE . . . IMPRISONED UNDER THAT SMOKING MOUNTAIN LIES **THE LORD OF THE LOCUSTS.**
LORD OF THE LOCUSTS? YOU DON'T EXPECT MY VILLAGERS TO BELIEVE THAT OLD **STICKEATERS** TALE ABOUT A DEVIL THAT THE DRAGONS TURNED TO **STONE?**
. . . YOU'RE SERIOUS!
THE EARTH TREMBLES, MY FRIEND. THE LORD OF THE LOCUSTS MAY SOON WALK AMONG US.
IF THE QUEEN AND HER GRANDDAUGHTER WERE TO FALL INTO THE WRONG HANDS . . .
BUT LUCIUS WOULD **NEVER** - -
BOOM

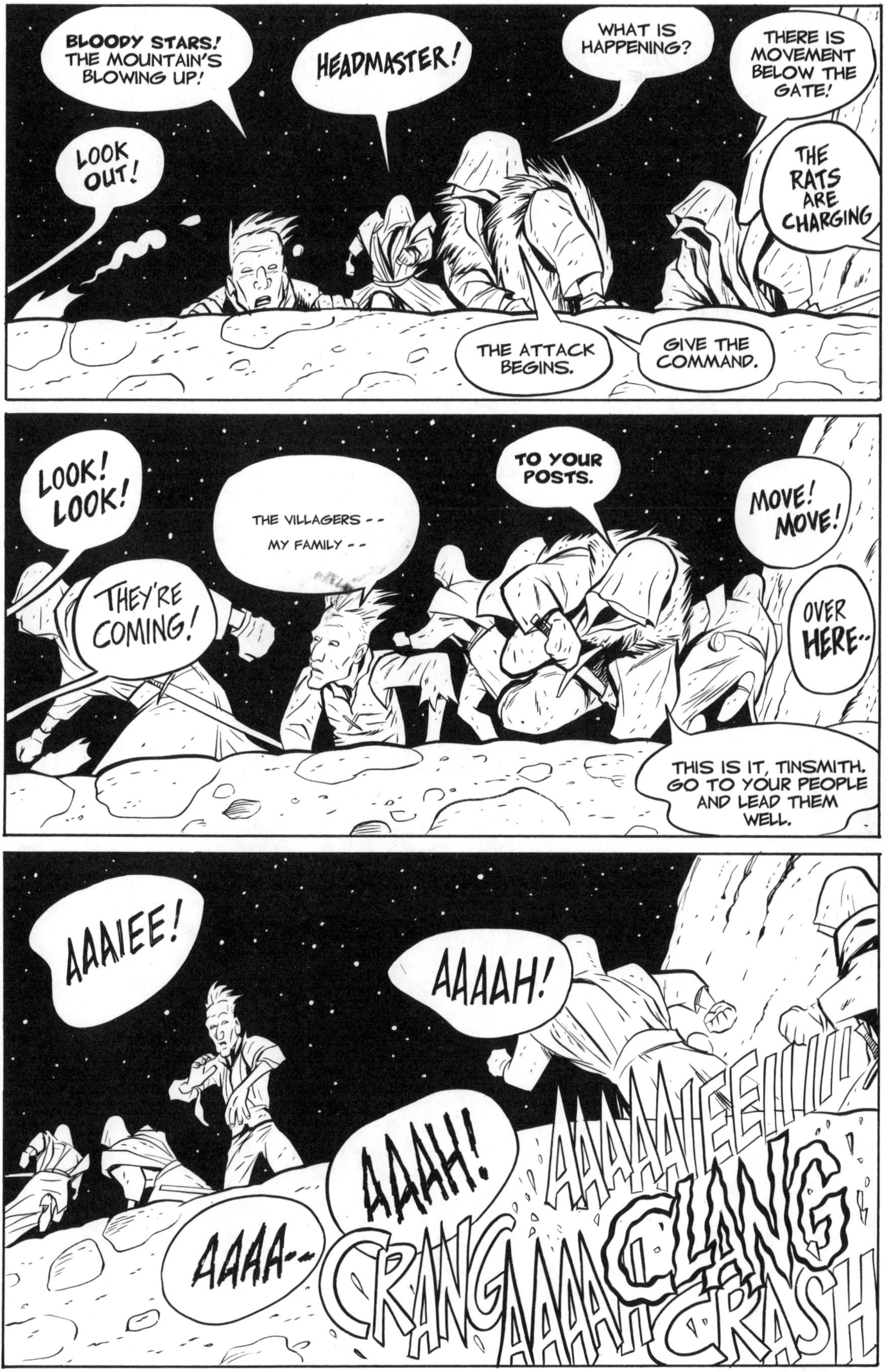
BLOODY STARS! THE MOUNTAIN'S BLOWING UP!
HEADMASTER!
WHAT IS HAPPENING?
THERE IS MOVEMENT BELOW THE GATE!
LOOK OUT!
THE RATS ARE CHARGING
THE ATTACK BEGINS.
GIVE THE COMMAND.
LOOK! LOOK!
THE VILLAGERS --
MY FAMILY --
TO YOUR POSTS.
MOVE! MOVE!
THEY'RE COMING!
OVER HERE..
THIS IS IT, TINSMITH. GO TO YOUR PEOPLE AND LEAD THEM WELL.
AAAIEE!
AAAAH!
AAAH!
AAAA--
CRANG
AAAAAIEEIIIUU
AAAAH
CLANG
CRASH

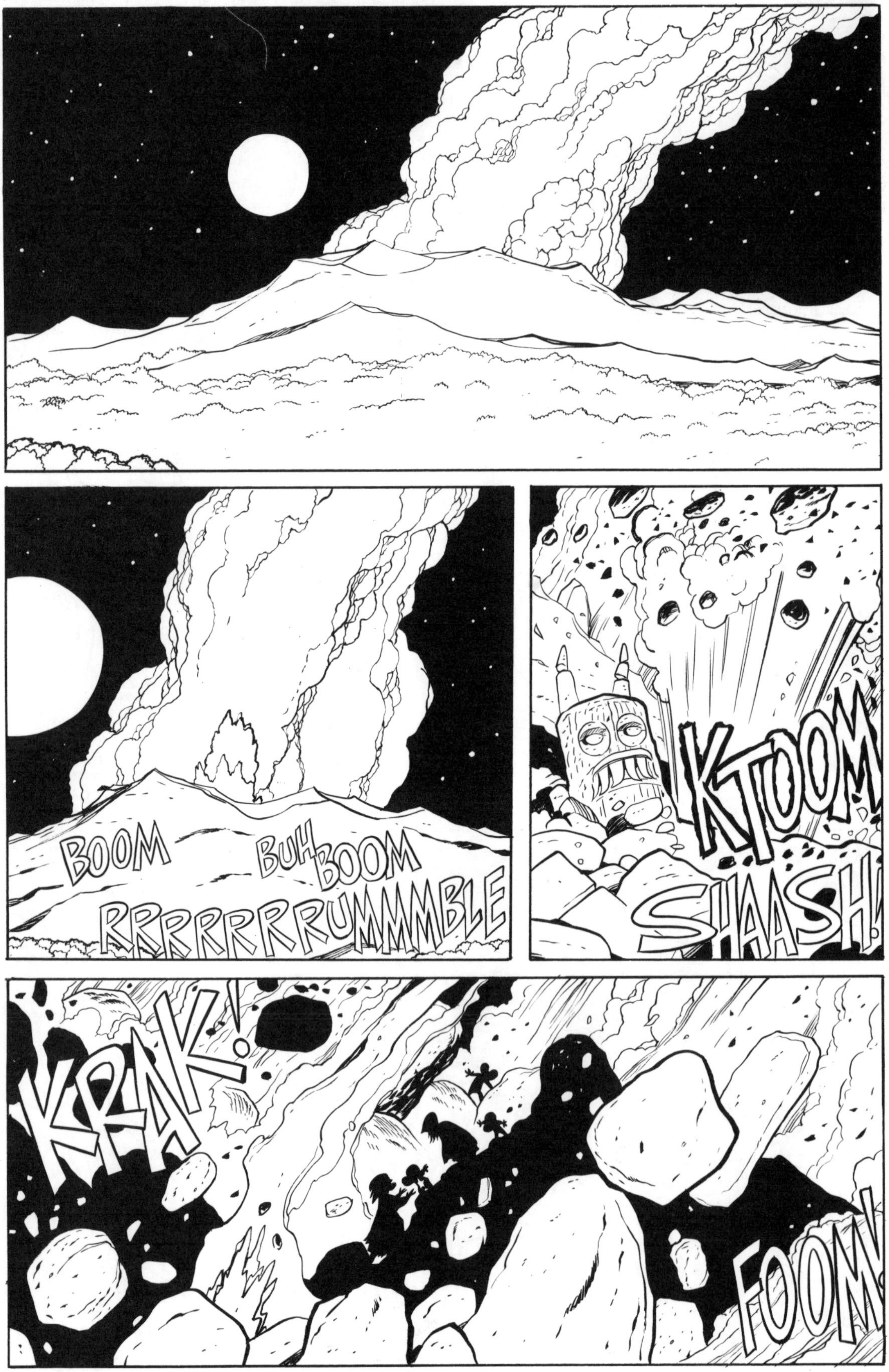
BOOM
BUH BOOM
RRRRRRRRUMMMBLE
KTOOM
SHAASH!
KRAK!
FOOM!

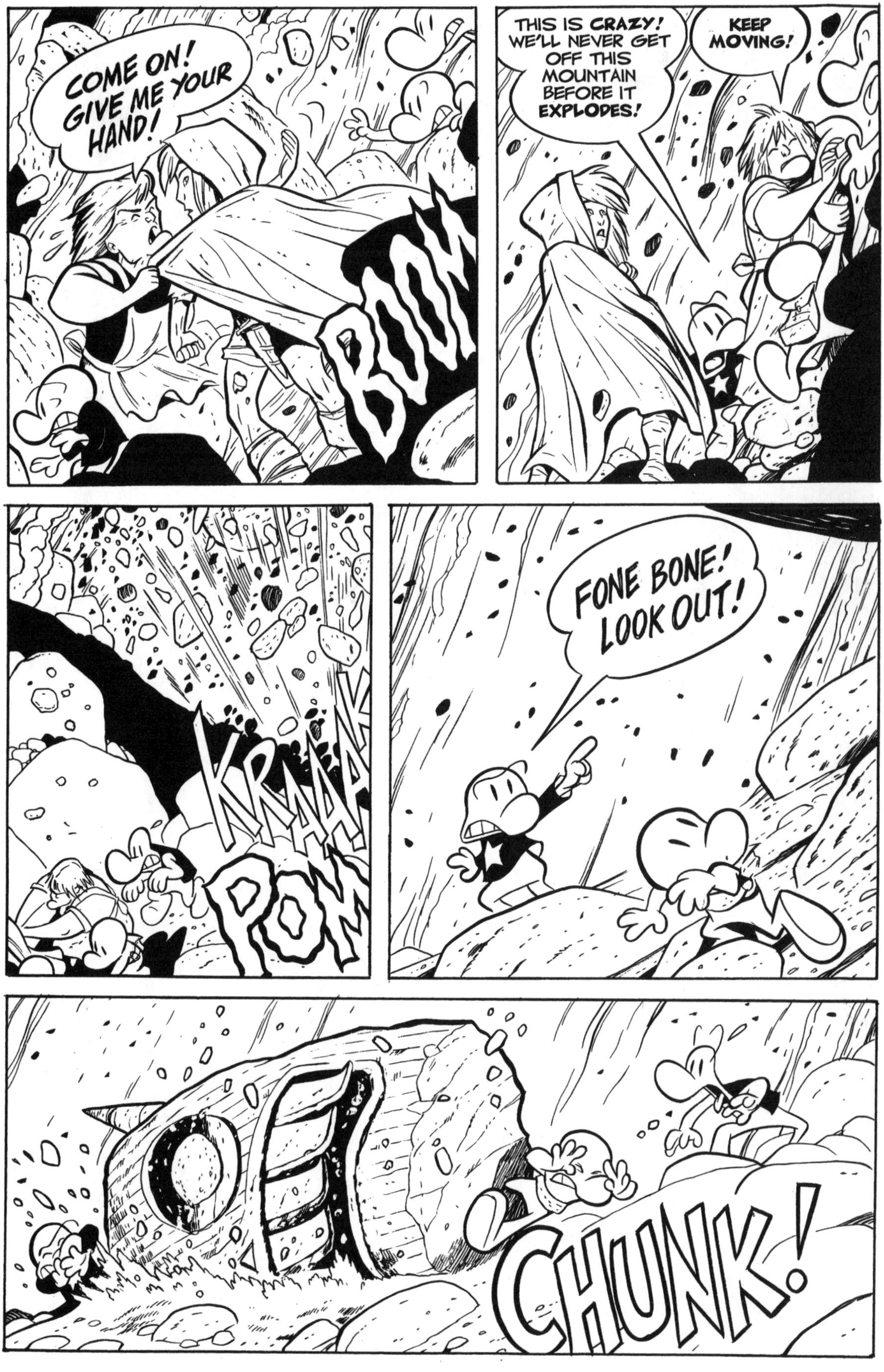
COME ON! GIVE ME YOUR HAND!
BOOM
THIS IS CRAZY! WE'LL NEVER GET OFF THIS MOUNTAIN BEFORE IT EXPLODES!
KEEP MOVING!
KRAAAK
POM
FONE BONE! LOOK OUT!
CHUNK!

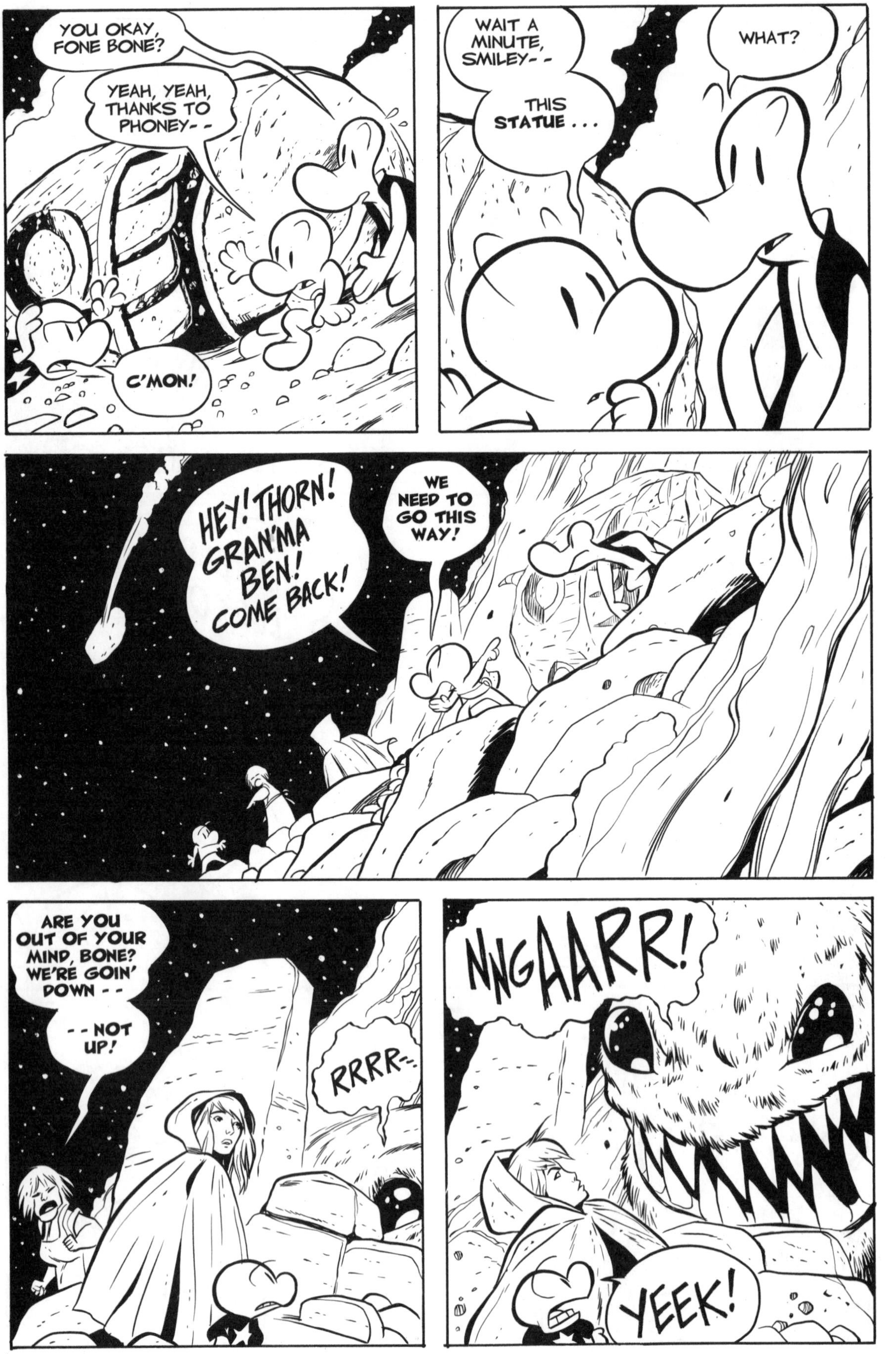
YOU OKAY, FONE BONE?
YEAH, YEAH, THANKS TO PHONEY- -
C'MON!
WAIT A MINUTE, SMILEY- -
THIS STATUE . . .
WHAT?
HEY! THORN! GRAN'MA BEN! COME BACK!
WE NEED TO GO THIS WAY!
ARE YOU OUT OF YOUR MIND, BONE? WE'RE GOIN' DOWN - -
- - NOT UP!
RRRR- -
NNGAARR!
YEEK!

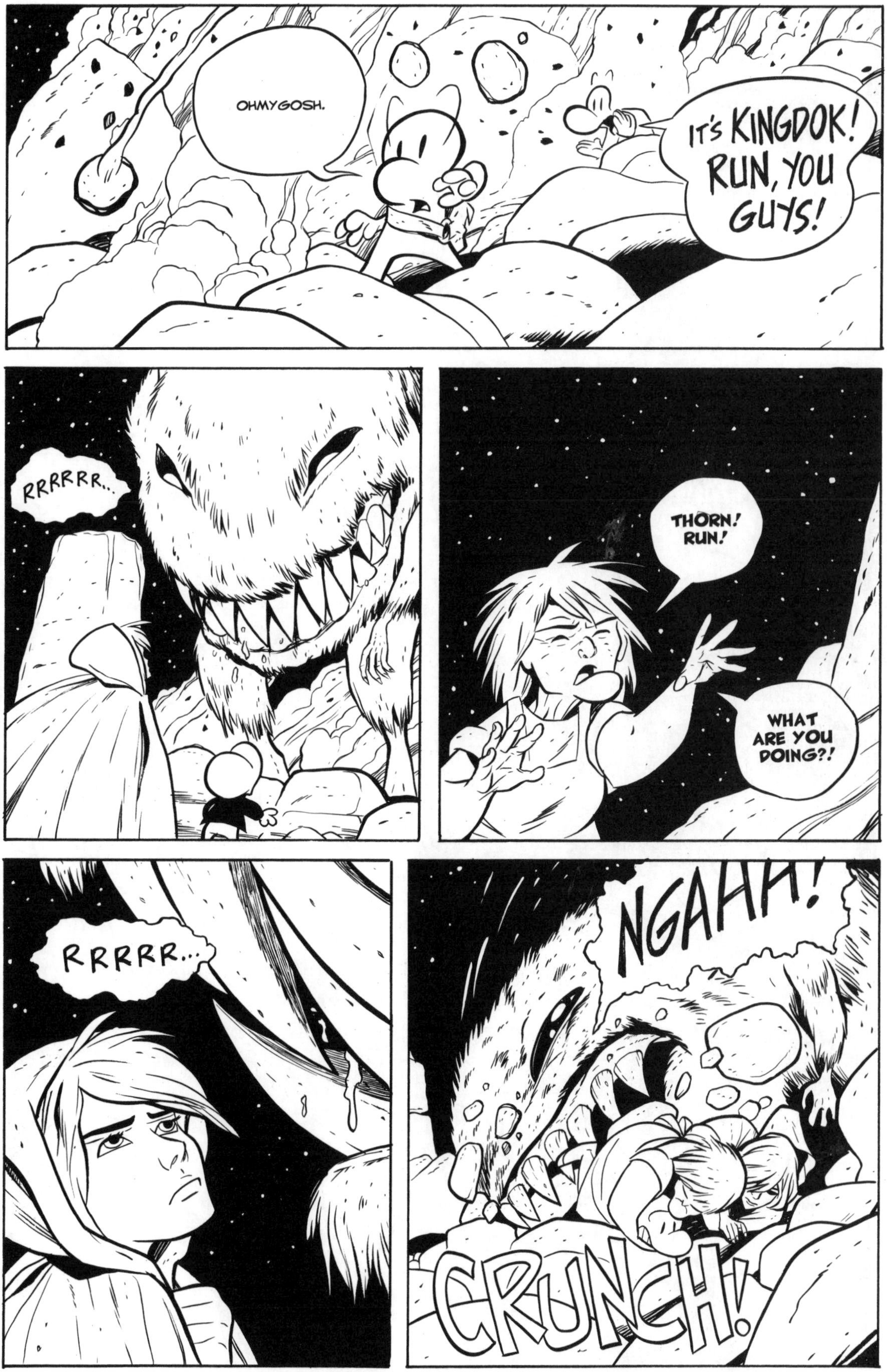
OHMYGOSH.
IT'S KINGDOK! RUN, YOU GUYS!
RRRRRR...
THORN! RUN!
WHAT ARE YOU DOING?!
RRRRR...
NGAHH!
CRUNCH!

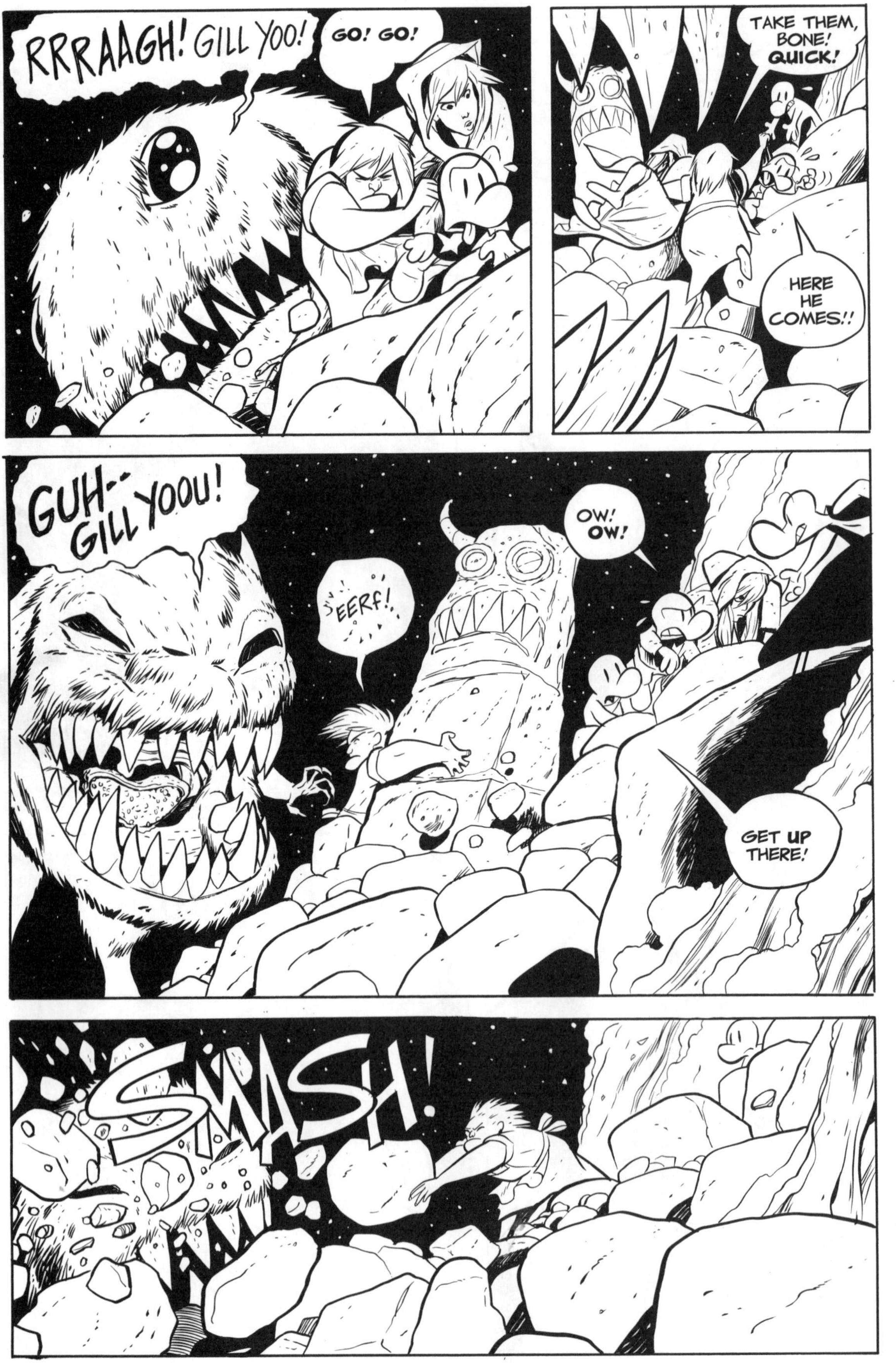
RRRAAGH! GILL YOO!
GO! GO!
TAKE THEM, BONE! QUICK!
HERE HE COMES!!
GUH-- GILL YOOU!
EERF!
OW! OW!
GET UP THERE!
SMASH!

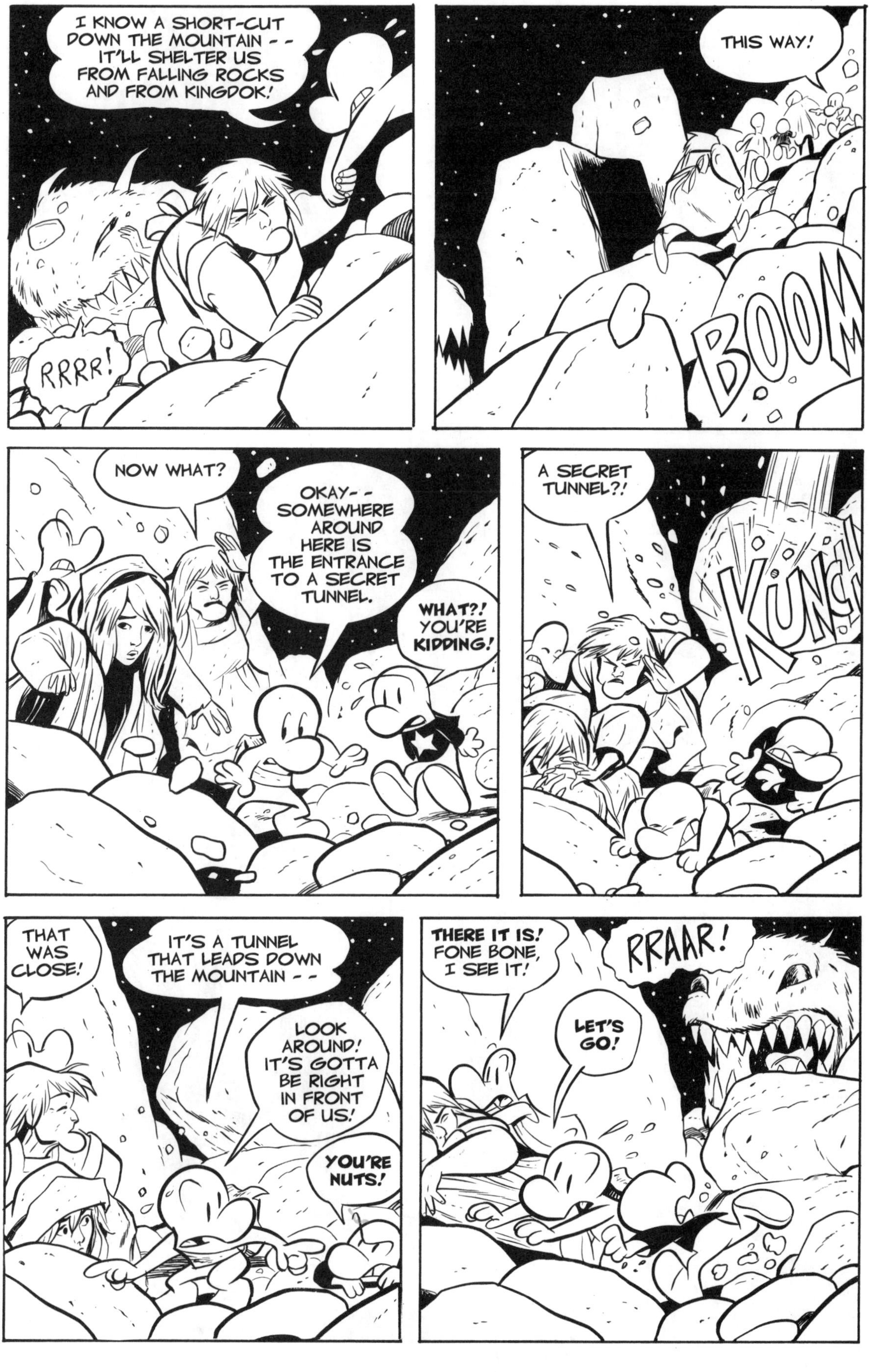
I KNOW A SHORT-CUT DOWN THE MOUNTAIN - - IT'LL SHELTER US FROM FALLING ROCKS AND FROM KINGDOK!
RRRR!
THIS WAY!
BOOM
NOW WHAT?
OKAY- - SOMEWHERE AROUND HERE IS THE ENTRANCE TO A SECRET TUNNEL.
WHAT?! YOU'RE KIDDING!
A SECRET TUNNEL?!
KUNCH
THAT WAS CLOSE!
IT'S A TUNNEL THAT LEADS DOWN THE MOUNTAIN - -
LOOK AROUND! IT'S GOTTA BE RIGHT IN FRONT OF US!
YOU'RE NUTS!
THERE IT IS! FONE BONE, I SEE IT!
RRAAR!
LET'S GO!

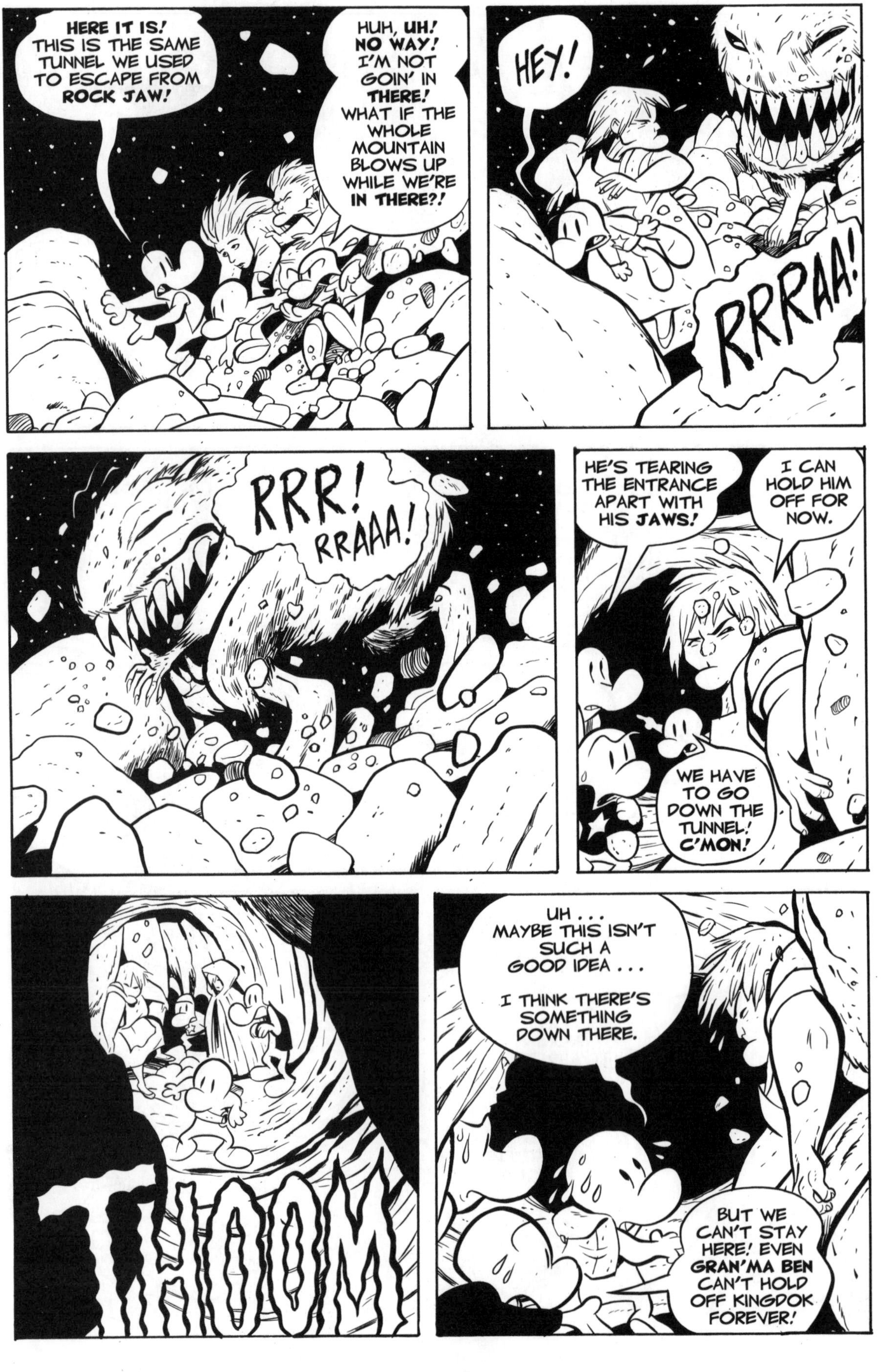
HERE IT IS! THIS IS THE SAME TUNNEL WE USED TO ESCAPE FROM ROCK JAW!
HUH, UH! NO WAY! I'M NOT GOIN' IN THERE! WHAT IF THE WHOLE MOUNTAIN BLOWS UP WHILE WE'RE IN THERE?!
HEY!
RRRAA!
RRR! RRAAA!
HE'S TEARING THE ENTRANCE APART WITH HIS JAWS!
I CAN HOLD HIM OFF FOR NOW.
WE HAVE TO GO DOWN THE TUNNEL! C'MON!
THOOM
UH . . . MAYBE THIS ISN'T SUCH A GOOD IDEA . . .
I THINK THERE'S SOMETHING DOWN THERE.
BUT WE CAN'T STAY HERE! EVEN GRAN'MA BEN CAN'T HOLD OFF KINGDOK FOREVER!

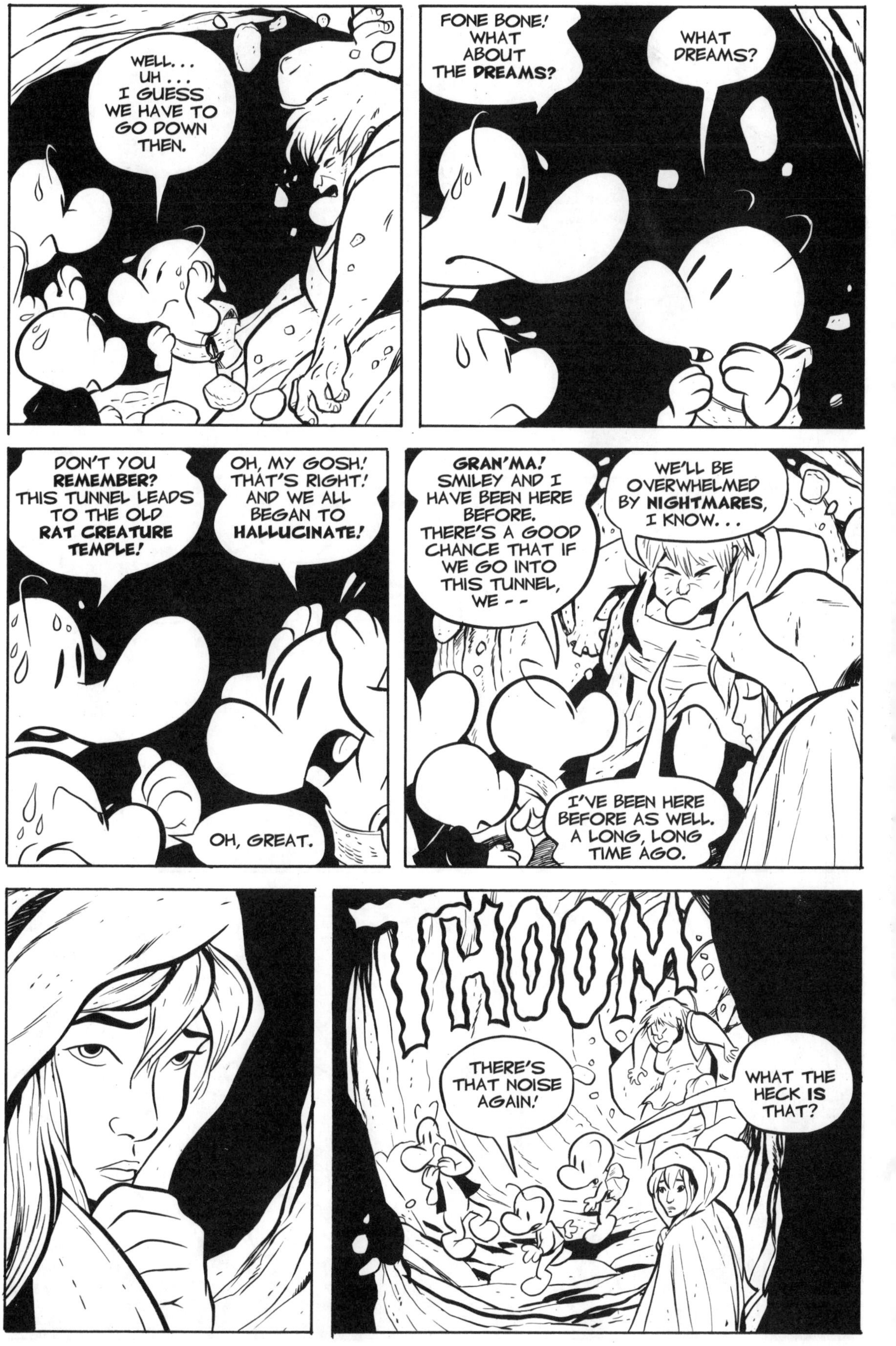
WELL. . . UH . . . I GUESS WE HAVE TO GO DOWN THEN.
FONE BONE! WHAT ABOUT THE DREAMS?
WHAT DREAMS?
DON'T YOU REMEMBER? THIS TUNNEL LEADS TO THE OLD RAT CREATURE TEMPLE!
OH, MY GOSH! THAT'S RIGHT! AND WE ALL BEGAN TO HALLUCINATE!
OH, GREAT.
GRAN'MA! SMILEY AND I HAVE BEEN HERE BEFORE. THERE'S A GOOD CHANCE THAT IF WE GO INTO THIS TUNNEL, WE --
WE'LL BE OVERWHELMED BY NIGHTMARES, I KNOW. . .
I'VE BEEN HERE BEFORE AS WELL. A LONG, LONG TIME AGO.
THOOM!
THERE'S THAT NOISE AGAIN!
WHAT THE HECK IS THAT?

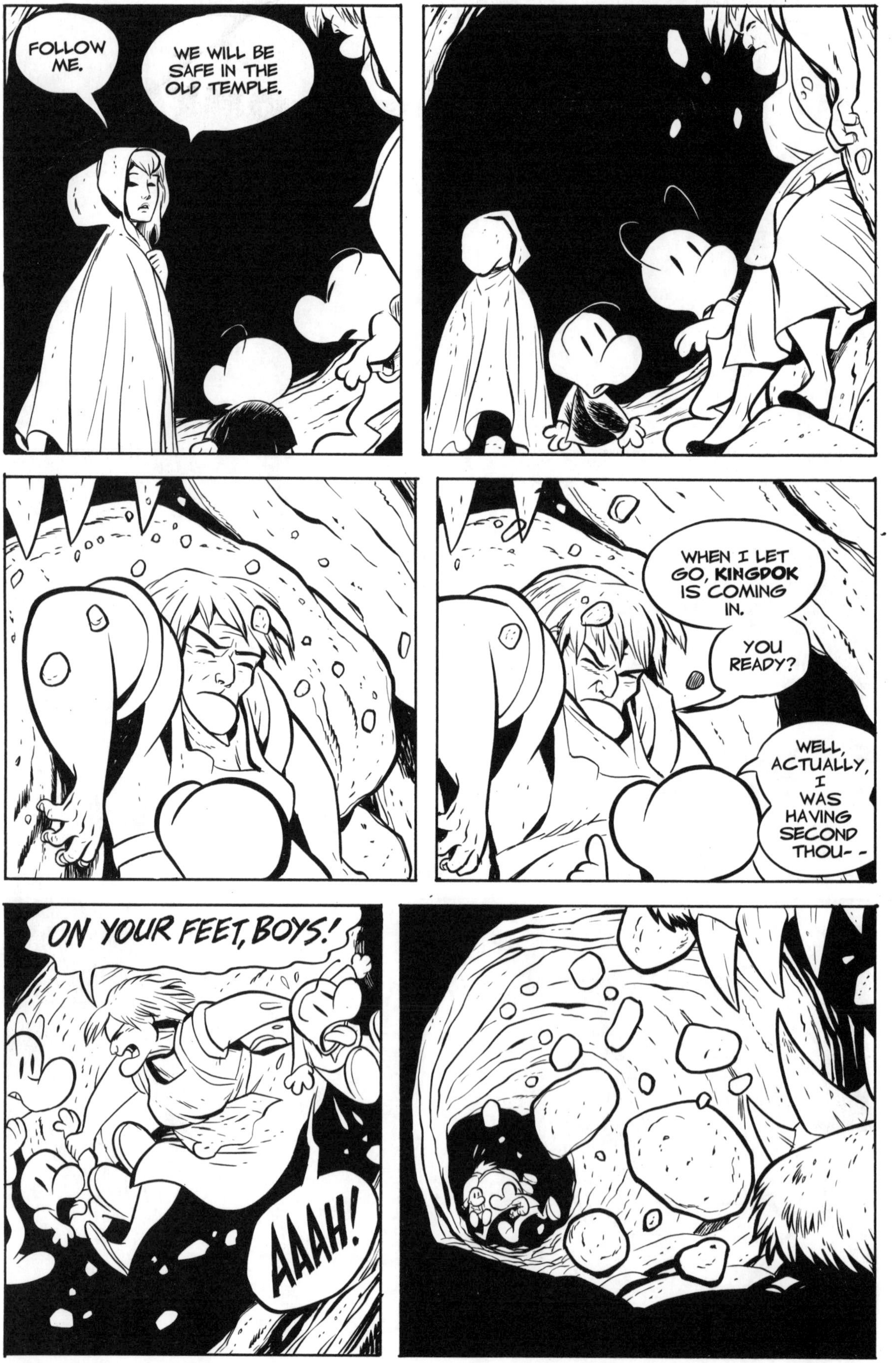
FOLLOW ME.
WE WILL BE SAFE IN THE OLD TEMPLE.
WHEN I LET GO, KINGDOK IS COMING IN.
YOU READY?
WELL, ACTUALLY, I WAS HAVING SECOND THOU- -
ON YOUR FEET, BOYS!
AAAH!

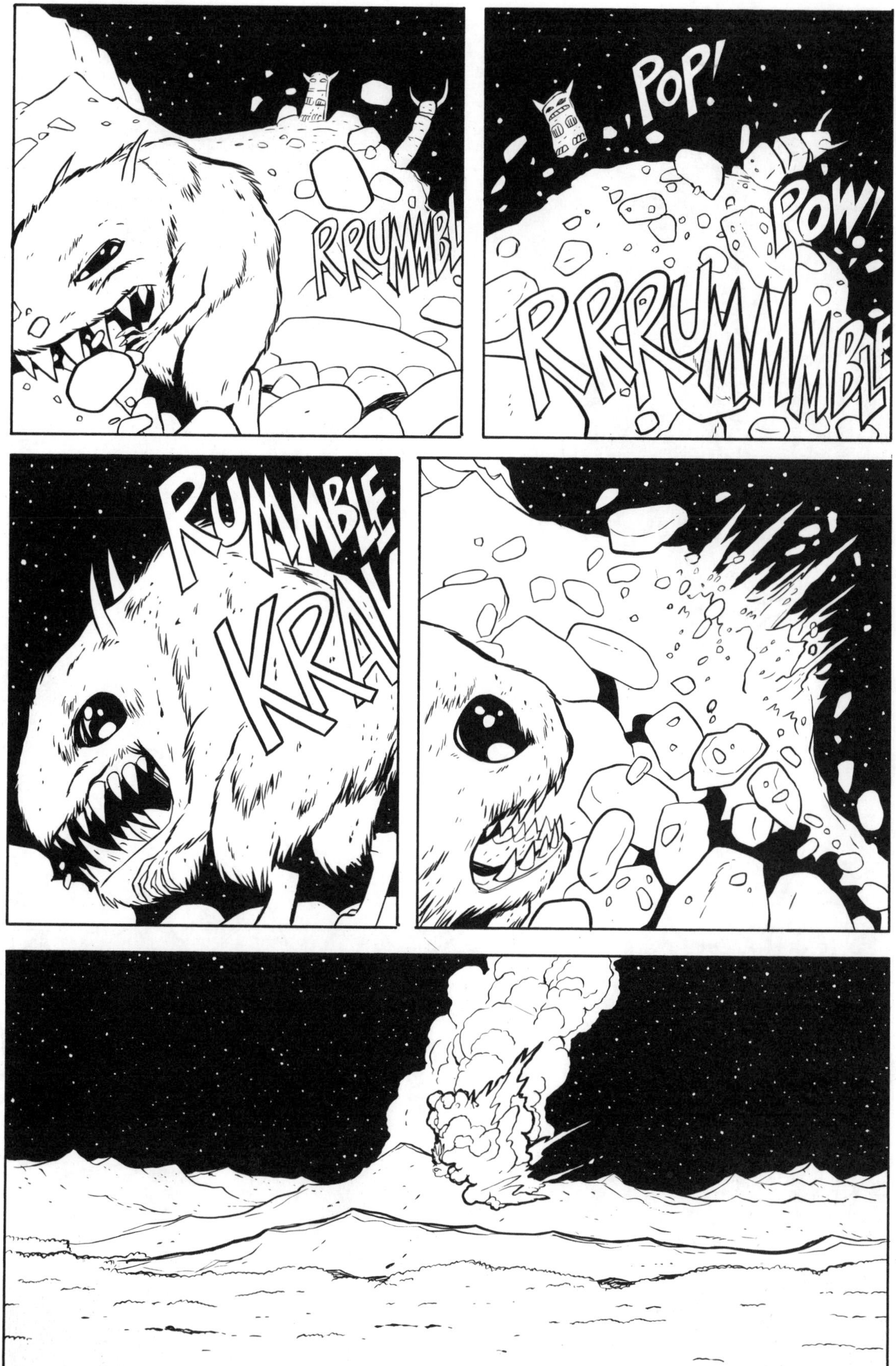
RRUMMBL
POP!
POW!
RRRUMMMMBLE
RUMMBLE
KRA

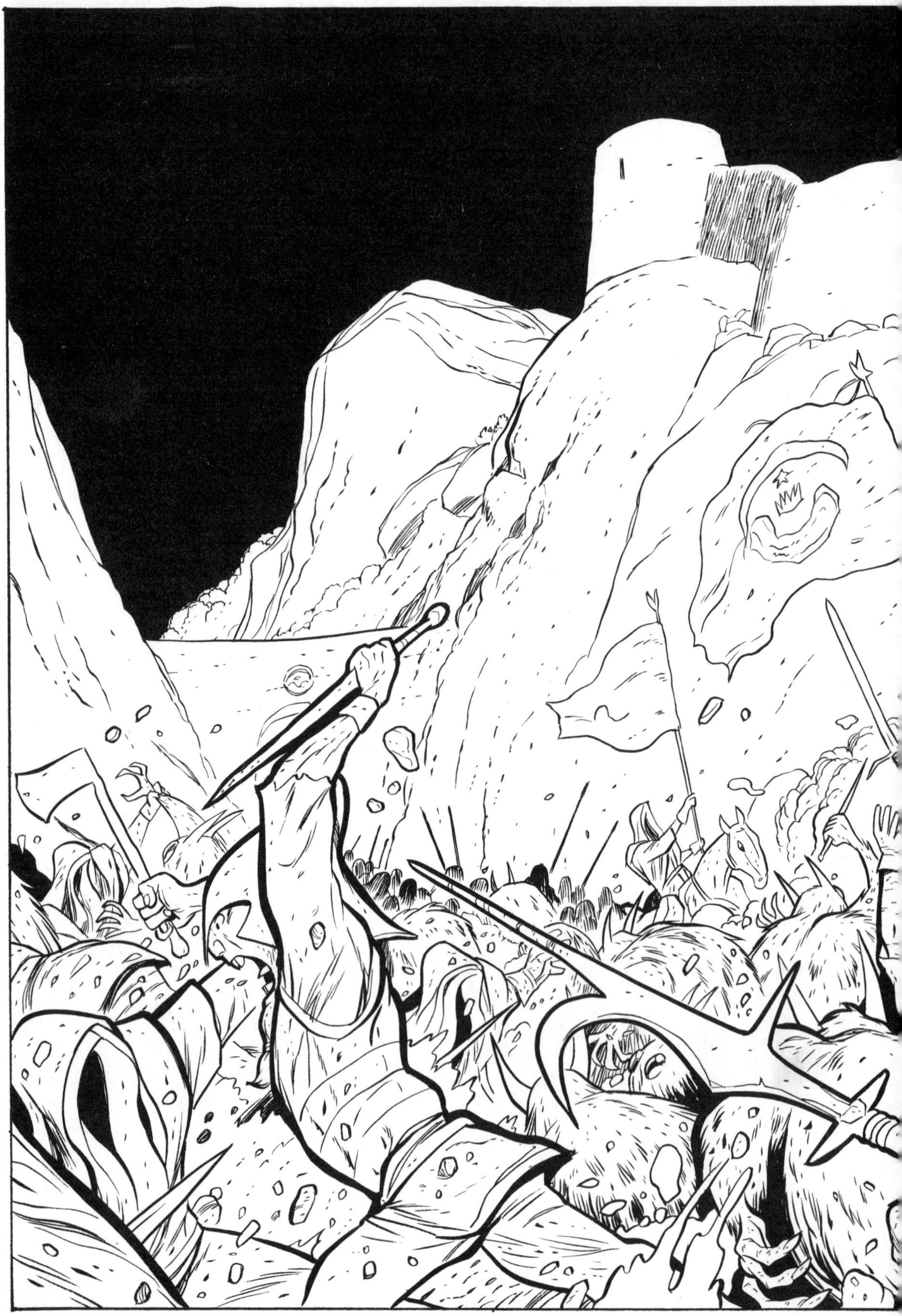

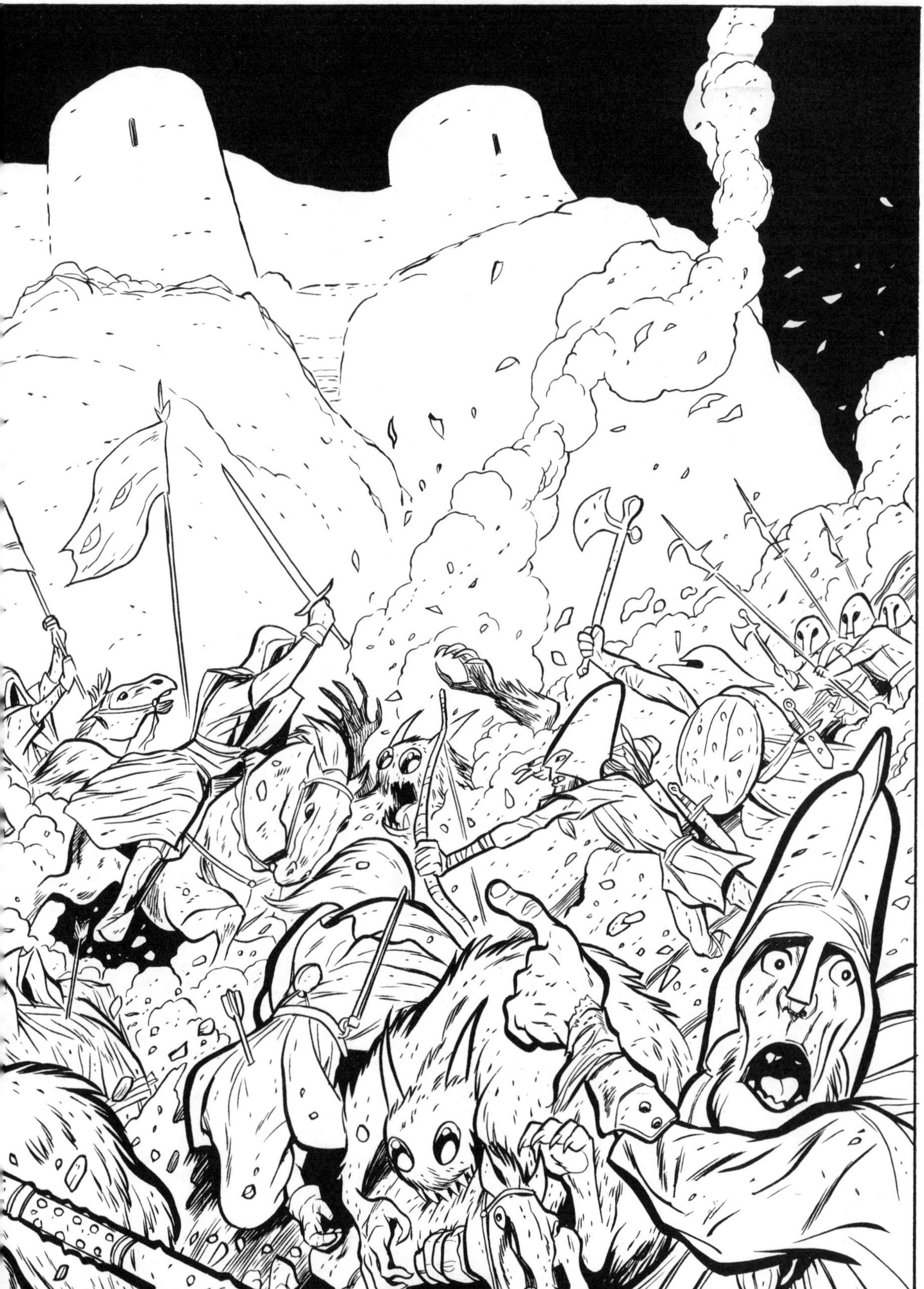

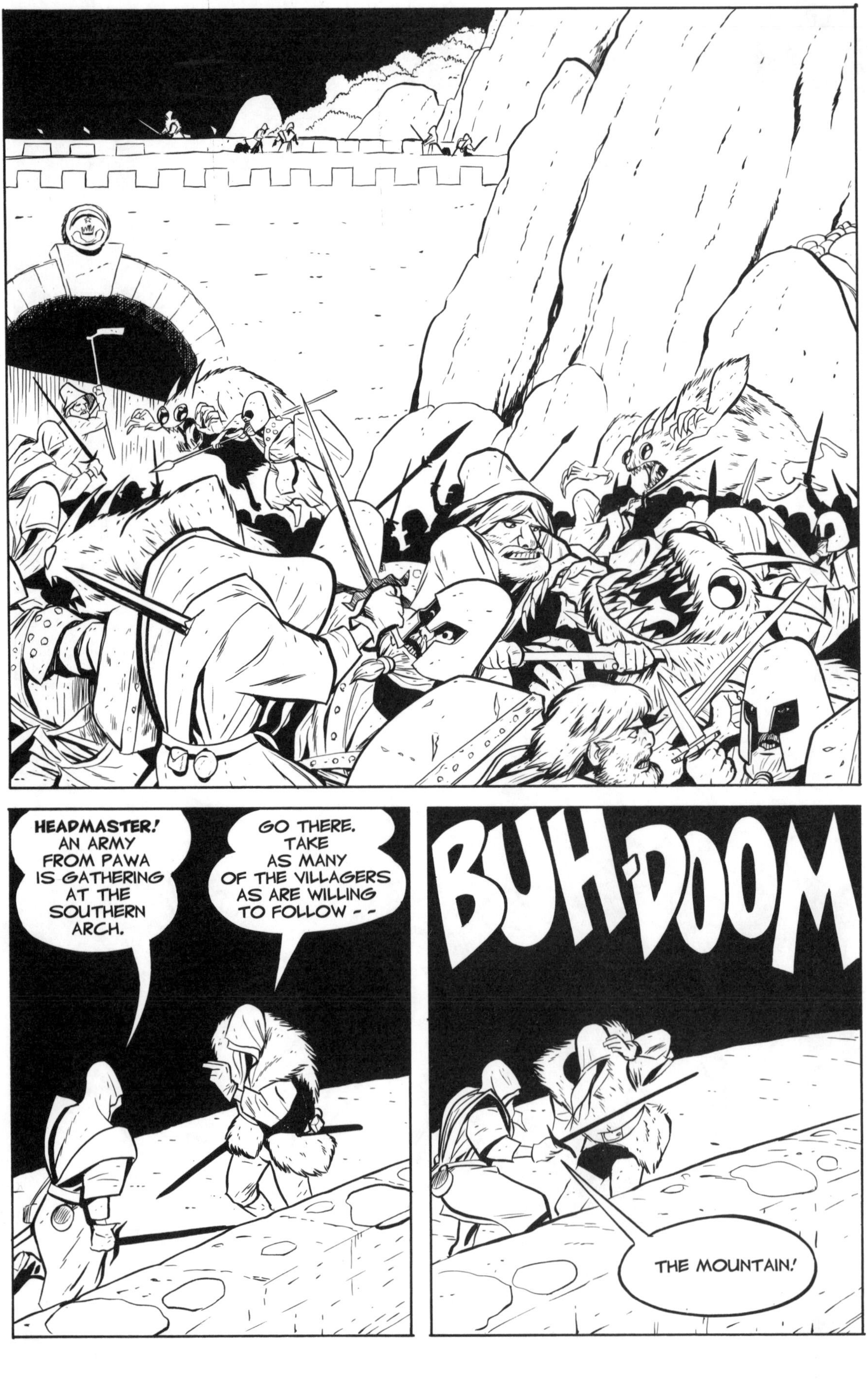
HEADMASTER! AN ARMY FROM PAWA IS GATHERING AT THE SOUTHERN ARCH.
GO THERE. TAKE AS MANY OF THE VILLAGERS AS ARE WILLING TO FOLLOW - -
BUH-DOOM
THE MOUNTAIN!

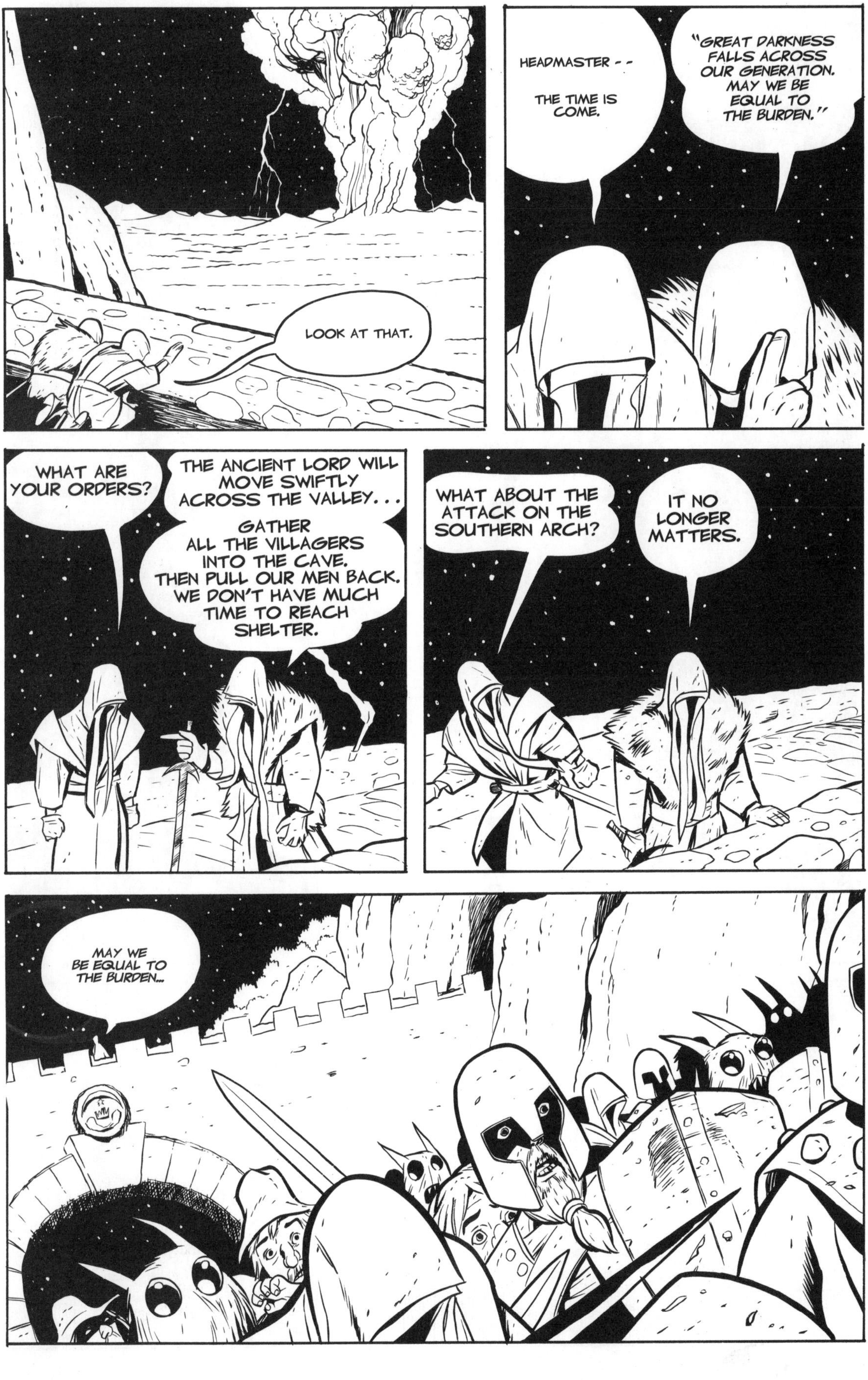
LOOK AT THAT.
HEADMASTER - - THE TIME IS COME.
"GREAT DARKNESS FALLS ACROSS OUR GENERATION. MAY WE BE EQUAL TO THE BURDEN."
WHAT ARE YOUR ORDERS?
THE ANCIENT LORD WILL MOVE SWIFTLY ACROSS THE VALLEY. . .
GATHER ALL THE VILLAGERS INTO THE CAVE. THEN PULL OUR MEN BACK. WE DON'T HAVE MUCH TIME TO REACH SHELTER.
WHAT ABOUT THE ATTACK ON THE SOUTHERN ARCH?
IT NO LONGER MATTERS.
MAY WE BE EQUAL TO THE BURDEN...

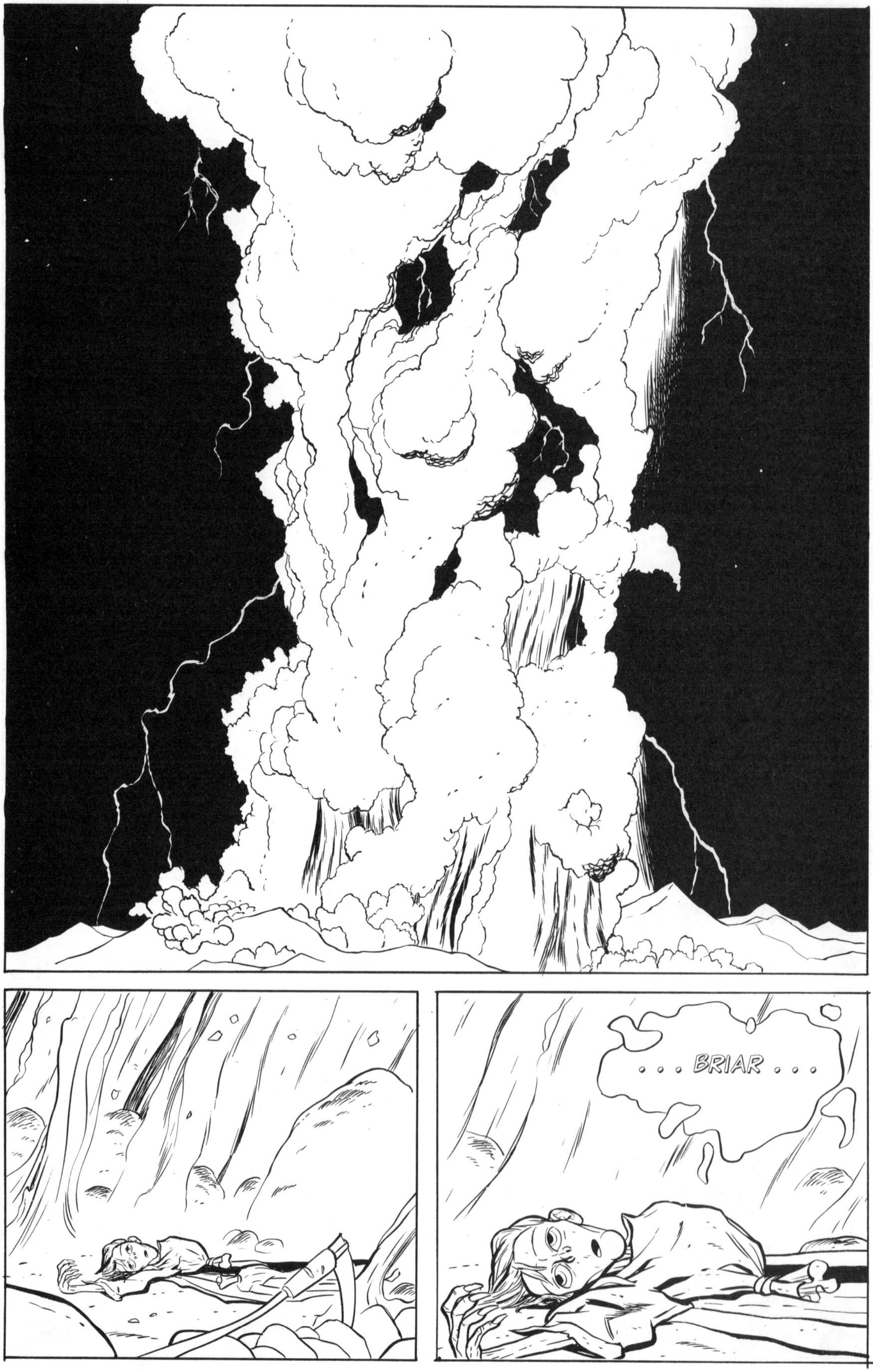
. . . BRIAR . . .

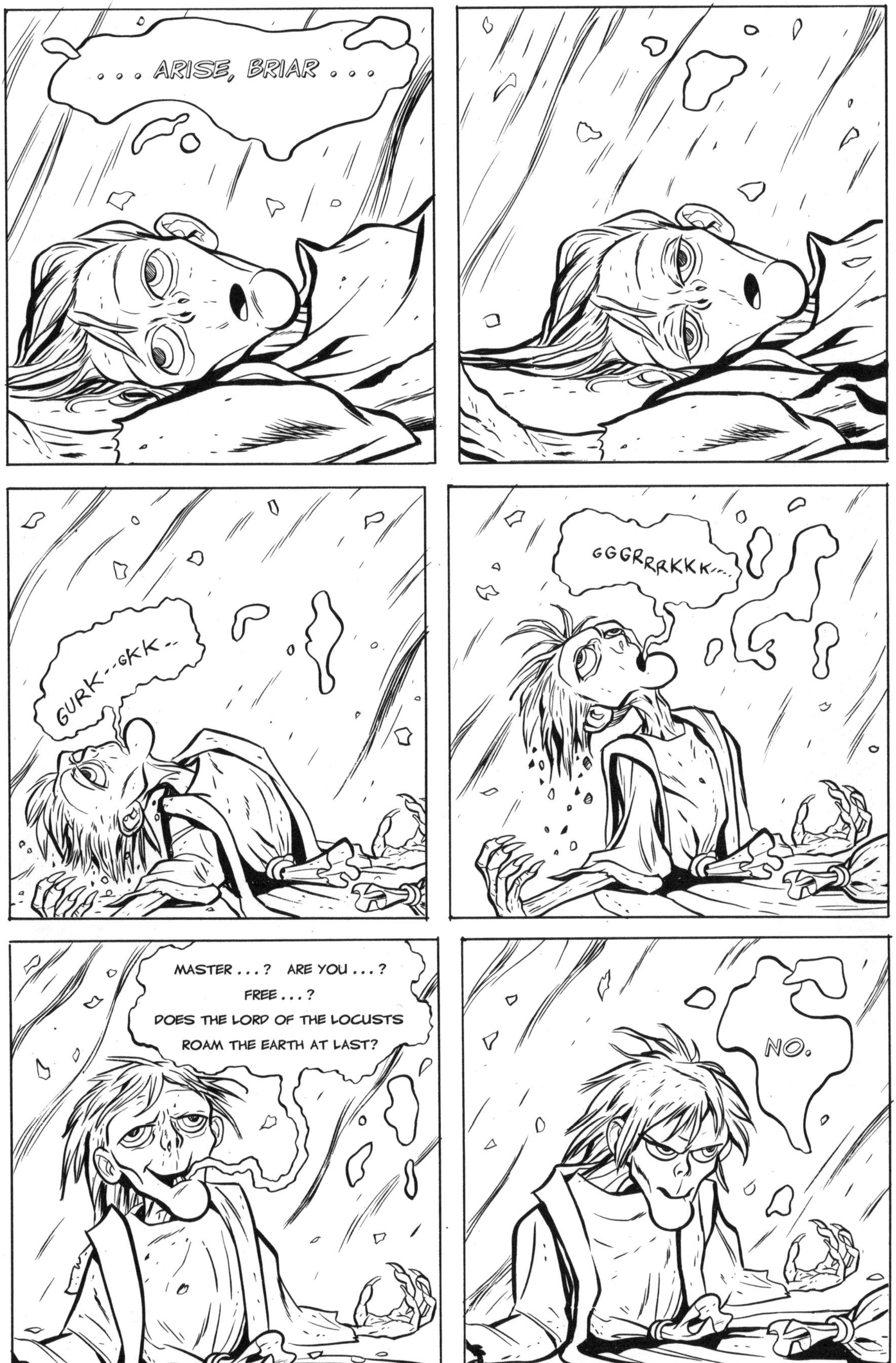
. . . ARISE, BRIAR . . .
GURK . . GKK . .
GGGRRRKKK . . .
MASTER . . . ? ARE YOU . . . ? FREE . . . ? DOES THE LORD OF THE LOCUSTS ROAM THE EARTH AT LAST?
NO.

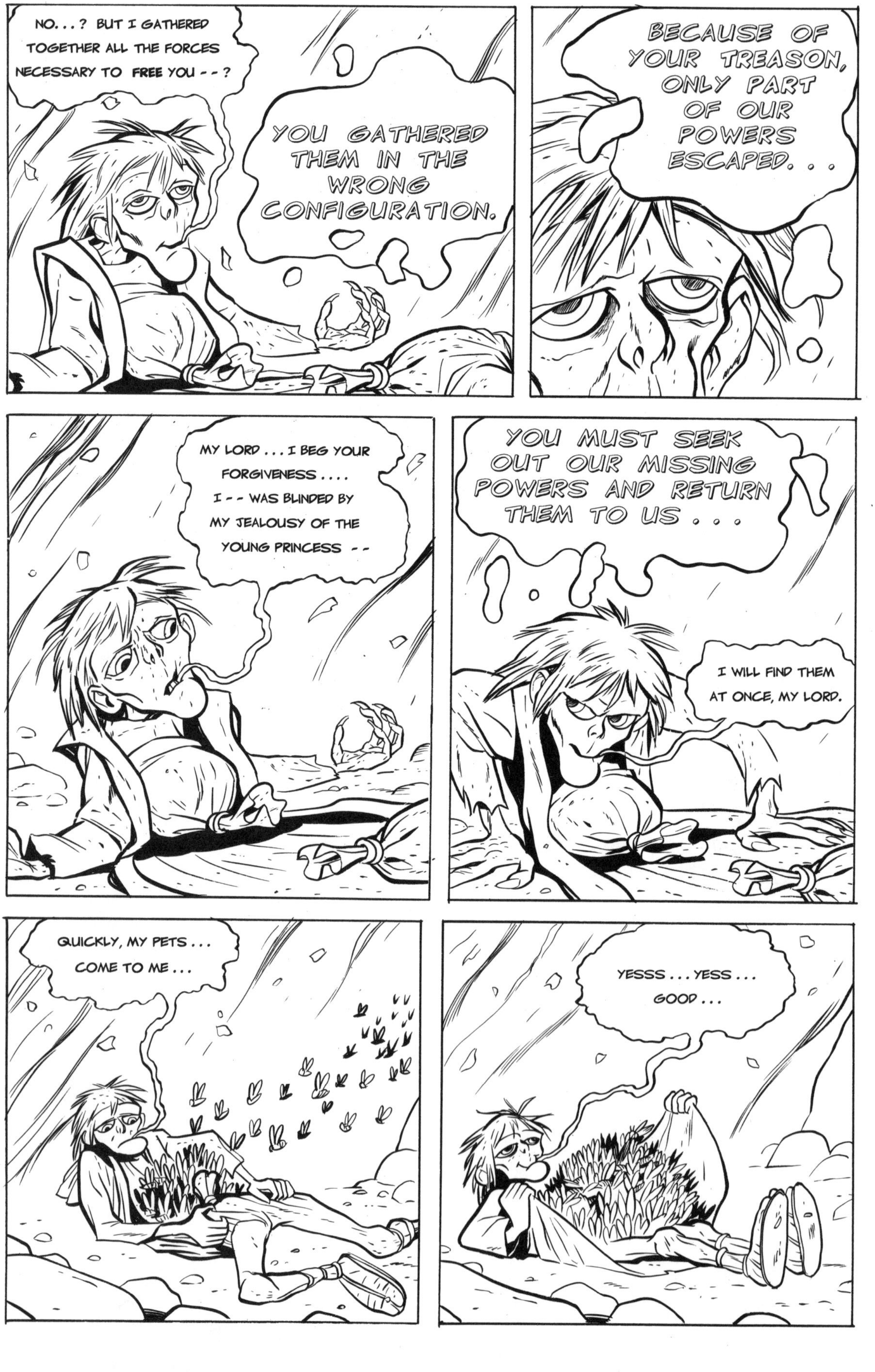
NO...? BUT I GATHERED TOGETHER ALL THE FORCES NECESSARY TO FREE YOU--?
YOU GATHERED THEM IN THE WRONG CONFIGURATION.
BECAUSE OF YOUR TREASON, ONLY PART OF OUR POWERS ESCAPED...
MY LORD... I BEG YOUR FORGIVENESS.... I-- WAS BLINDED BY MY JEALOUSY OF THE YOUNG PRINCESS--
YOU MUST SEEK OUT OUR MISSING POWERS AND RETURN THEM TO US...
I WILL FIND THEM AT ONCE, MY LORD.
QUICKLY, MY PETS... COME TO ME...
YESSS... YESS... GOOD...

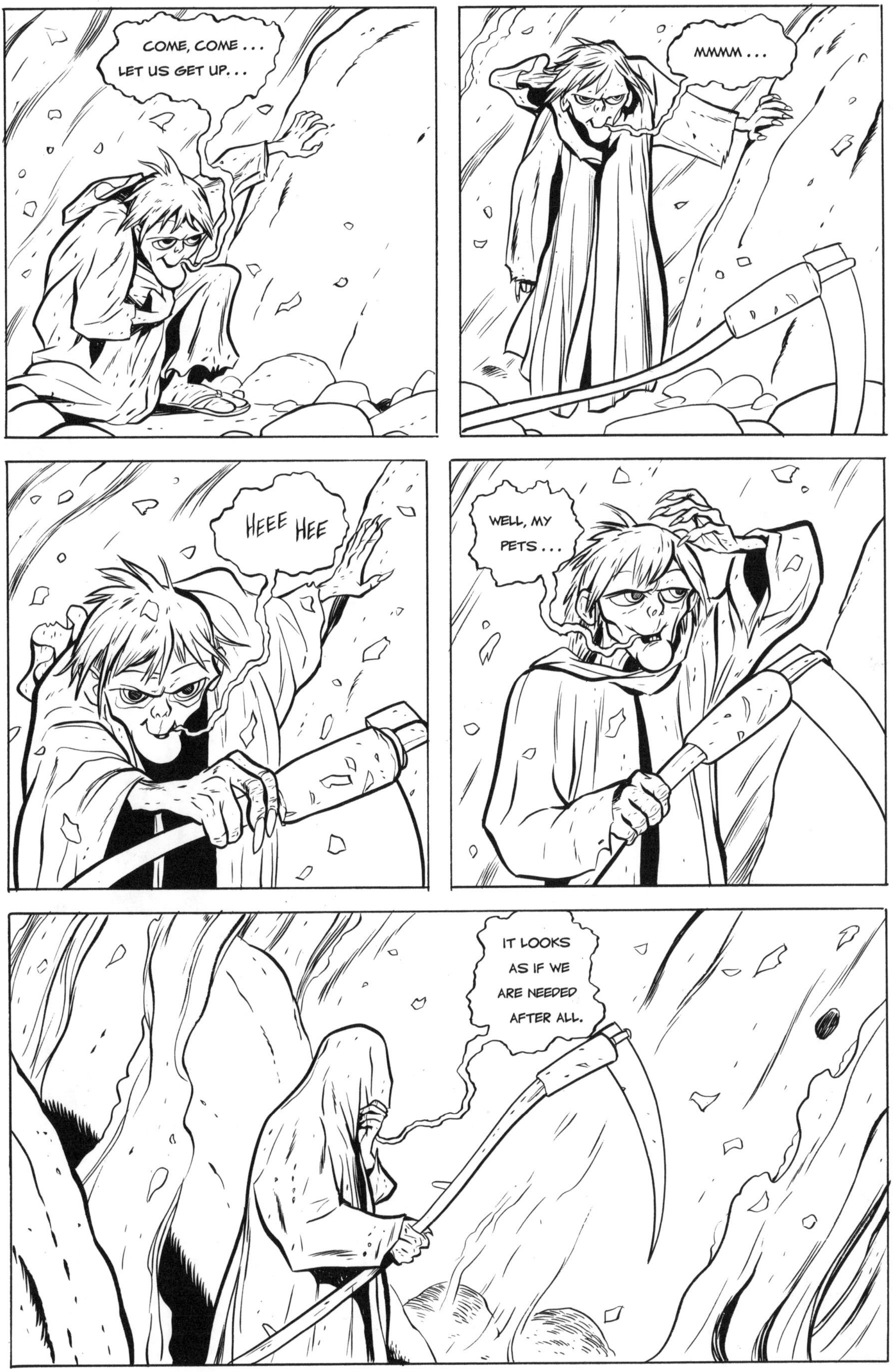
COME, COME . . .
LET US GET UP. . .
MMMM . . .
HEEE HEE
WELL, MY PETS . . .
IT LOOKS AS IF WE ARE NEEDED AFTER ALL.

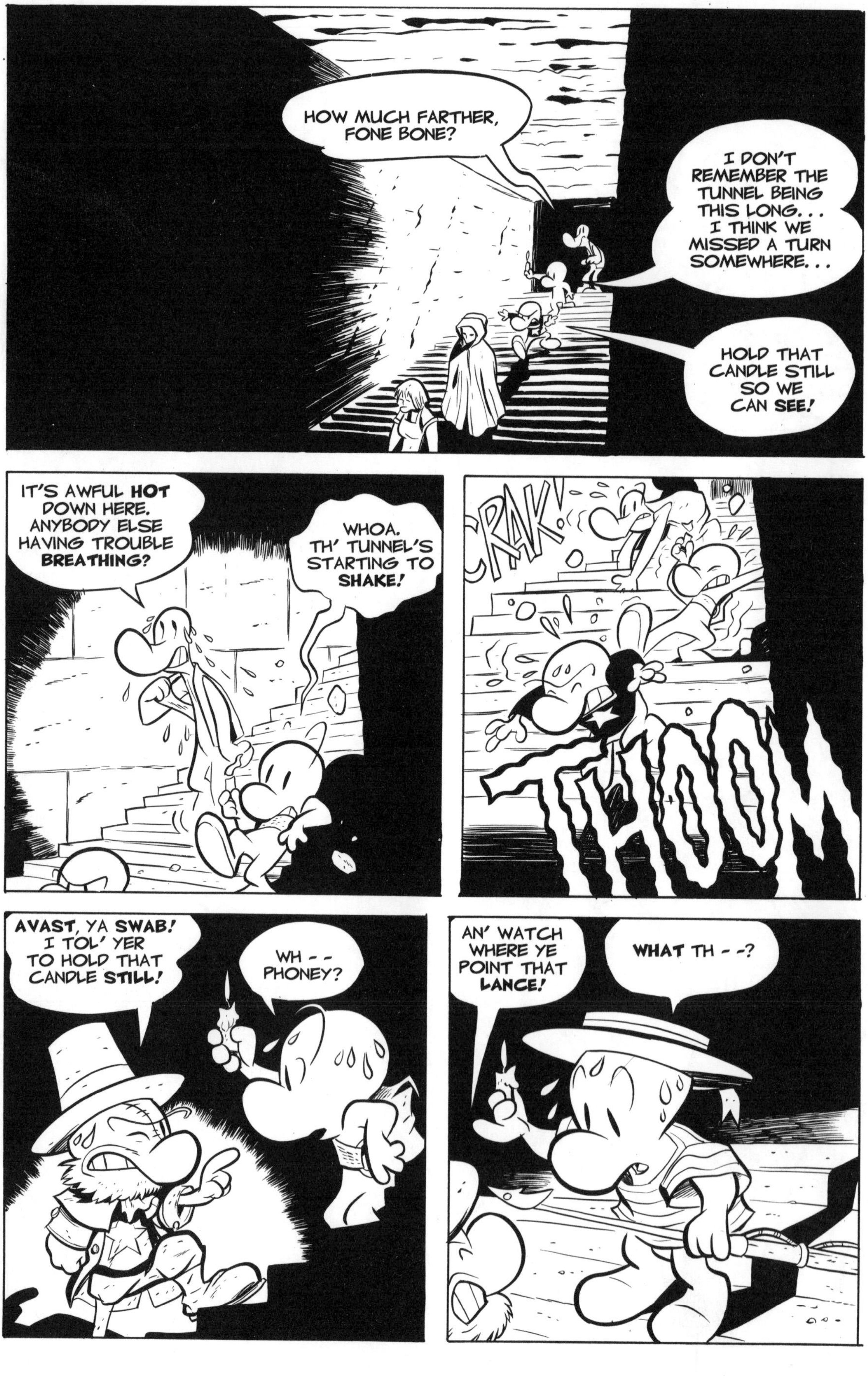
HOW MUCH FARTHER, FONE BONE?
I DON'T REMEMBER THE TUNNEL BEING THIS LONG... I THINK WE MISSED A TURN SOMEWHERE...
HOLD THAT CANDLE STILL SO WE CAN SEE!
IT'S AWFUL HOT DOWN HERE. ANYBODY ELSE HAVING TROUBLE BREATHING?
WHOA. TH' TUNNEL'S STARTING TO SHAKE!
CRAK!
THOOM
AVAST, YA SWAB! I TOL' YER TO HOLD THAT CANDLE STILL!
WH -- PHONEY?
AN' WATCH WHERE YE POINT THAT LANCE!
WHAT TH --?

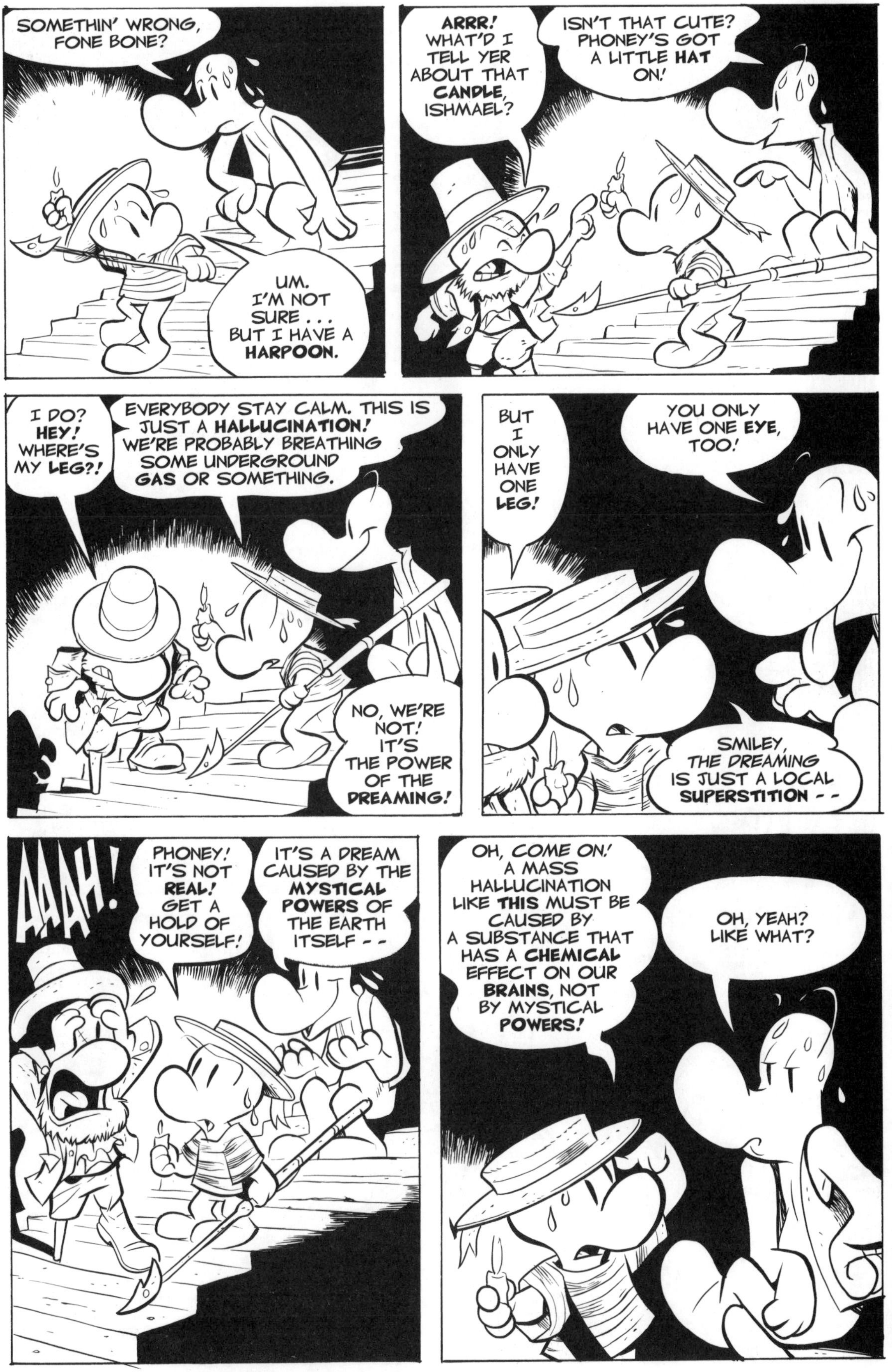
SOMETHIN' WRONG, FONE BONE?
UM. I'M NOT SURE . . . BUT I HAVE A HARPOON.
ARRR! WHAT'D I TELL YER ABOUT THAT CANDLE, ISHMAEL?
ISN'T THAT CUTE? PHONEY'S GOT A LITTLE HAT ON!
I DO? HEY! WHERE'S MY LEG?!
EVERYBODY STAY CALM. THIS IS JUST A HALLUCINATION! WE'RE PROBABLY BREATHING SOME UNDERGROUND GAS OR SOMETHING.
NO, WE'RE NOT! IT'S THE POWER OF THE DREAMING!
BUT I ONLY HAVE ONE LEG!
YOU ONLY HAVE ONE EYE, TOO!
SMILEY, THE DREAMING IS JUST A LOCAL SUPERSTITION - -
AAAH!
PHONEY! IT'S NOT REAL! GET A HOLD OF YOURSELF!
IT'S A DREAM CAUSED BY THE MYSTICAL POWERS OF THE EARTH ITSELF - -
OH, COME ON! A MASS HALLUCINATION LIKE THIS MUST BE CAUSED BY A SUBSTANCE THAT HAS A CHEMICAL EFFECT ON OUR BRAINS, NOT BY MYSTICAL POWERS!
OH, YEAH? LIKE WHAT?

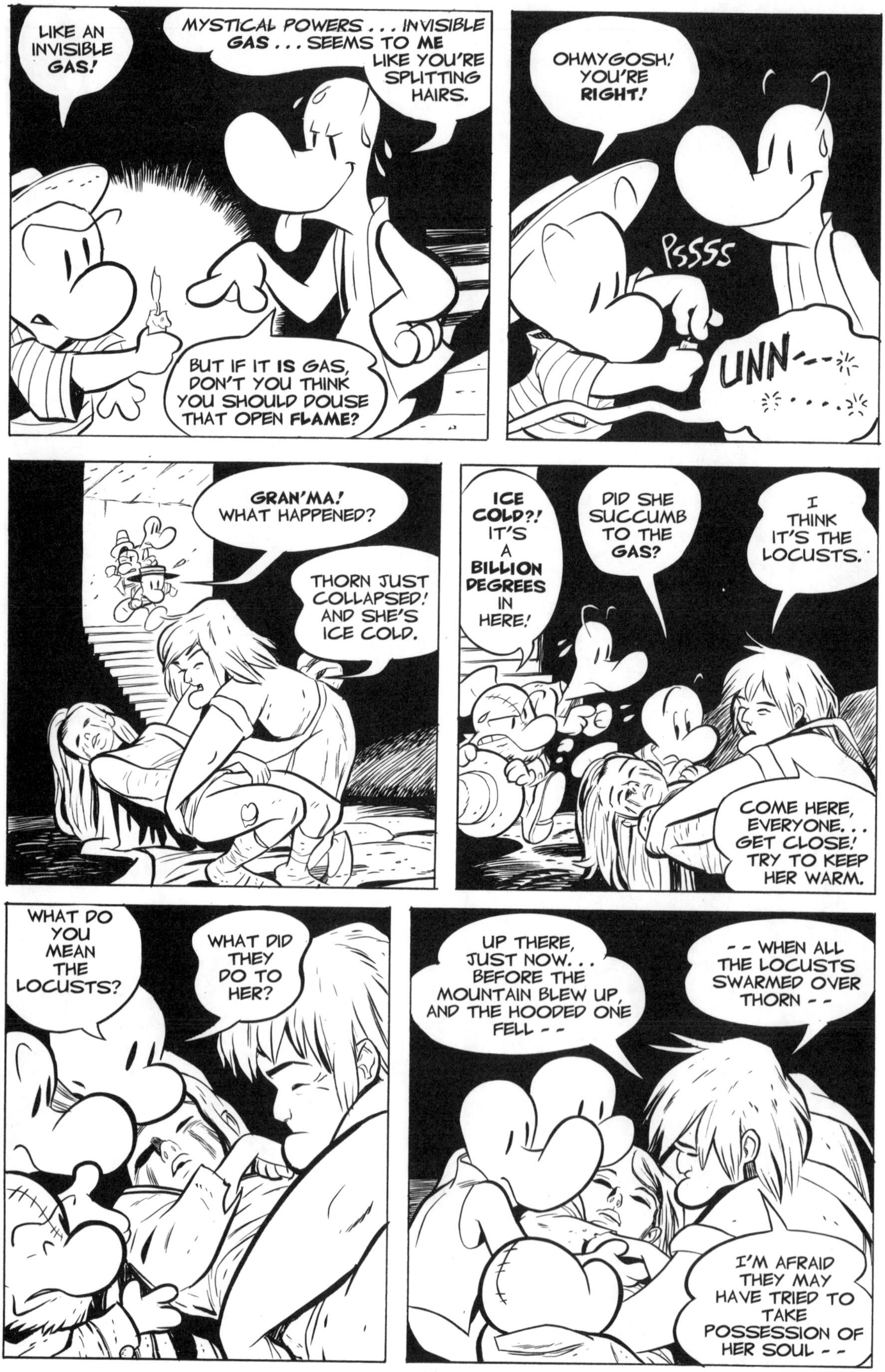
LIKE AN INVISIBLE GAS!
MYSTICAL POWERS . . . INVISIBLE GAS . . . SEEMS TO ME LIKE YOU'RE SPLITTING HAIRS.
BUT IF IT IS GAS, DON'T YOU THINK YOU SHOULD DOUSE THAT OPEN FLAME?
OHMYGOSH! YOU'RE RIGHT!
PSSSS
UNN- - - . . . .
GRAN'MA! WHAT HAPPENED?
THORN JUST COLLAPSED! AND SHE'S ICE COLD.
ICE COLD?! IT'S A BILLION DEGREES IN HERE!
DID SHE SUCCUMB TO THE GAS?
I THINK IT'S THE LOCUSTS.
COME HERE, EVERYONE. . . GET CLOSE! TRY TO KEEP HER WARM.
WHAT DO YOU MEAN THE LOCUSTS?
WHAT DID THEY DO TO HER?
UP THERE, JUST NOW. . . BEFORE THE MOUNTAIN BLEW UP, AND THE HOODED ONE FELL - -
- - WHEN ALL THE LOCUSTS SWARMED OVER THORN - -
I'M AFRAID THEY MAY HAVE TRIED TO TAKE POSSESSION OF HER SOUL - -

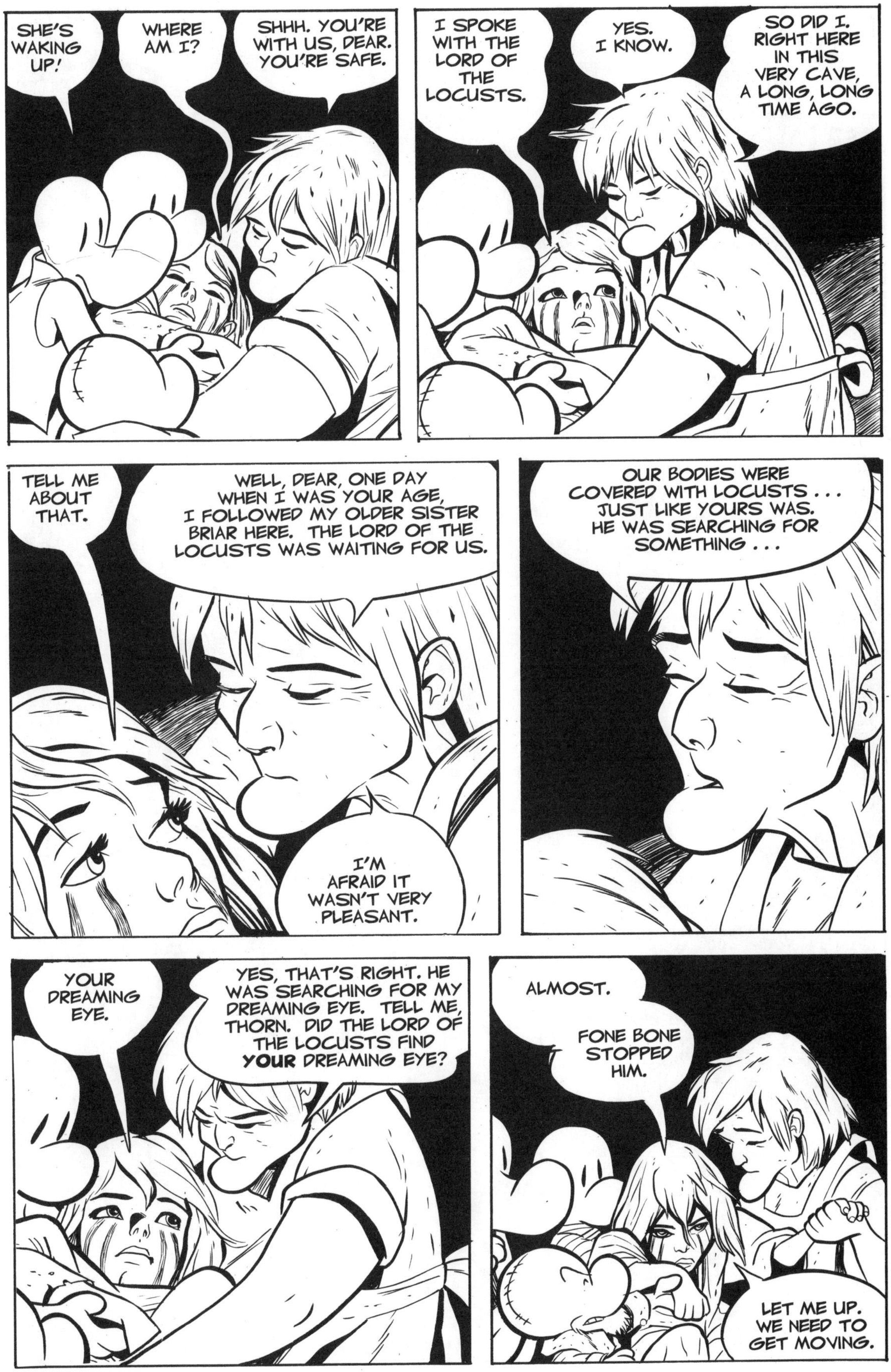
SHE'S WAKING UP!
WHERE AM I?
SHHH. YOU'RE WITH US, DEAR. YOU'RE SAFE.
I SPOKE WITH THE LORD OF THE LOCUSTS.
YES. I KNOW.
SO DID I. RIGHT HERE IN THIS VERY CAVE, A LONG, LONG TIME AGO.
TELL ME ABOUT THAT.
WELL, DEAR, ONE DAY WHEN I WAS YOUR AGE, I FOLLOWED MY OLDER SISTER BRIAR HERE. THE LORD OF THE LOCUSTS WAS WAITING FOR US.
I'M AFRAID IT WASN'T VERY PLEASANT.
OUR BODIES WERE COVERED WITH LOCUSTS . . . JUST LIKE YOURS WAS. HE WAS SEARCHING FOR SOMETHING . . .
YOUR DREAMING EYE.
YES, THAT'S RIGHT. HE WAS SEARCHING FOR MY DREAMING EYE. TELL ME, THORN. DID THE LORD OF THE LOCUSTS FIND **YOUR** DREAMING EYE?
ALMOST.
FONE BONE STOPPED HIM.
LET ME UP. WE NEED TO GET MOVING.

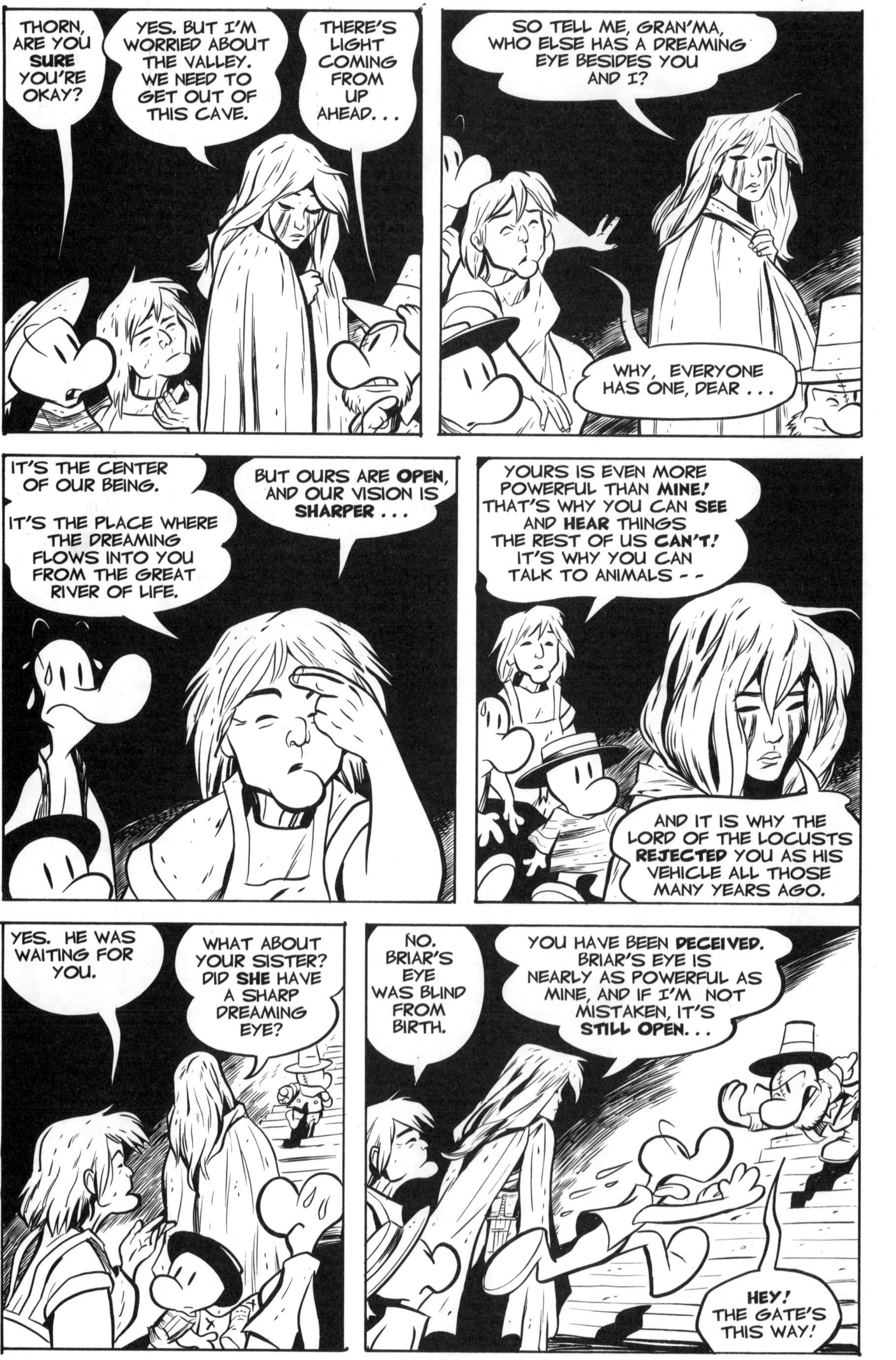
THORN, ARE YOU **SURE** YOU'RE OKAY?
YES. BUT I'M WORRIED ABOUT THE VALLEY. WE NEED TO GET OUT OF THIS CAVE.
THERE'S LIGHT COMING FROM UP AHEAD...
SO TELL ME, GRAN'MA, WHO ELSE HAS A DREAMING EYE BESIDES YOU AND I?
WHY, EVERYONE HAS ONE, DEAR...
IT'S THE CENTER OF OUR BEING.
IT'S THE PLACE WHERE THE DREAMING FLOWS INTO YOU FROM THE GREAT RIVER OF LIFE.
BUT OURS ARE **OPEN**, AND OUR VISION IS **SHARPER**...
YOURS IS EVEN MORE POWERFUL THAN **MINE!** THAT'S WHY YOU CAN **SEE** AND **HEAR** THINGS THE REST OF US **CAN'T!** IT'S WHY YOU CAN TALK TO ANIMALS --
AND IT IS WHY THE LORD OF THE LOCUSTS **REJECTED** YOU AS HIS VEHICLE ALL THOSE MANY YEARS AGO.
YES. HE WAS WAITING FOR YOU.
WHAT ABOUT YOUR SISTER? DID **SHE** HAVE A SHARP DREAMING EYE?
NO. BRIAR'S EYE WAS BLIND FROM BIRTH.
YOU HAVE BEEN **DECEIVED.** BRIAR'S EYE IS NEARLY AS POWERFUL AS MINE, AND IF I'M NOT MISTAKEN, IT'S **STILL OPEN...**
HEY! THE GATE'S THIS WAY!

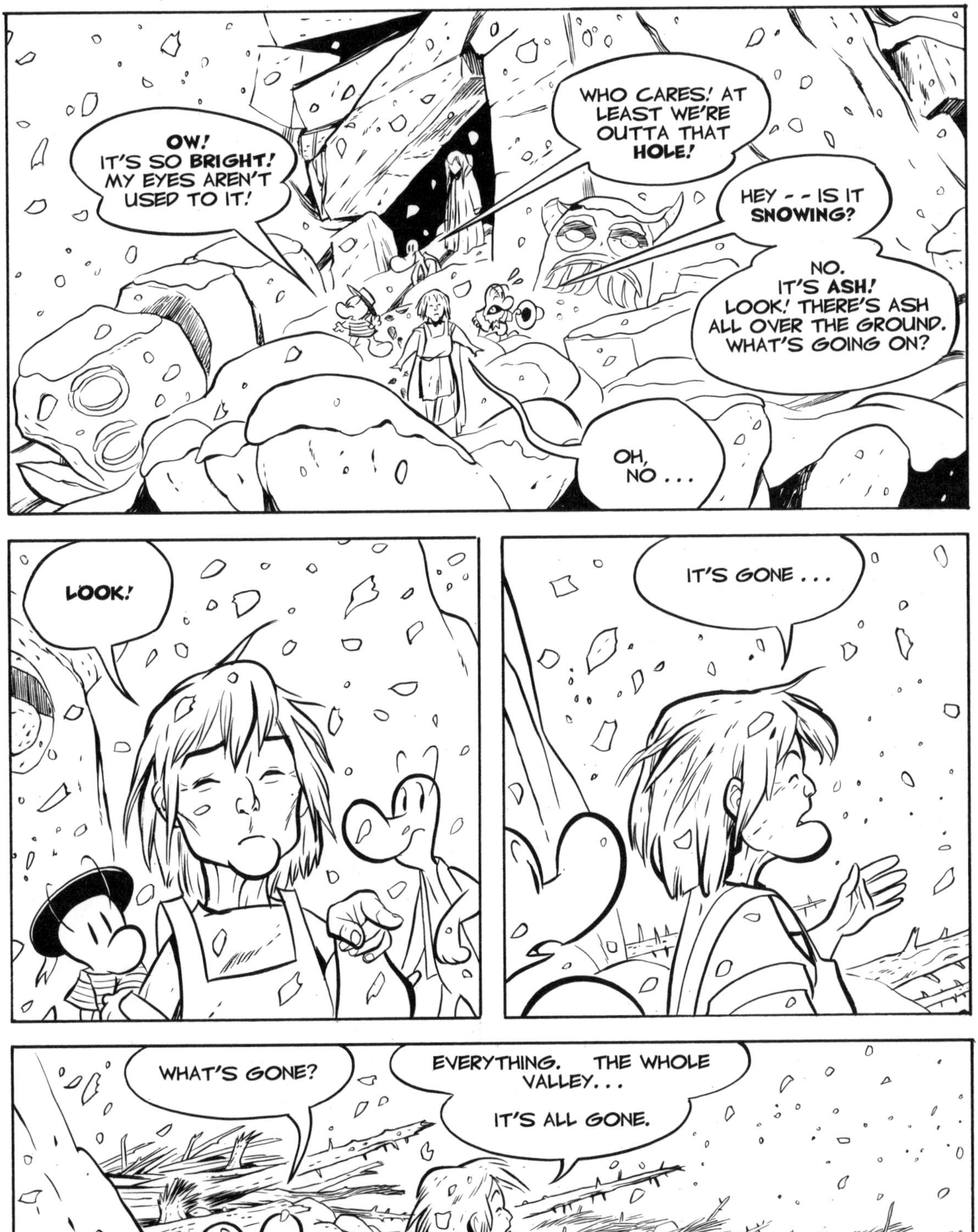
OW! IT'S SO BRIGHT! MY EYES AREN'T USED TO IT!
WHO CARES! AT LEAST WE'RE OUTTA THAT HOLE!
HEY - - IS IT SNOWING?
NO. IT'S ASH! LOOK! THERE'S ASH ALL OVER THE GROUND. WHAT'S GOING ON?
OH, NO . . .
LOOK!
IT'S GONE . . .
WHAT'S GONE?
EVERYTHING. THE WHOLE VALLEY . . .
IT'S ALL GONE.

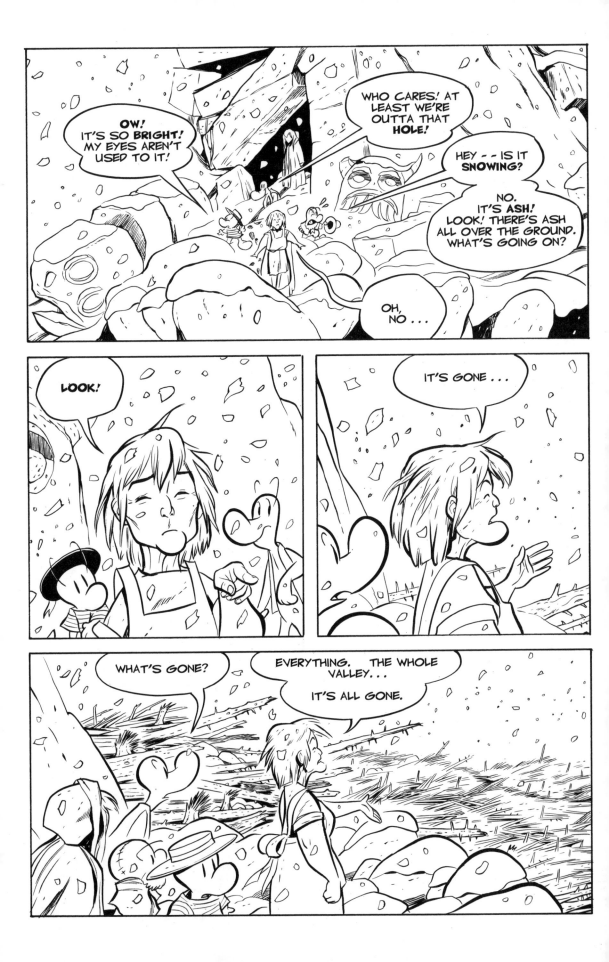

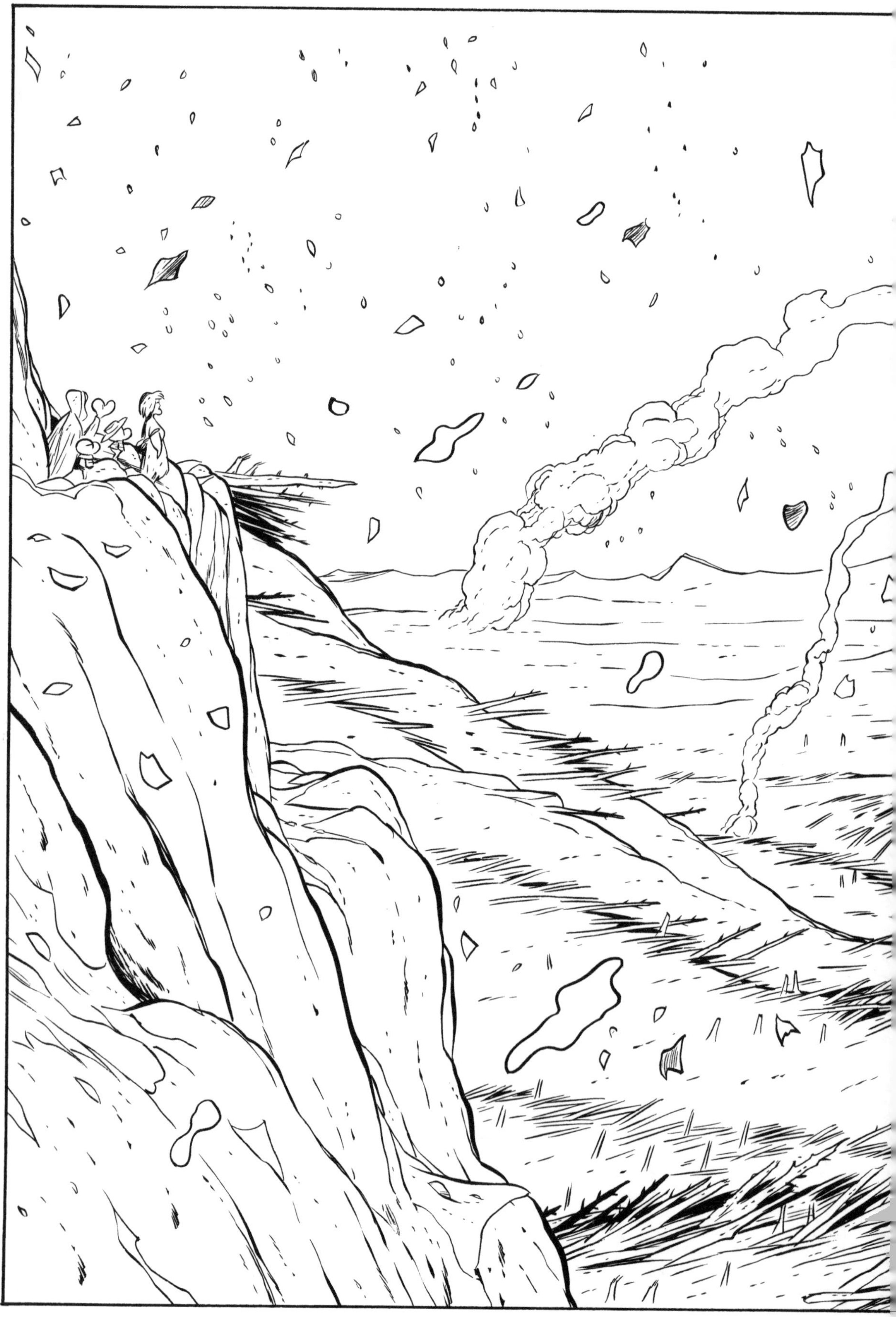

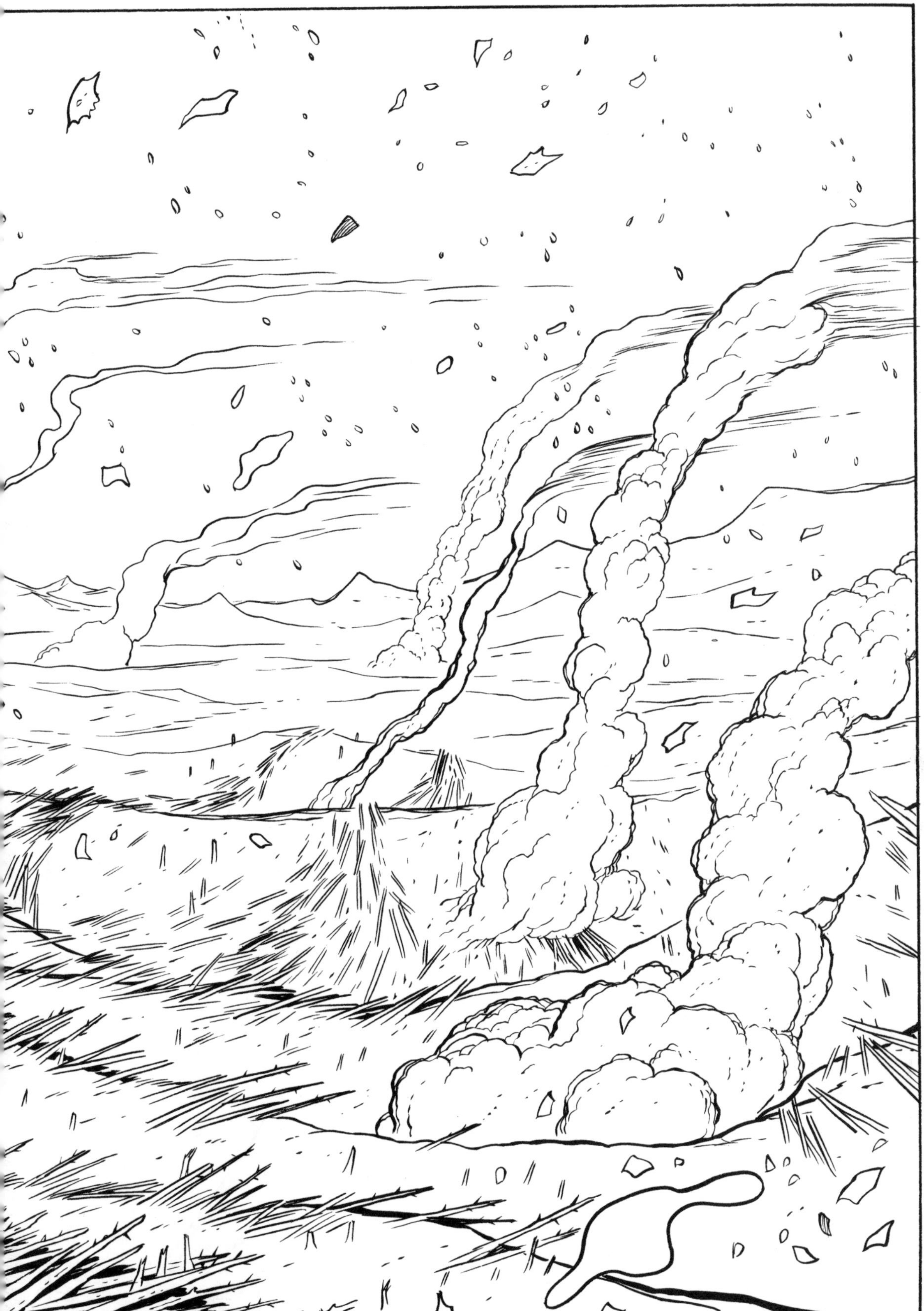

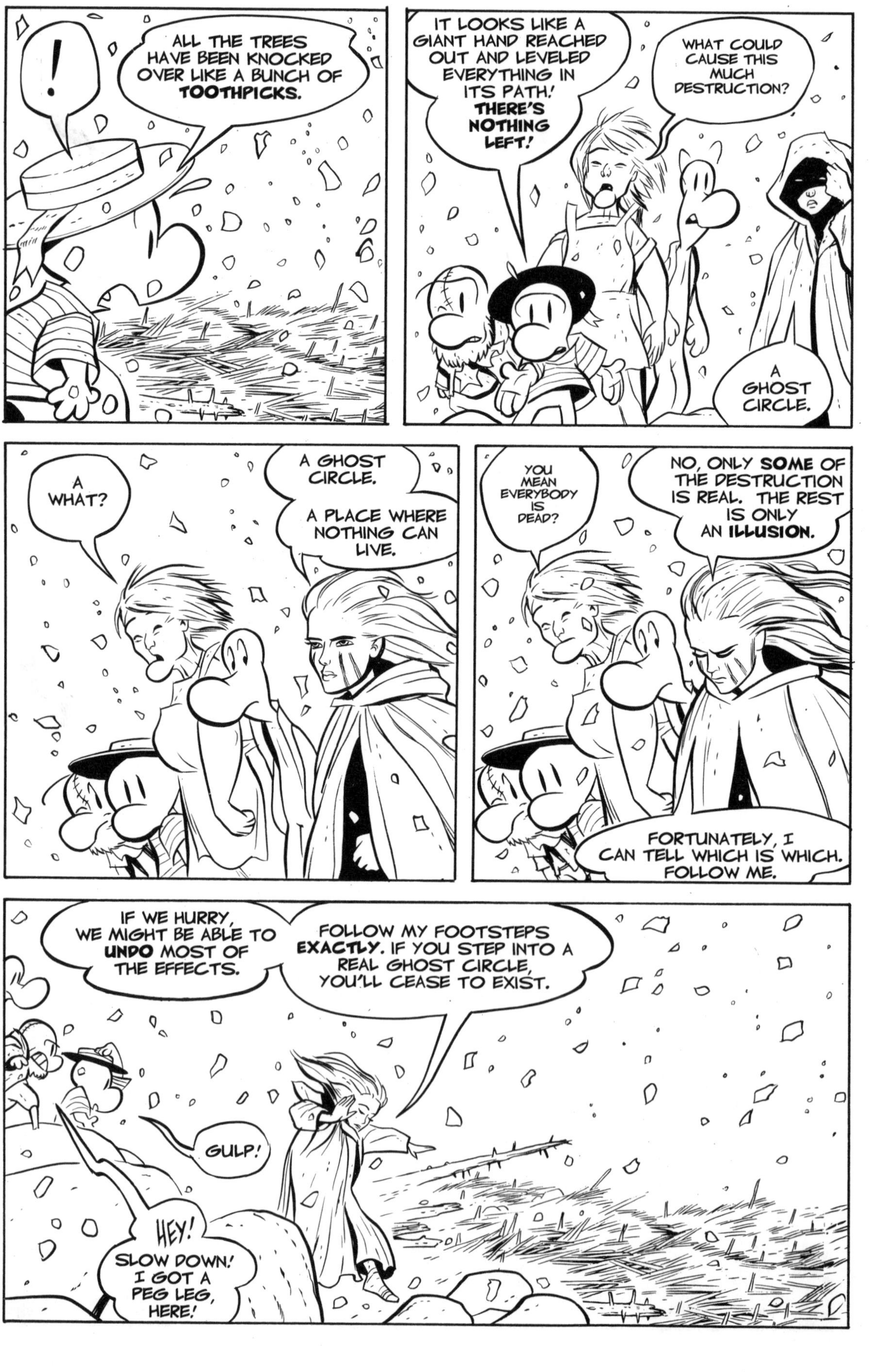
!
ALL THE TREES HAVE BEEN KNOCKED OVER LIKE A BUNCH OF TOOTHPICKS.
IT LOOKS LIKE A GIANT HAND REACHED OUT AND LEVELED EVERYTHING IN ITS PATH! THERE'S NOTHING LEFT!
WHAT COULD CAUSE THIS MUCH DESTRUCTION?
A GHOST CIRCLE.
A WHAT?
A GHOST CIRCLE.
A PLACE WHERE NOTHING CAN LIVE.
YOU MEAN EVERYBODY IS DEAD?
NO, ONLY SOME OF THE DESTRUCTION IS REAL. THE REST IS ONLY AN ILLUSION.
FORTUNATELY, I CAN TELL WHICH IS WHICH. FOLLOW ME.
IF WE HURRY, WE MIGHT BE ABLE TO UNDO MOST OF THE EFFECTS.
FOLLOW MY FOOTSTEPS EXACTLY. IF YOU STEP INTO A REAL GHOST CIRCLE, YOU'LL CEASE TO EXIST.
GULP!
HEY!
SLOW DOWN! I GOT A PEG LEG, HERE!

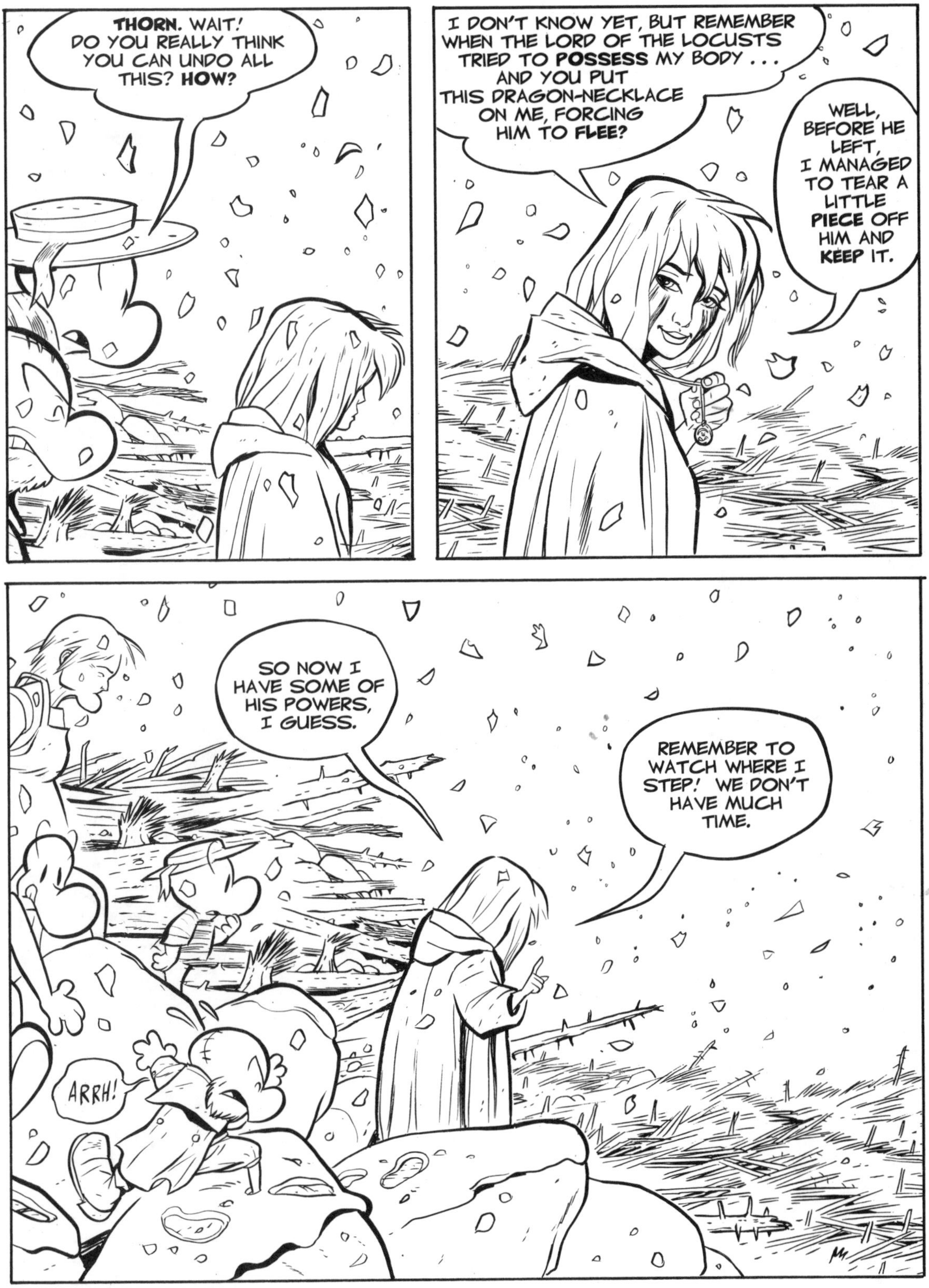
THORN. WAIT! DO YOU REALLY THINK YOU CAN UNDO ALL THIS? HOW?
I DON'T KNOW YET, BUT REMEMBER WHEN THE LORD OF THE LOCUSTS TRIED TO POSSESS MY BODY . . . AND YOU PUT THIS DRAGON-NECKLACE ON ME, FORCING HIM TO FLEE?
WELL, BEFORE HE LEFT, I MANAGED TO TEAR A LITTLE PIECE OFF HIM AND KEEP IT.
SO NOW I HAVE SOME OF HIS POWERS, I GUESS.
REMEMBER TO WATCH WHERE I STEP! WE DON'T HAVE MUCH TIME.
ARRH!

NEXT: GHOST CIRCLES

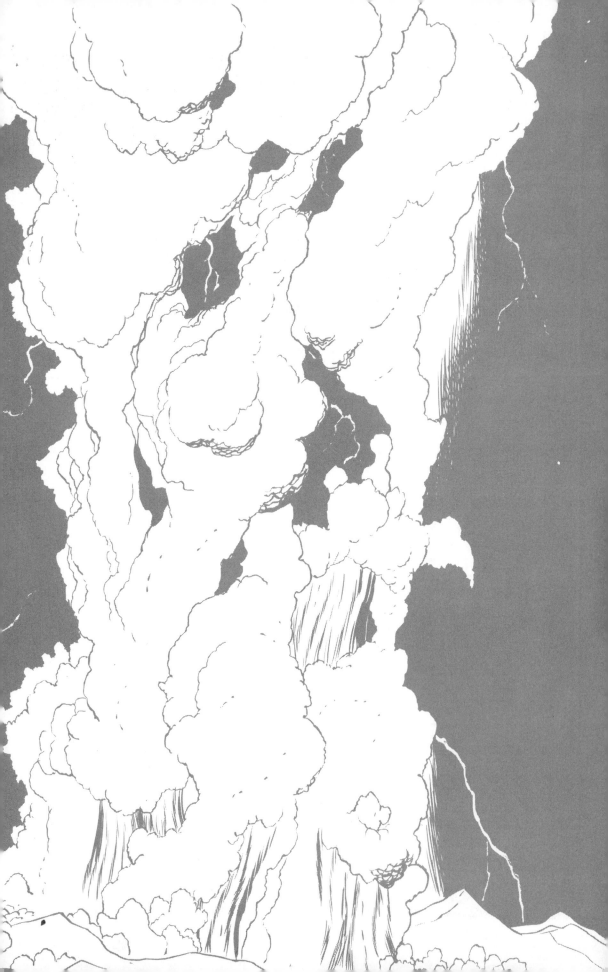

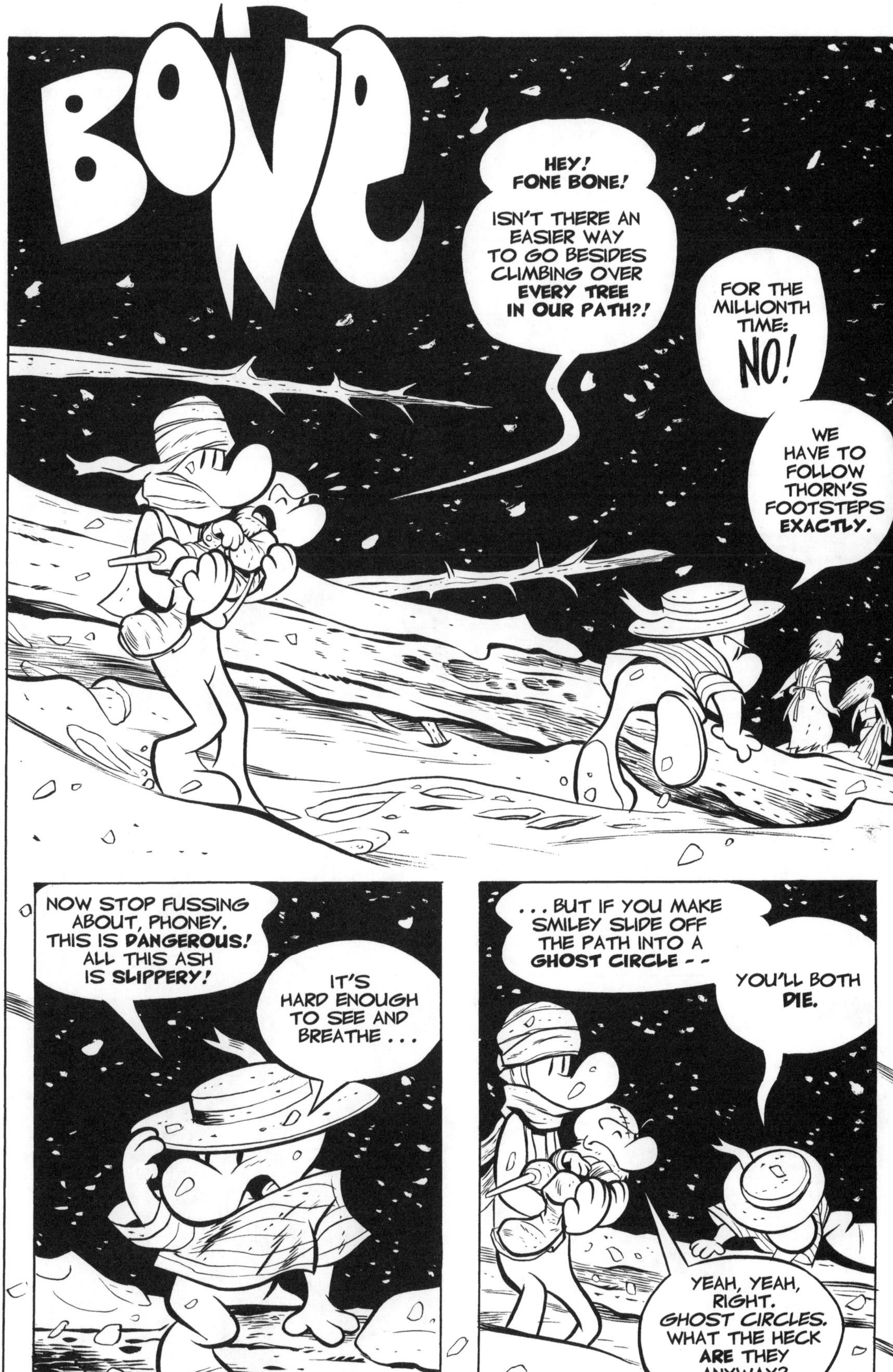
BONE
HEY! FONE BONE!
ISN'T THERE AN EASIER WAY TO GO BESIDES CLIMBING OVER EVERY TREE IN OUR PATH?!
FOR THE MILLIONTH TIME: NO!
WE HAVE TO FOLLOW THORN'S FOOTSTEPS EXACTLY.
NOW STOP FUSSING ABOUT, PHONEY. THIS IS DANGEROUS! ALL THIS ASH IS SLIPPERY!
IT'S HARD ENOUGH TO SEE AND BREATHE . . .
. . . BUT IF YOU MAKE SMILEY SLIDE OFF THE PATH INTO A GHOST CIRCLE - -
YOU'LL BOTH DIE.
YEAH, YEAH, RIGHT. GHOST CIRCLES. WHAT THE HECK ARE THEY ANYWAY?

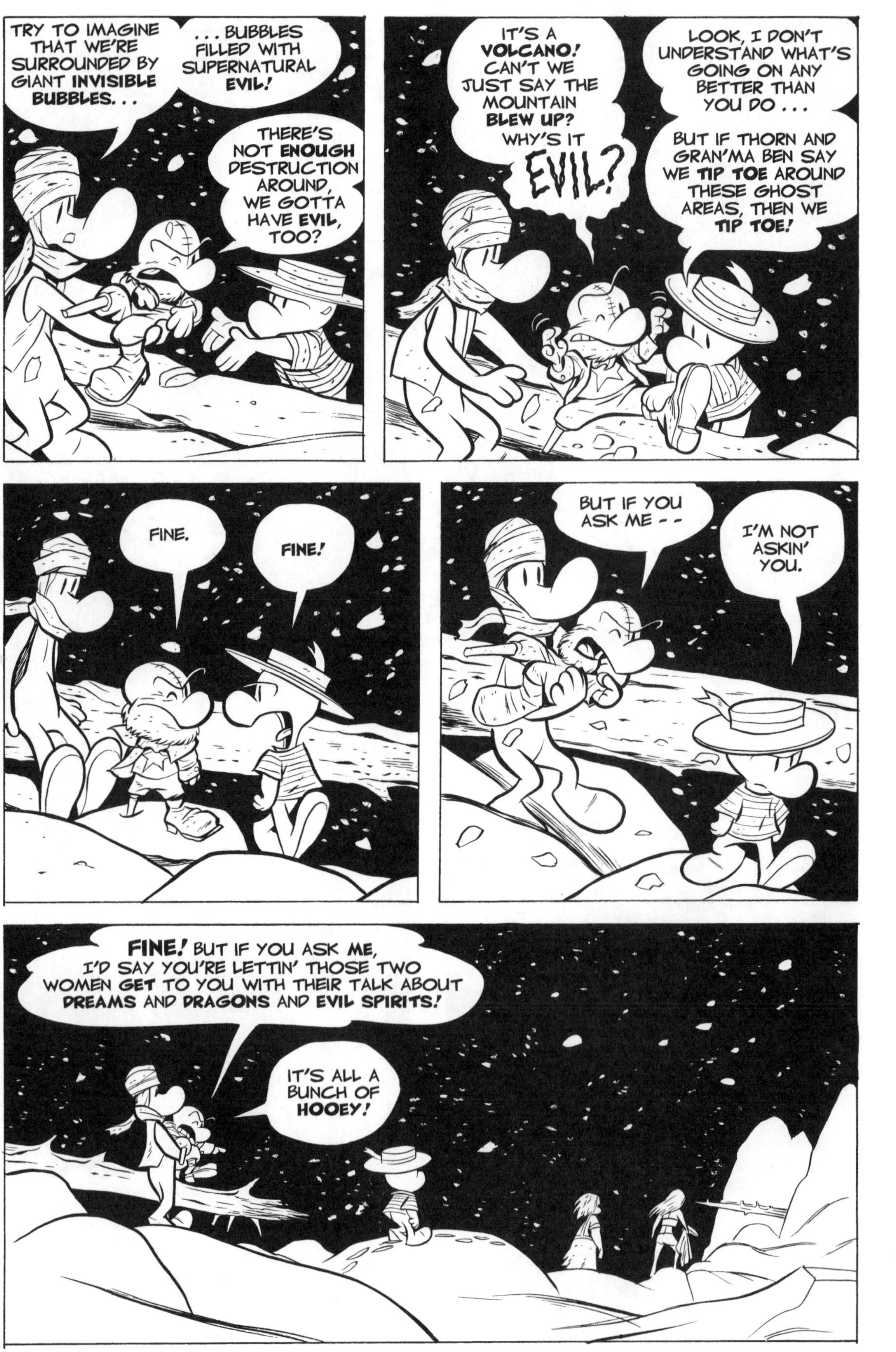
TRY TO IMAGINE THAT WE'RE SURROUNDED BY GIANT INVISIBLE BUBBLES...
...BUBBLES FILLED WITH SUPERNATURAL EVIL!
THERE'S NOT ENOUGH DESTRUCTION AROUND, WE GOTTA HAVE EVIL, TOO?
IT'S A VOLCANO! CAN'T WE JUST SAY THE MOUNTAIN BLEW UP? WHY'S IT EVIL?
LOOK, I DON'T UNDERSTAND WHAT'S GOING ON ANY BETTER THAN YOU DO...
BUT IF THORN AND GRAN'MA BEN SAY WE TIP TOE AROUND THESE GHOST AREAS, THEN WE TIP TOE!
FINE.
FINE!
BUT IF YOU ASK ME --
I'M NOT ASKIN' YOU.
FINE! BUT IF YOU ASK ME, I'D SAY YOU'RE LETTIN' THOSE TWO WOMEN GET TO YOU WITH THEIR TALK ABOUT DREAMS AND DRAGONS AND EVIL SPIRITS!
IT'S ALL A BUNCH OF HOOEY!

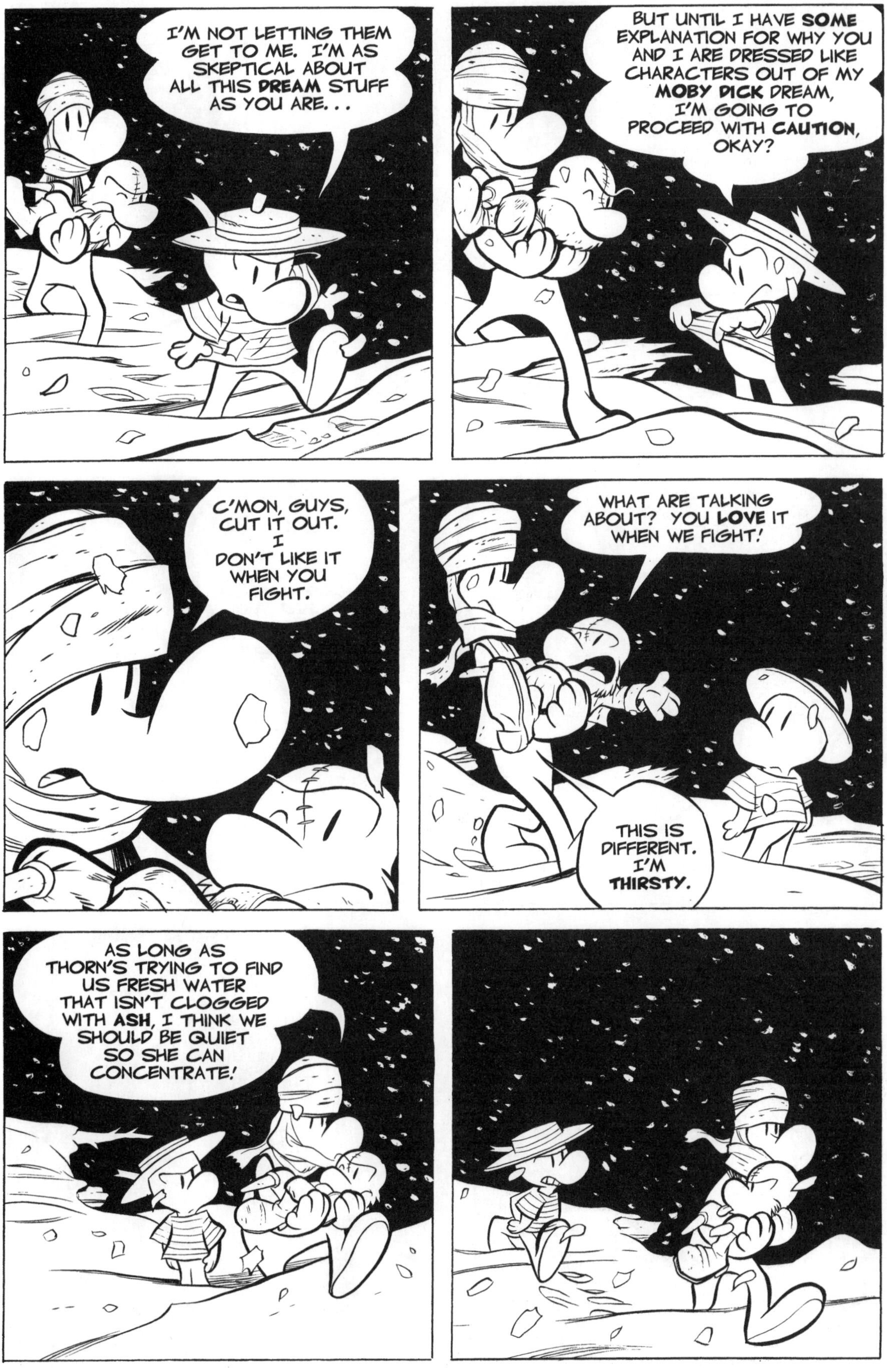
I'M NOT LETTING THEM GET TO ME. I'M AS SKEPTICAL ABOUT ALL THIS DREAM STUFF AS YOU ARE. . .
BUT UNTIL I HAVE SOME EXPLANATION FOR WHY YOU AND I ARE DRESSED LIKE CHARACTERS OUT OF MY MOBY DICK DREAM, I'M GOING TO PROCEED WITH CAUTION, OKAY?
C'MON, GUYS, CUT IT OUT. I DON'T LIKE IT WHEN YOU FIGHT.
WHAT ARE TALKING ABOUT? YOU LOVE IT WHEN WE FIGHT!
THIS IS DIFFERENT. I'M THIRSTY.
AS LONG AS THORN'S TRYING TO FIND US FRESH WATER THAT ISN'T CLOGGED WITH ASH, I THINK WE SHOULD BE QUIET SO SHE CAN CONCENTRATE!

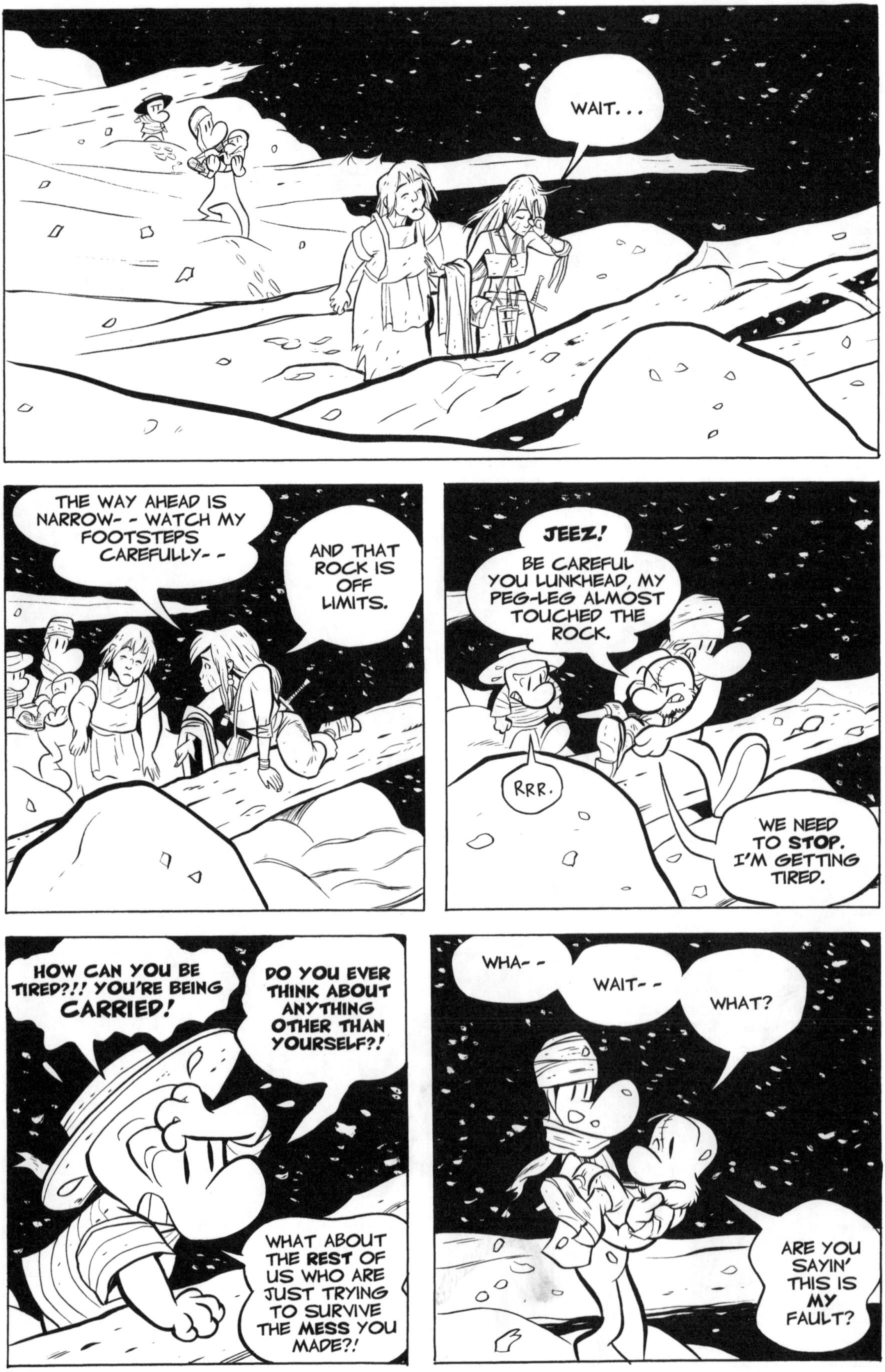
WAIT. . .
THE WAY AHEAD IS NARROW- - WATCH MY FOOTSTEPS CAREFULLY- -
AND THAT ROCK IS OFF LIMITS.
JEEZ! BE CAREFUL YOU LUNKHEAD, MY PEG-LEG ALMOST TOUCHED THE ROCK.
RRR.
WE NEED TO STOP. I'M GETTING TIRED.
HOW CAN YOU BE TIRED?!! YOU'RE BEING CARRIED!
DO YOU EVER THINK ABOUT ANYTHING OTHER THAN YOURSELF?!
WHAT ABOUT THE REST OF US WHO ARE JUST TRYING TO SURVIVE THE MESS YOU MADE?!
WHA- -
WAIT- -
WHAT?
ARE YOU SAYIN' THIS IS MY FAULT?

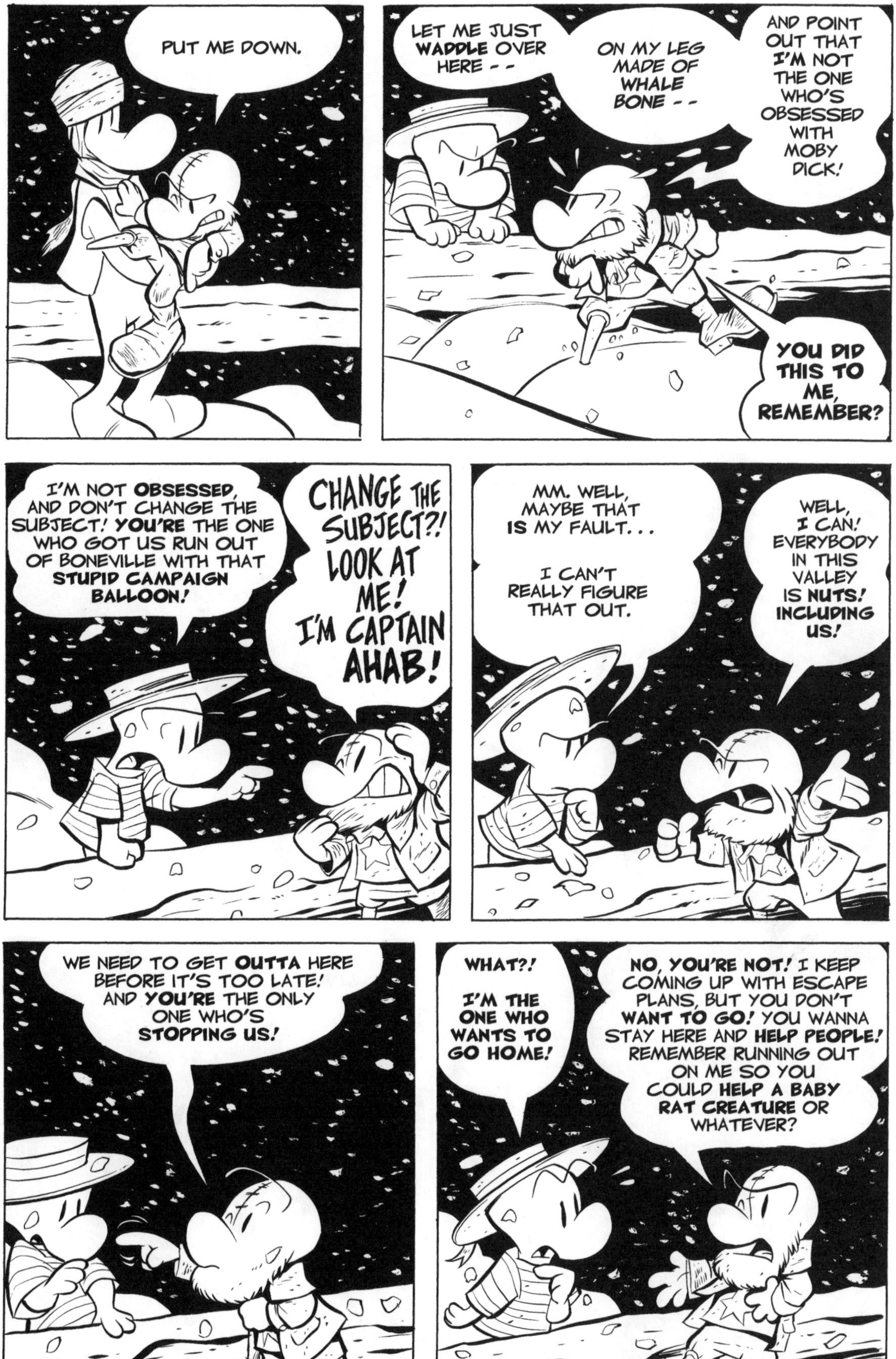
PUT ME DOWN.
LET ME JUST WADDLE OVER HERE - -
ON MY LEG MADE OF WHALE BONE - -
AND POINT OUT THAT I'M NOT THE ONE WHO'S OBSESSED WITH MOBY DICK!
YOU DID THIS TO ME, REMEMBER?
I'M NOT OBSESSED, AND DON'T CHANGE THE SUBJECT! YOU'RE THE ONE WHO GOT US RUN OUT OF BONEVILLE WITH THAT STUPID CAMPAIGN BALLOON!
CHANGE THE SUBJECT?! LOOK AT ME! I'M CAPTAIN AHAB!
MM. WELL, MAYBE THAT IS MY FAULT...
I CAN'T REALLY FIGURE THAT OUT.
WELL, I CAN! EVERYBODY IN THIS VALLEY IS NUTS! INCLUDING US!
WE NEED TO GET OUTTA HERE BEFORE IT'S TOO LATE! AND YOU'RE THE ONLY ONE WHO'S STOPPING US!
WHAT?!
I'M THE ONE WHO WANTS TO GO HOME!
NO, YOU'RE NOT! I KEEP COMING UP WITH ESCAPE PLANS, BUT YOU DON'T WANT TO GO! YOU WANNA STAY HERE AND HELP PEOPLE! REMEMBER RUNNING OUT ON ME SO YOU COULD HELP A BABY RAT CREATURE OR WHATEVER?

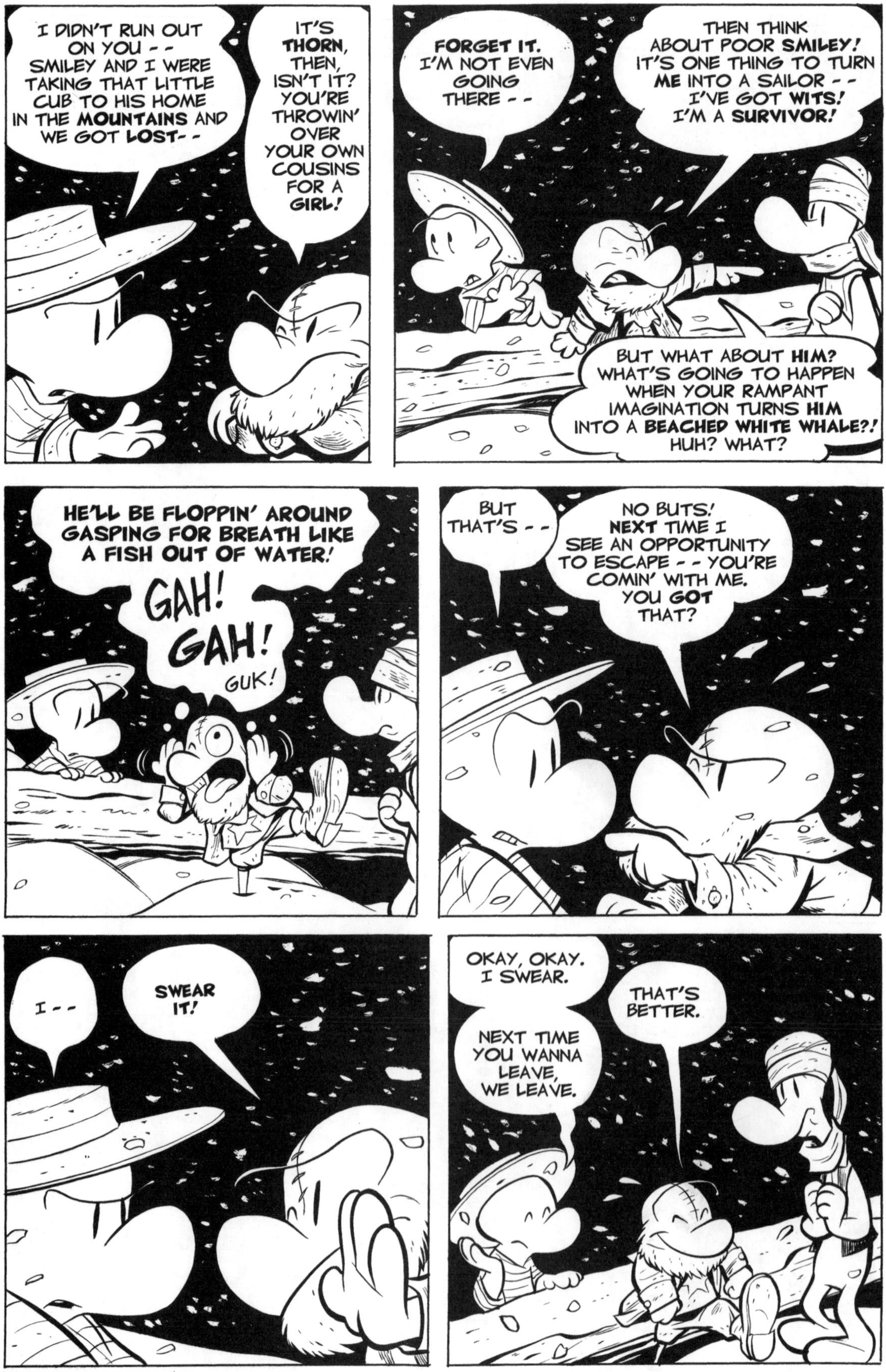
I DIDN'T RUN OUT ON YOU - - SMILEY AND I WERE TAKING THAT LITTLE CUB TO HIS HOME IN THE MOUNTAINS AND WE GOT LOST- -
IT'S THORN, THEN, ISN'T IT? YOU'RE THROWIN' OVER YOUR OWN COUSINS FOR A GIRL!
FORGET IT. I'M NOT EVEN GOING THERE - -
THEN THINK ABOUT POOR SMILEY! IT'S ONE THING TO TURN ME INTO A SAILOR - - I'VE GOT WITS! I'M A SURVIVOR!
BUT WHAT ABOUT HIM? WHAT'S GOING TO HAPPEN WHEN YOUR RAMPANT IMAGINATION TURNS HIM INTO A BEACHED WHITE WHALE?! HUH? WHAT?
HE'LL BE FLOPPIN' AROUND GASPING FOR BREATH LIKE A FISH OUT OF WATER!
GAH! GAH! GUK!
BUT THAT'S - -
NO BUTS! NEXT TIME I SEE AN OPPORTUNITY TO ESCAPE - - YOU'RE COMIN' WITH ME. YOU GOT THAT?
I - -
SWEAR IT!
OKAY, OKAY. I SWEAR.
NEXT TIME YOU WANNA LEAVE, WE LEAVE.
THAT'S BETTER.

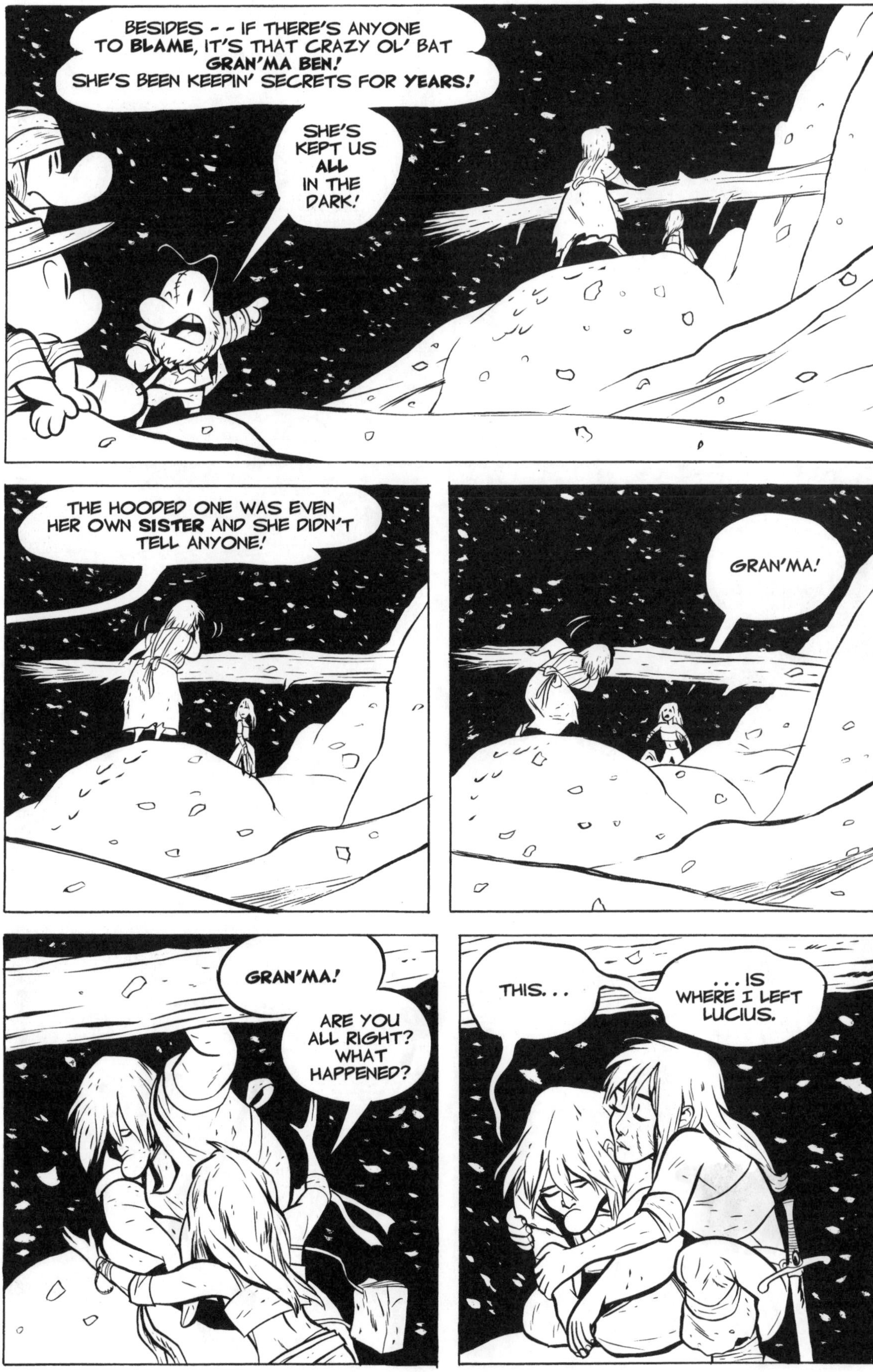
BESIDES - - IF THERE'S ANYONE TO BLAME, IT'S THAT CRAZY OL' BAT GRAN'MA BEN! SHE'S BEEN KEEPIN' SECRETS FOR YEARS!
SHE'S KEPT US ALL IN THE DARK!
THE HOODED ONE WAS EVEN HER OWN SISTER AND SHE DIDN'T TELL ANYONE!
GRAN'MA!
GRAN'MA!
ARE YOU ALL RIGHT? WHAT HAPPENED?
THIS. . .
. . . IS WHERE I LEFT LUCIUS.

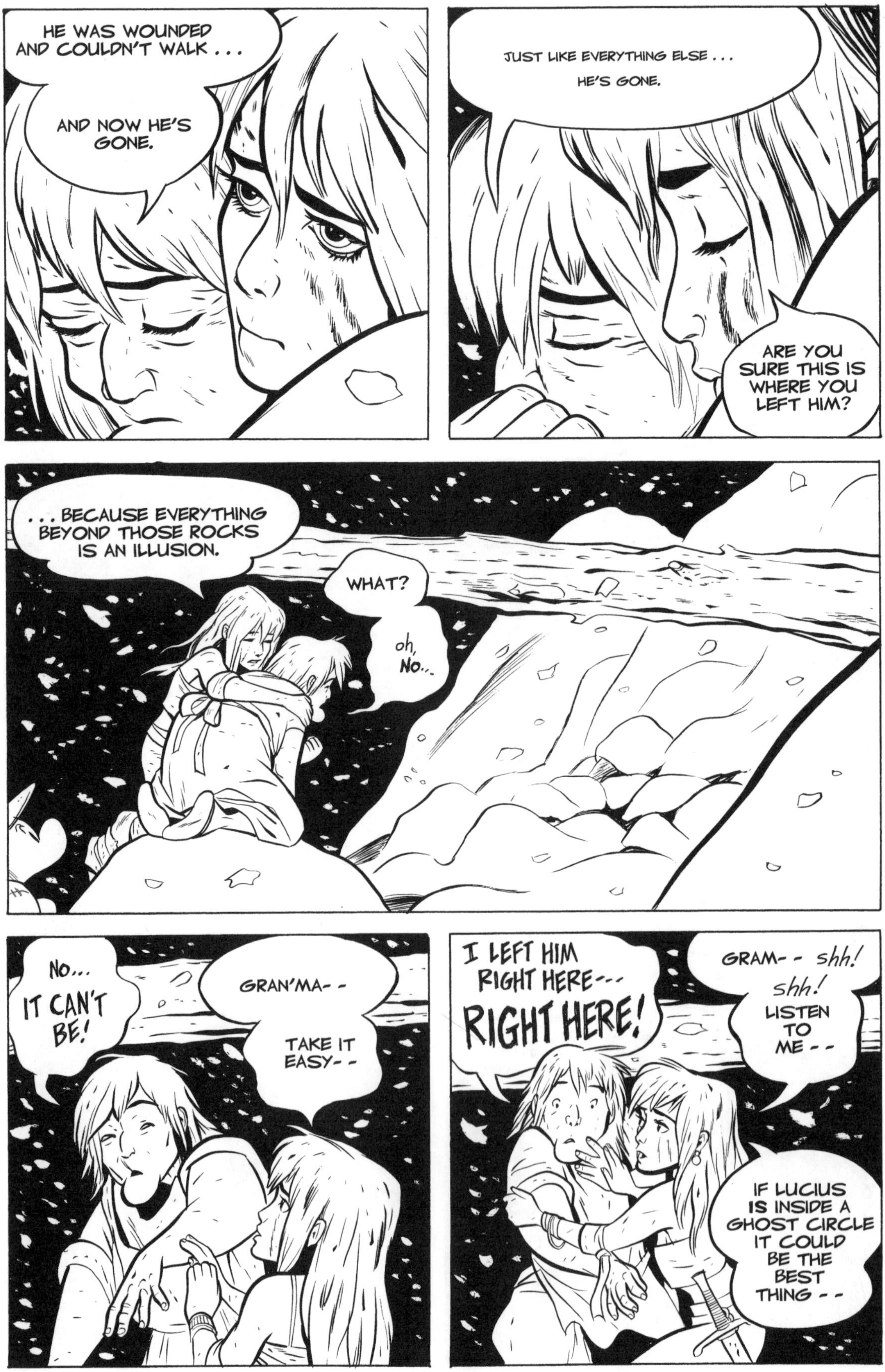
HE WAS WOUNDED AND COULDN'T WALK . . .
AND NOW HE'S GONE.
JUST LIKE EVERYTHING ELSE . . .
HE'S GONE.
ARE YOU SURE THIS IS WHERE YOU LEFT HIM?
. . . BECAUSE EVERYTHING BEYOND THOSE ROCKS IS AN ILLUSION.
WHAT?
oh, NO...
NO... IT CAN'T BE!
GRAN'MA- -
TAKE IT EASY- -
I LEFT HIM RIGHT HERE--- RIGHT HERE!
GRAM- - shh! shh! LISTEN TO ME - -
IF LUCIUS IS INSIDE A GHOST CIRCLE IT COULD BE THE BEST THING - -

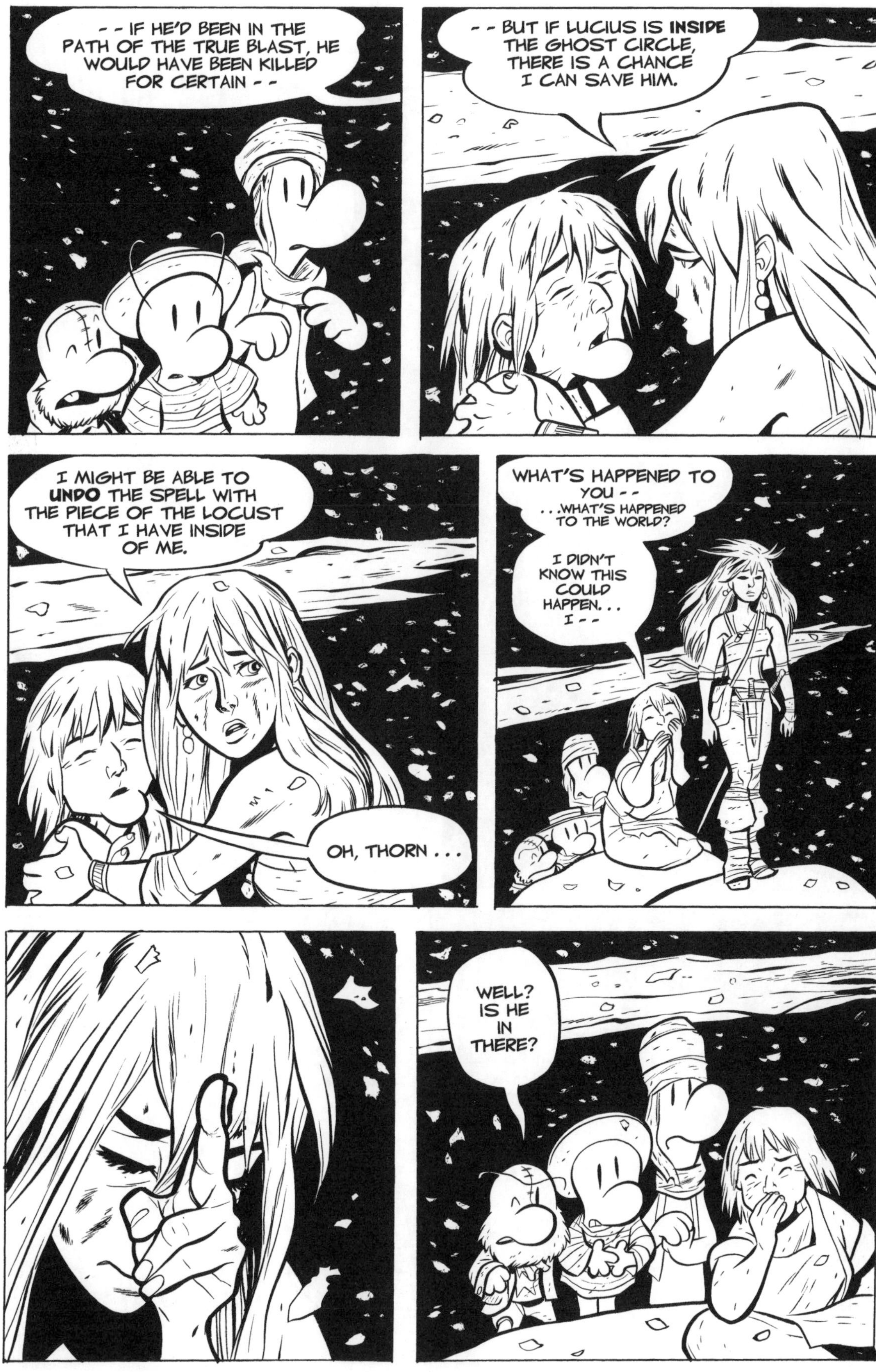
-- IF HE'D BEEN IN THE PATH OF THE TRUE BLAST, HE WOULD HAVE BEEN KILLED FOR CERTAIN --
-- BUT IF LUCIUS IS INSIDE THE GHOST CIRCLE, THERE IS A CHANCE I CAN SAVE HIM.
I MIGHT BE ABLE TO UNDO THE SPELL WITH THE PIECE OF THE LOCUST THAT I HAVE INSIDE OF ME.
OH, THORN...
WHAT'S HAPPENED TO YOU -- ...WHAT'S HAPPENED TO THE WORLD?
I DIDN'T KNOW THIS COULD HAPPEN... I --
WELL? IS HE IN THERE?

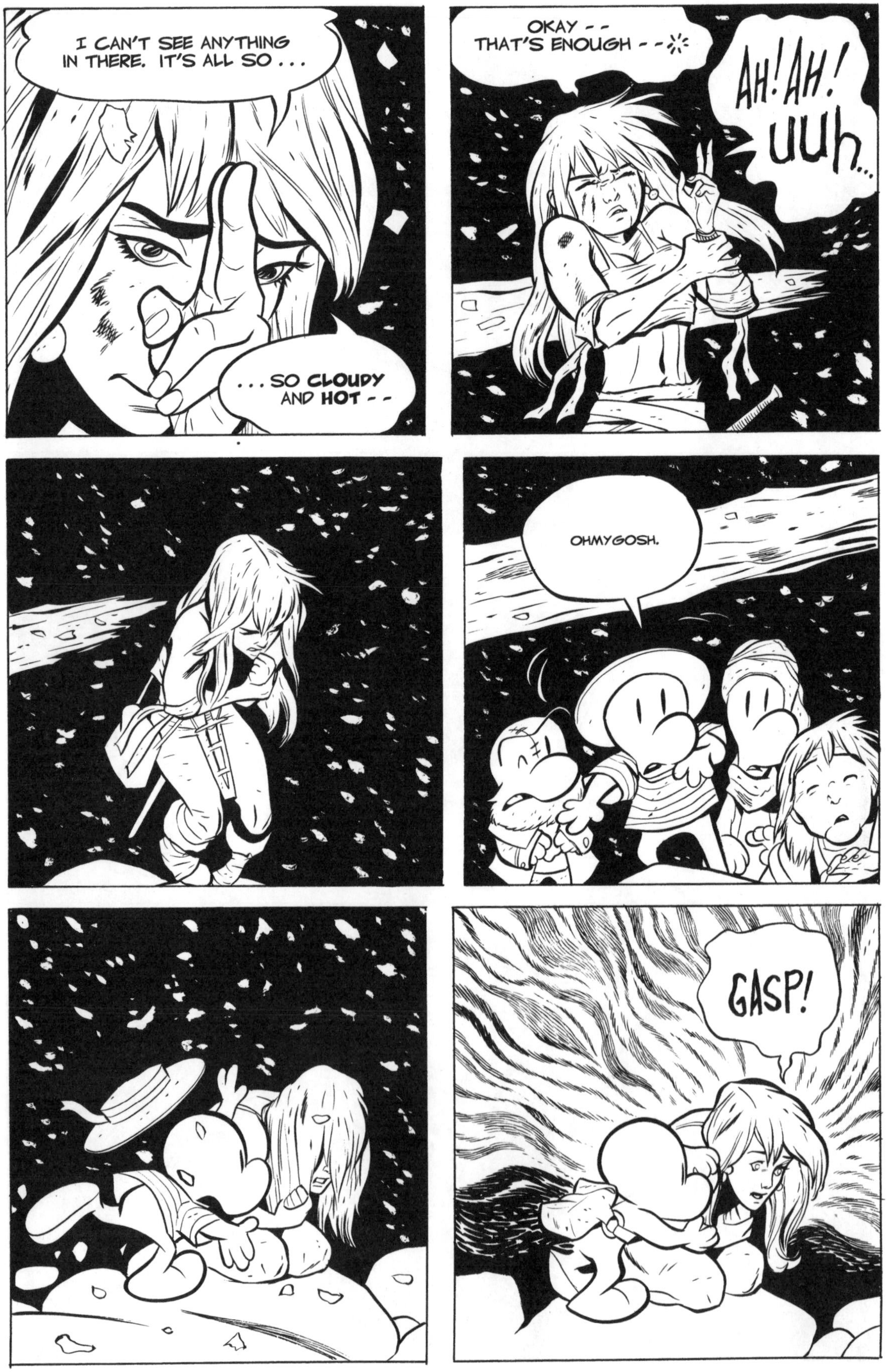
I CAN'T SEE ANYTHING IN THERE. IT'S ALL SO . . .
. . . SO **CLOUDY** AND **HOT** - -
OKAY - - THAT'S ENOUGH - -
AH! AH! uuh...
OHMYGOSH.
GASP!

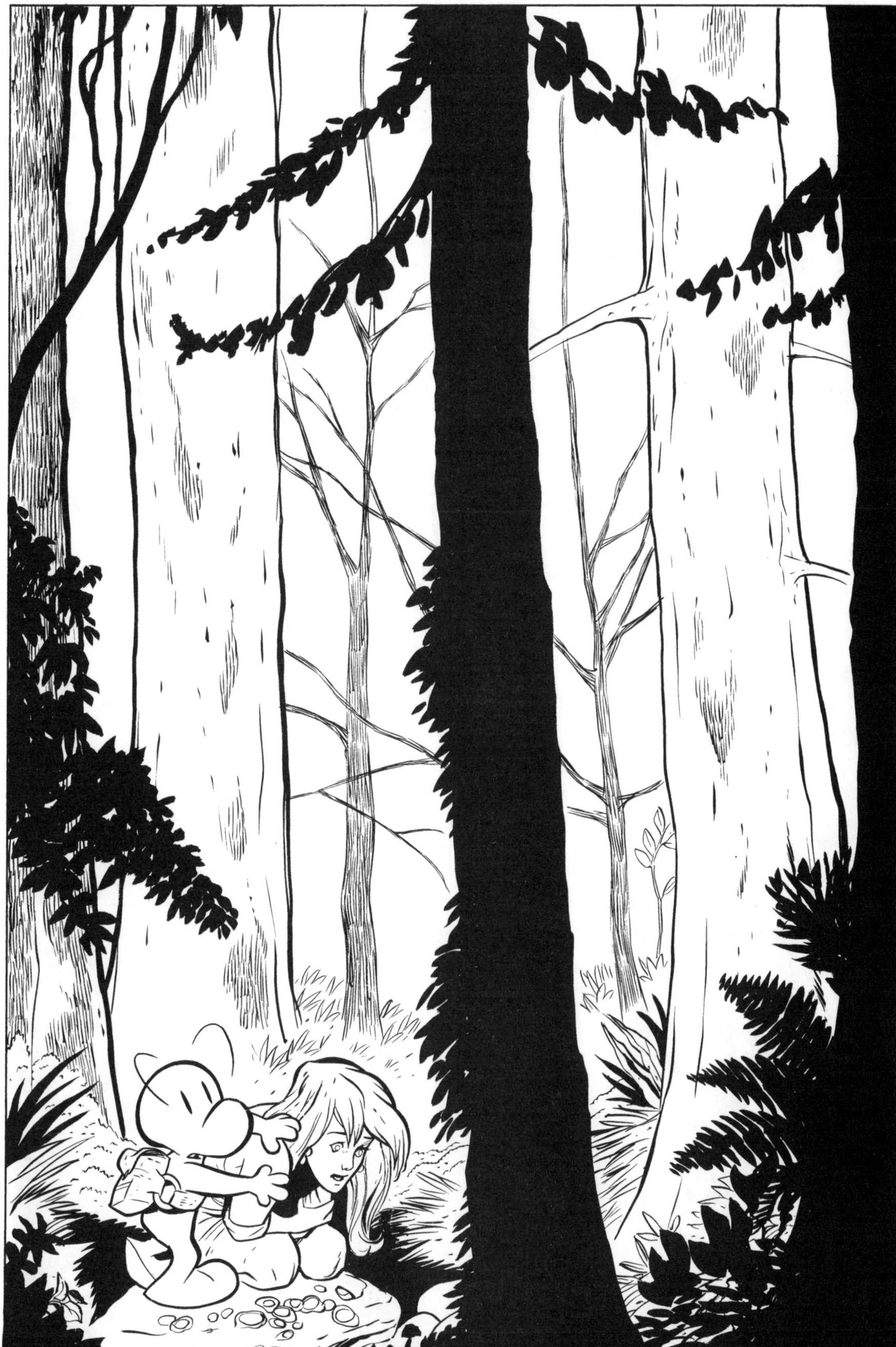

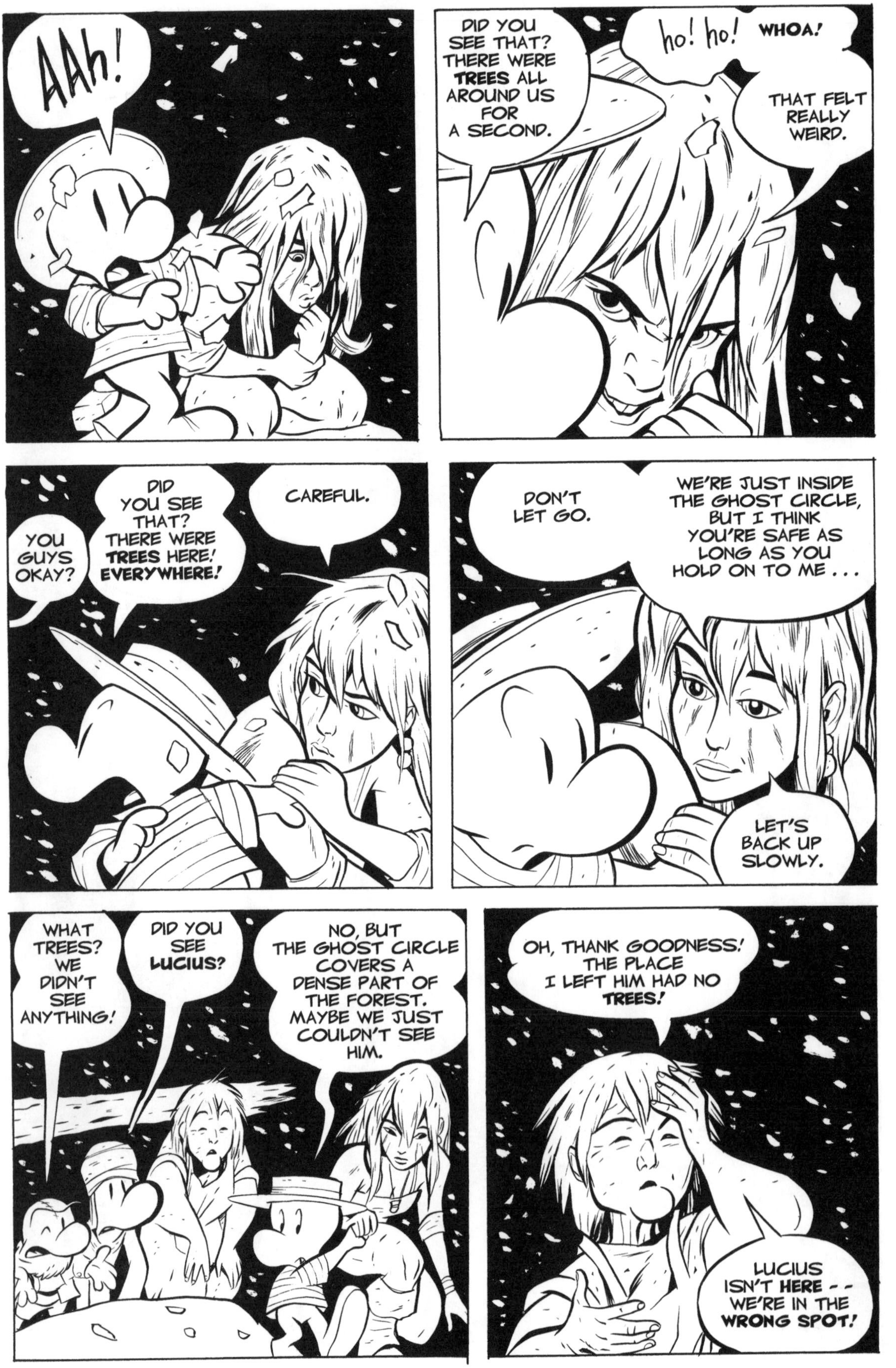
AAh!
DID YOU SEE THAT? THERE WERE TREES ALL AROUND US FOR A SECOND.
ho! ho! WHOA!
THAT FELT REALLY WEIRD.
YOU GUYS OKAY?
DID YOU SEE THAT? THERE WERE TREES HERE! EVERYWHERE!
CAREFUL.
DON'T LET GO.
WE'RE JUST INSIDE THE GHOST CIRCLE, BUT I THINK YOU'RE SAFE AS LONG AS YOU HOLD ON TO ME . . .
LET'S BACK UP SLOWLY.
WHAT TREES? WE DIDN'T SEE ANYTHING!
DID YOU SEE LUCIUS?
NO, BUT THE GHOST CIRCLE COVERS A DENSE PART OF THE FOREST. MAYBE WE JUST COULDN'T SEE HIM.
OH, THANK GOODNESS! THE PLACE I LEFT HIM HAD NO TREES!
LUCIUS ISN'T HERE - - WE'RE IN THE WRONG SPOT!

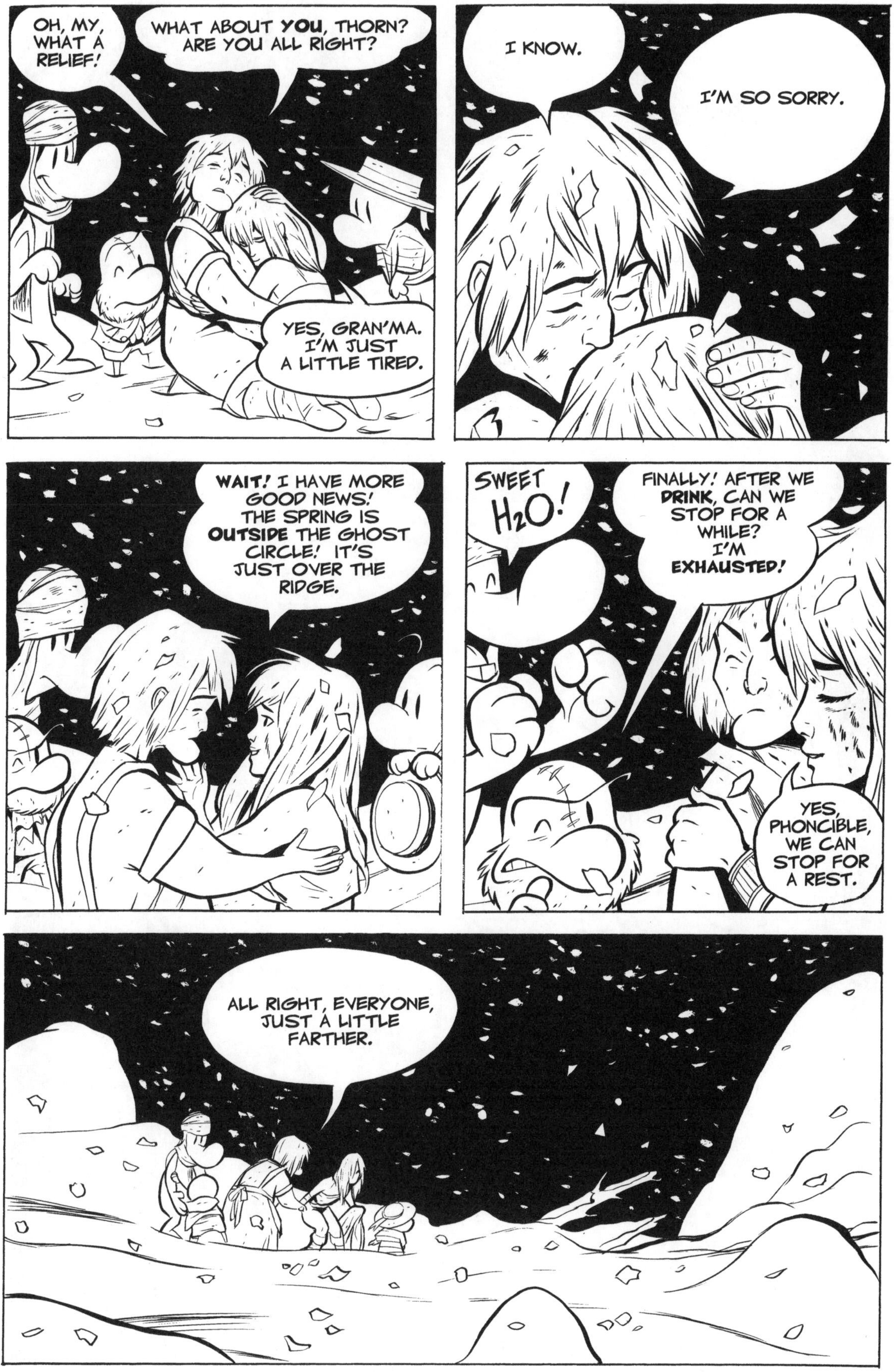
OH, MY, WHAT A RELIEF!
WHAT ABOUT **YOU**, THORN? ARE YOU ALL RIGHT?
YES, GRAN'MA. I'M JUST A LITTLE TIRED.
I KNOW.
I'M SO SORRY.
WAIT! I HAVE MORE GOOD NEWS! THE SPRING IS **OUTSIDE** THE GHOST CIRCLE! IT'S JUST OVER THE RIDGE.
SWEET H2O!
FINALLY! AFTER WE **DRINK**, CAN WE STOP FOR A WHILE? I'M **EXHAUSTED!**
YES, PHONCIBLE, WE CAN STOP FOR A REST.
ALL RIGHT, EVERYONE, JUST A LITTLE FARTHER.

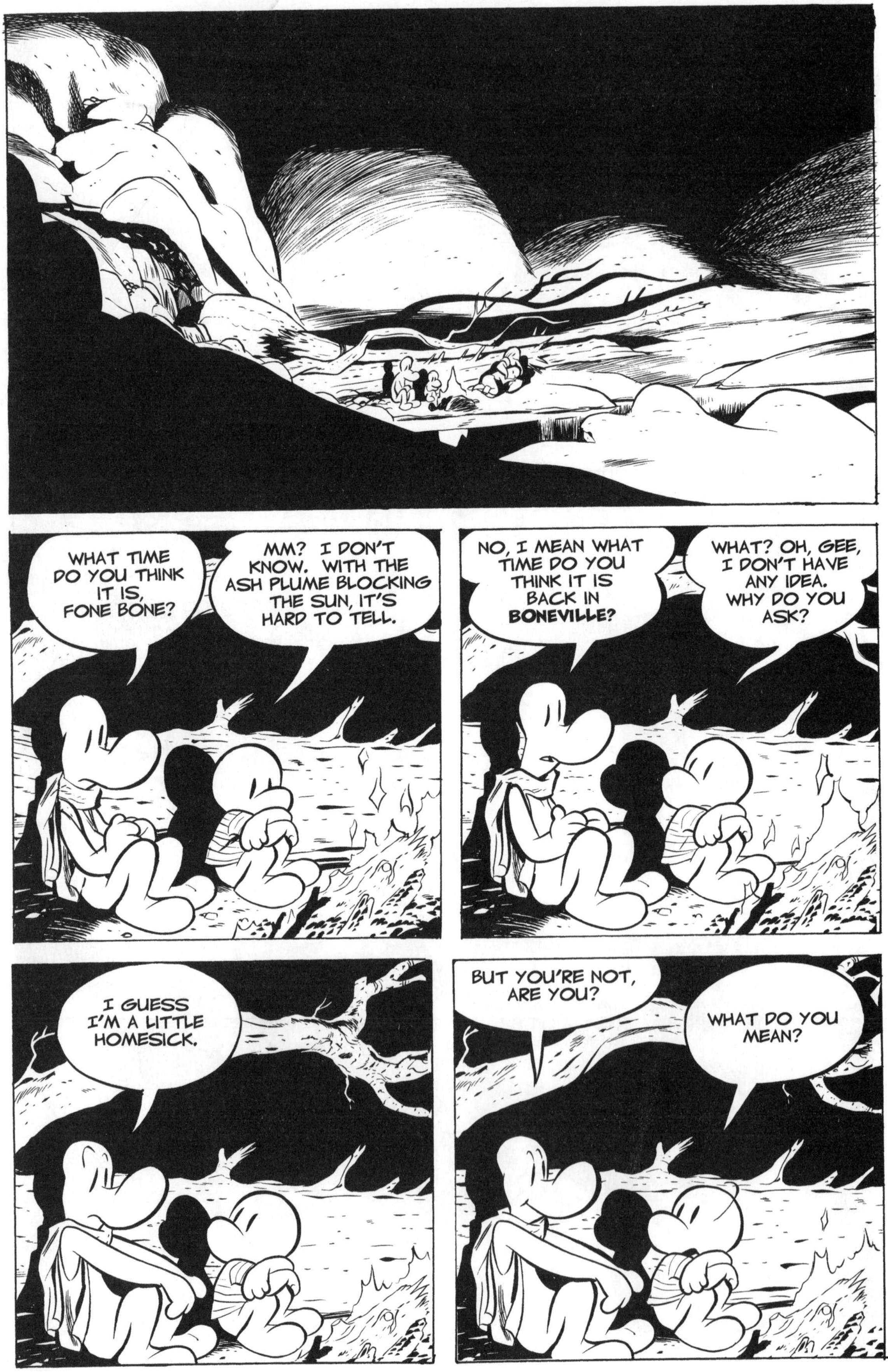
WHAT TIME DO YOU THINK IT IS, FONE BONE?
MM? I DON'T KNOW. WITH THE ASH PLUME BLOCKING THE SUN, IT'S HARD TO TELL.
NO, I MEAN WHAT TIME DO YOU THINK IT IS BACK IN **BONEVILLE?**
WHAT? OH, GEE, I DON'T HAVE ANY IDEA. WHY DO YOU ASK?
I GUESS I'M A LITTLE HOMESICK.
BUT YOU'RE NOT, ARE YOU?
WHAT DO YOU MEAN?

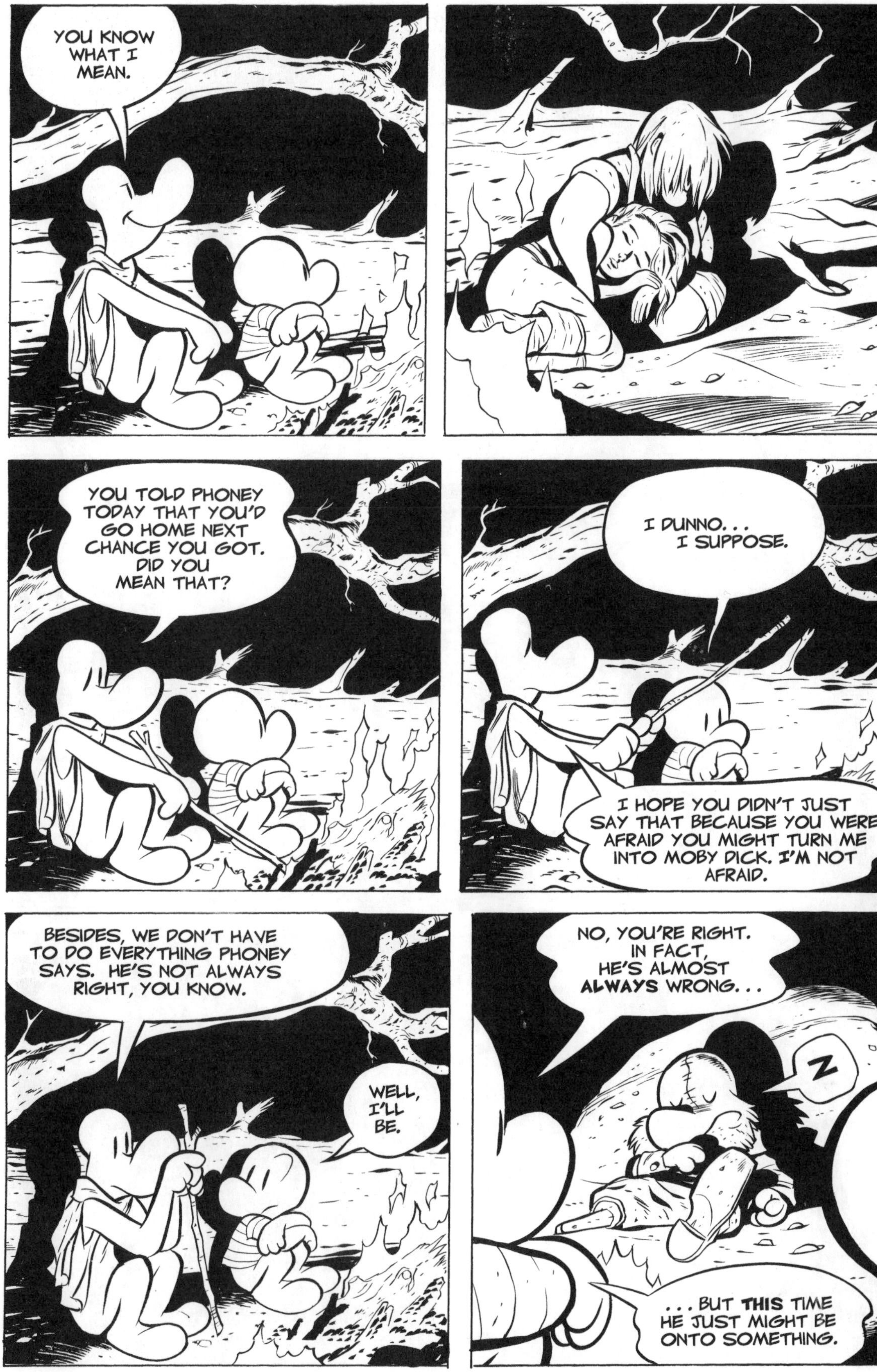
YOU KNOW WHAT I MEAN.
YOU TOLD PHONEY TODAY THAT YOU'D GO HOME NEXT CHANCE YOU GOT. DID YOU MEAN THAT?
I DUNNO... I SUPPOSE.
I HOPE YOU DIDN'T JUST SAY THAT BECAUSE YOU WERE AFRAID YOU MIGHT TURN ME INTO MOBY DICK. I'M NOT AFRAID.
BESIDES, WE DON'T HAVE TO DO EVERYTHING PHONEY SAYS. HE'S NOT ALWAYS RIGHT, YOU KNOW.
WELL, I'LL BE.
NO, YOU'RE RIGHT. IN FACT, HE'S ALMOST ALWAYS WRONG...
Z
...BUT THIS TIME HE JUST MIGHT BE ONTO SOMETHING.

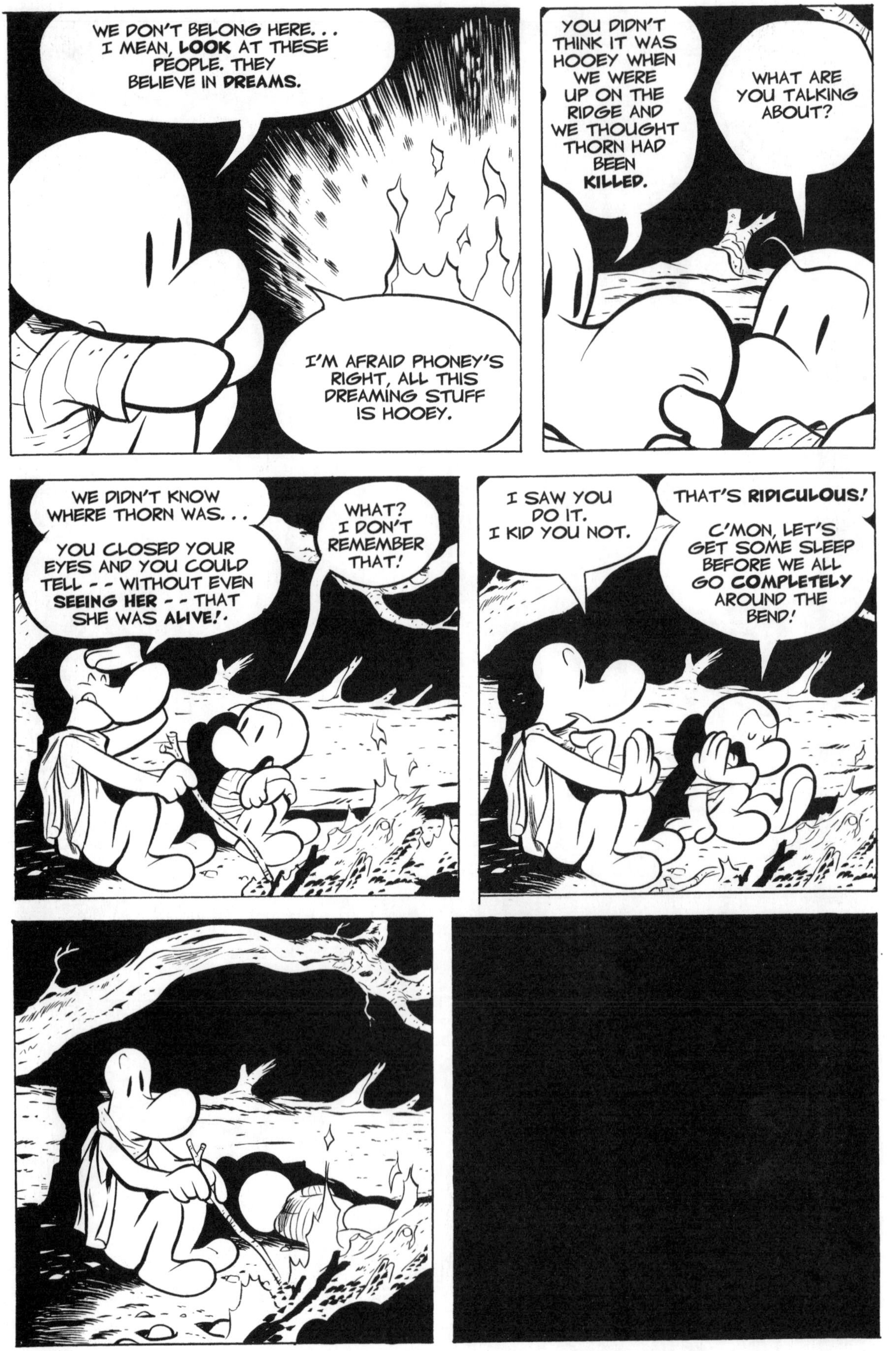
WE DON'T BELONG HERE. . . I MEAN, **LOOK** AT THESE PEOPLE. THEY BELIEVE IN **DREAMS.**
I'M AFRAID PHONEY'S RIGHT, ALL THIS DREAMING STUFF IS HOOEY.
YOU DIDN'T THINK IT WAS HOOEY WHEN WE WERE UP ON THE RIDGE AND WE THOUGHT THORN HAD BEEN **KILLED.**
WHAT ARE YOU TALKING ABOUT?
WE DIDN'T KNOW WHERE THORN WAS. . .
YOU CLOSED YOUR EYES AND YOU COULD TELL - - WITHOUT EVEN **SEEING HER** - - THAT SHE WAS **ALIVE!**.
WHAT? I DON'T REMEMBER THAT!
I SAW YOU DO IT. I KID YOU NOT.
THAT'S **RIDICULOUS!**
C'MON, LET'S GET SOME SLEEP BEFORE WE ALL GO **COMPLETELY** AROUND THE BEND!

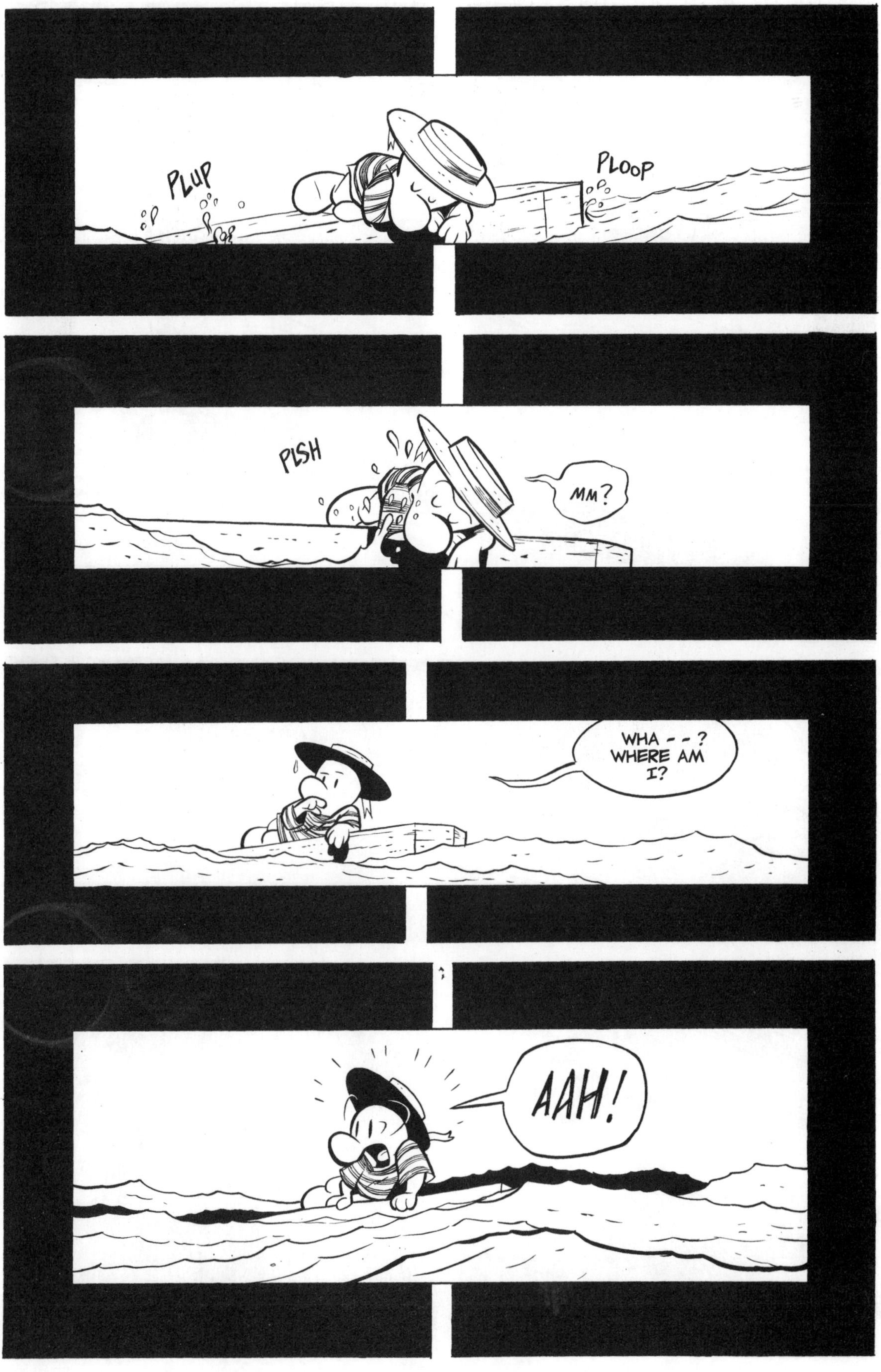
PLUP
PLOOP
PLSH
MM?
WHA - - ? WHERE AM I?
AAH!

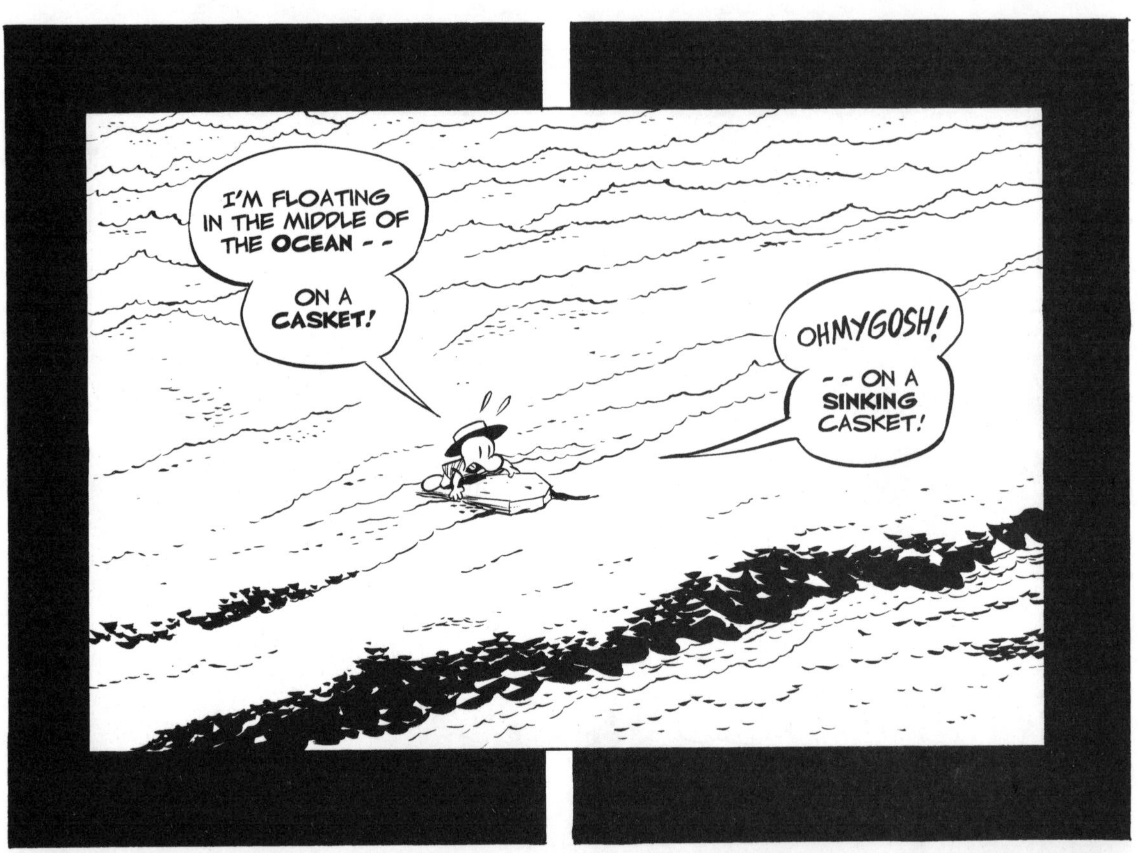
I'M FLOATING IN THE MIDDLE OF THE OCEAN - -
ON A CASKET!
OHMYGOSH!
- - ON A SINKING CASKET!
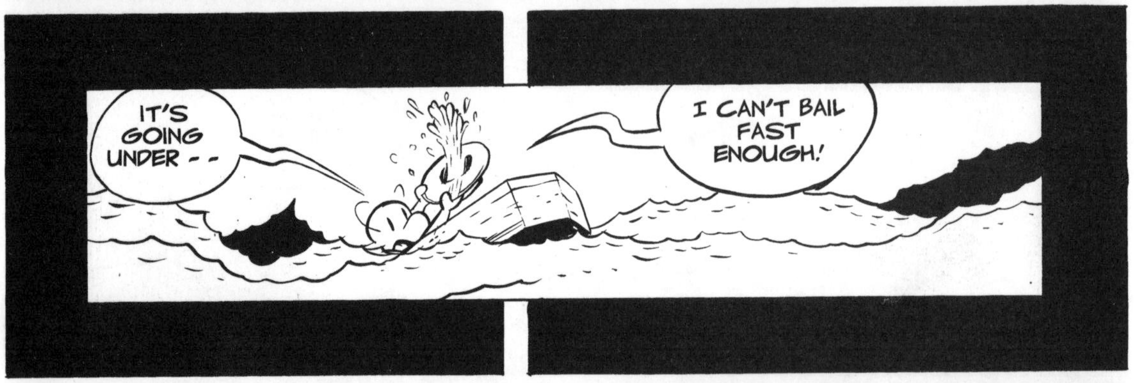
IT'S GOING UNDER - -
I CAN'T BAIL FAST ENOUGH!
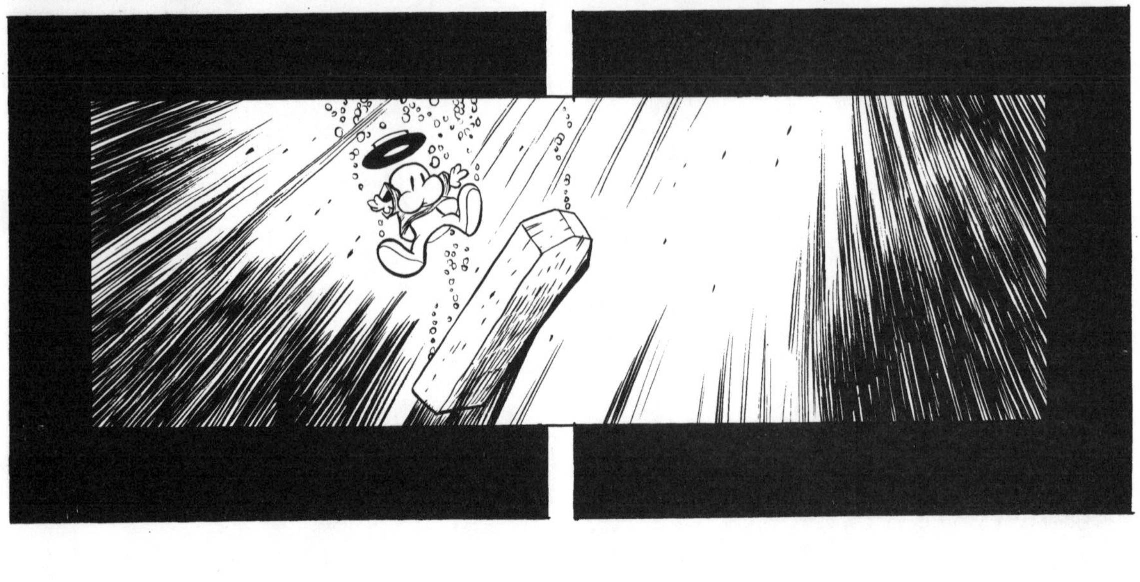

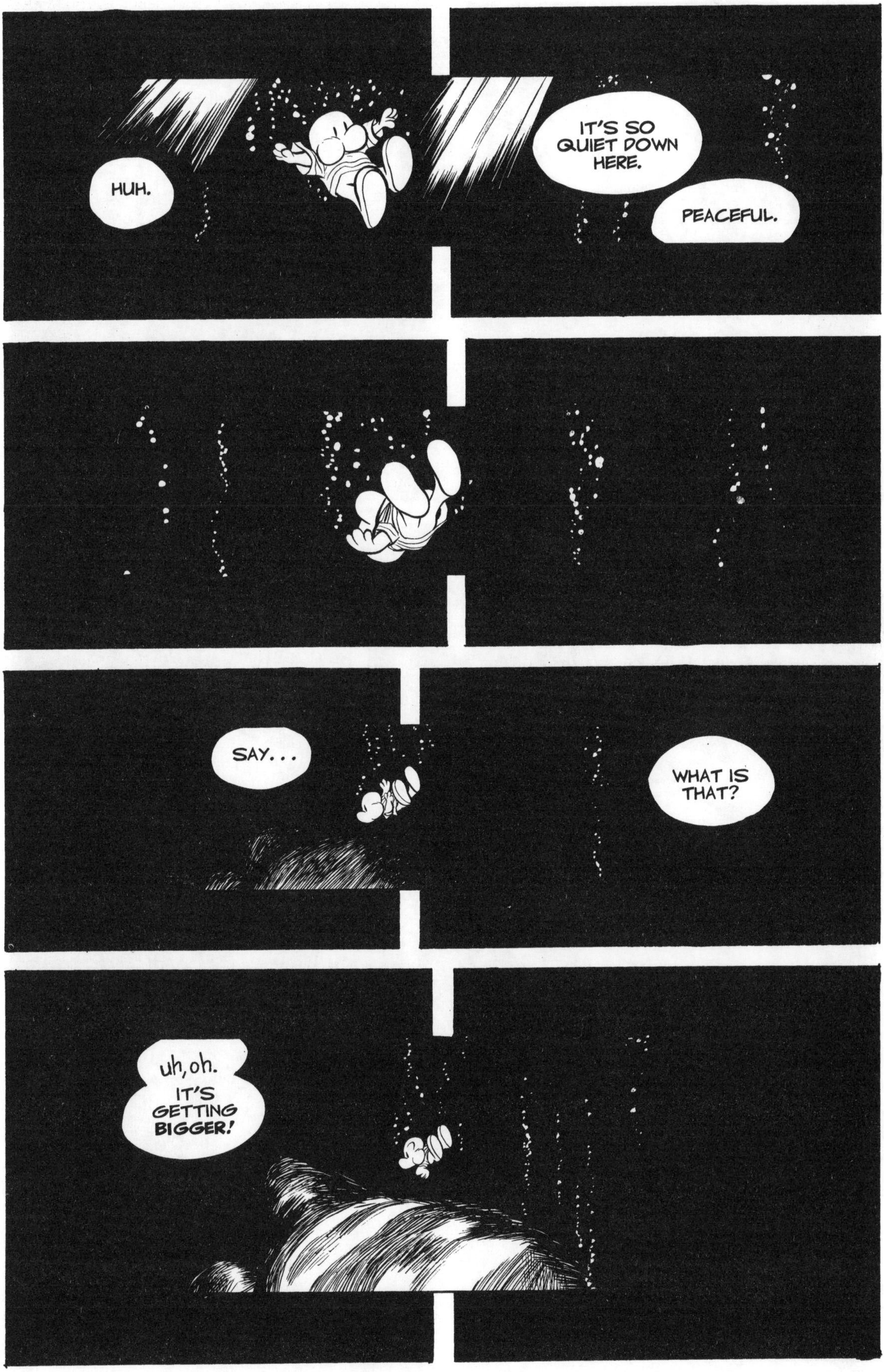
HUH.
IT'S SO QUIET DOWN HERE.
PEACEFUL.
SAY...
WHAT IS THAT?
uh, oh. IT'S GETTING BIGGER!

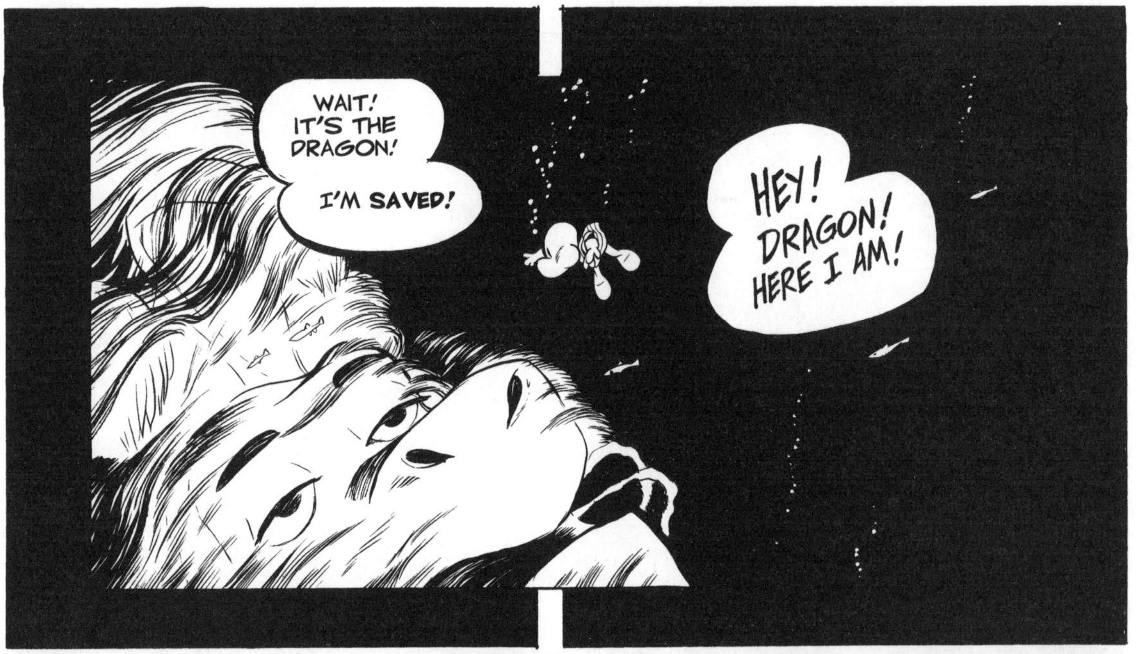
WAIT! IT'S THE DRAGON!
I'M SAVED!
HEY! DRAGON! HERE I AM!

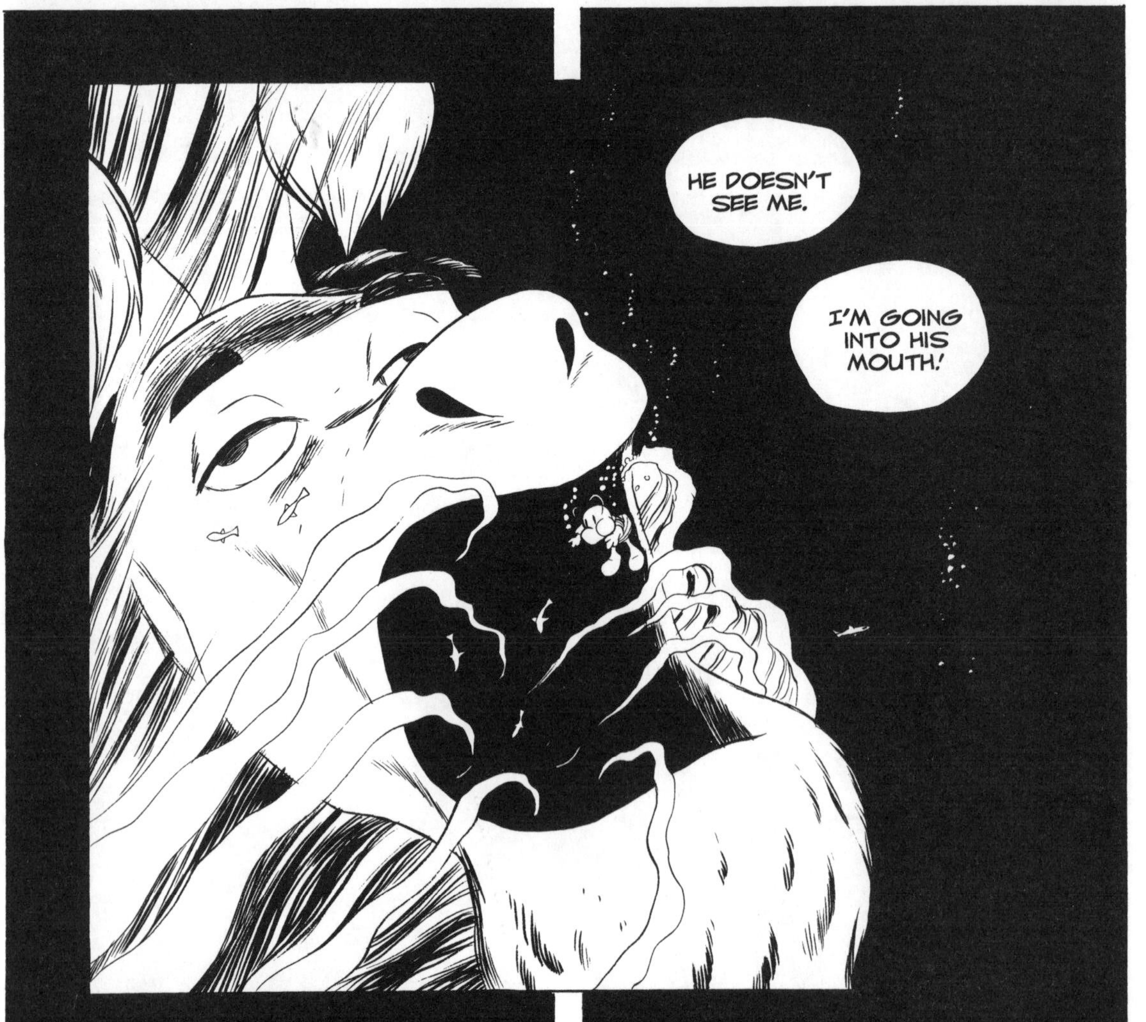
HE DOESN'T SEE ME.
I'M GOING INTO HIS MOUTH!

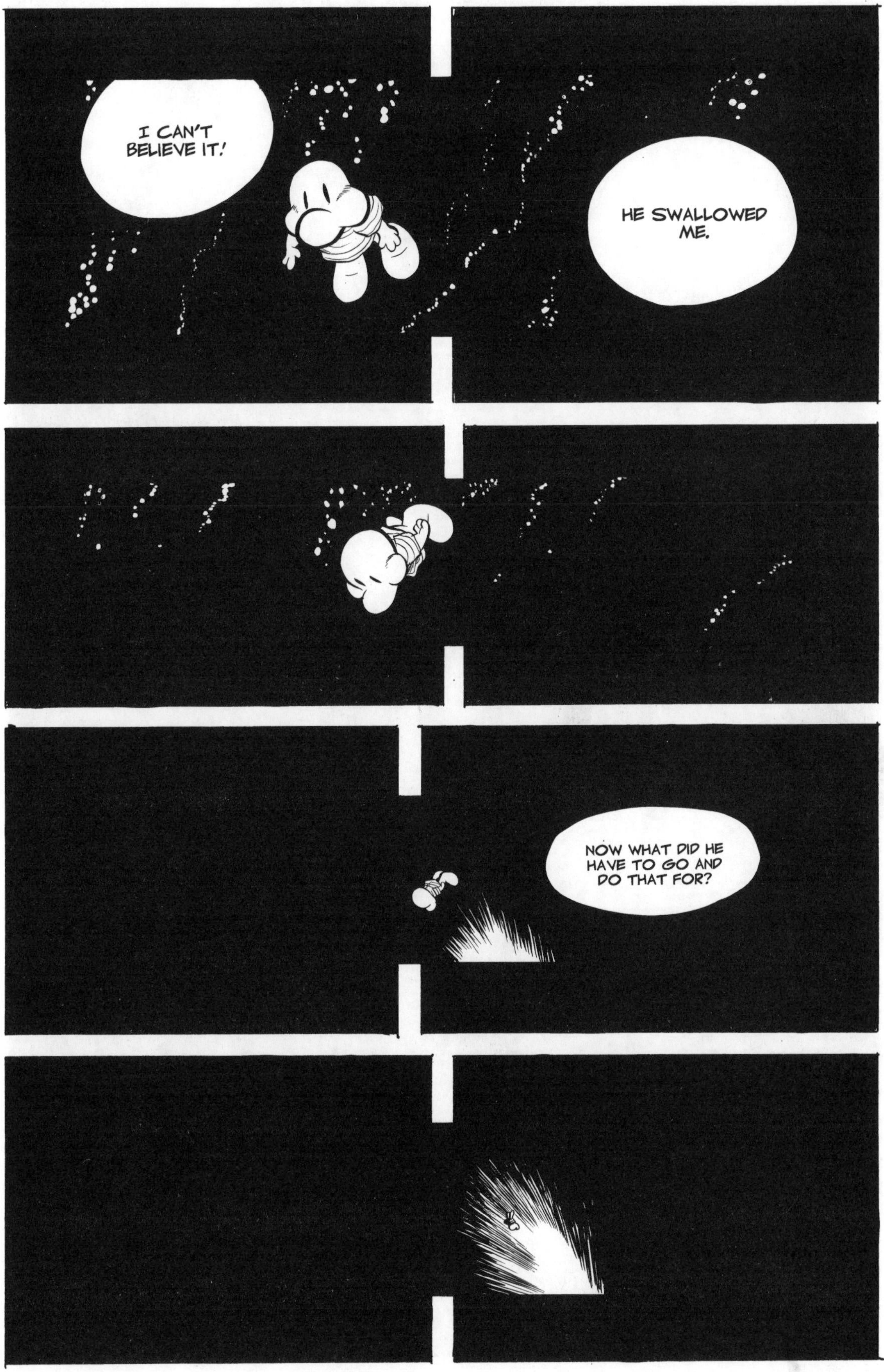
I CAN'T BELIEVE IT!
HE SWALLOWED ME.
NOW WHAT DID HE HAVE TO GO AND DO THAT FOR?

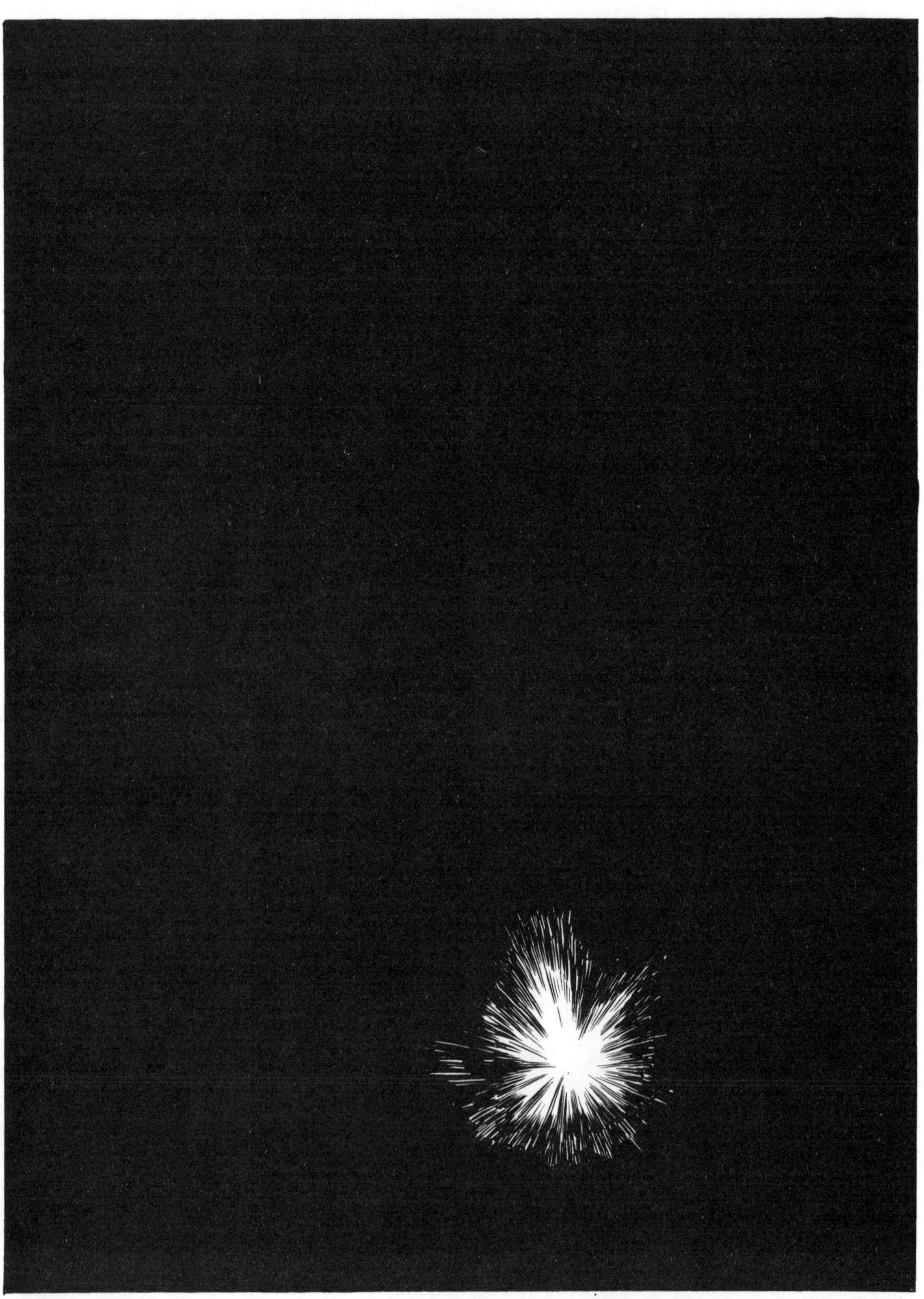

NEXT: A LITTLE NIGHT MUSIC

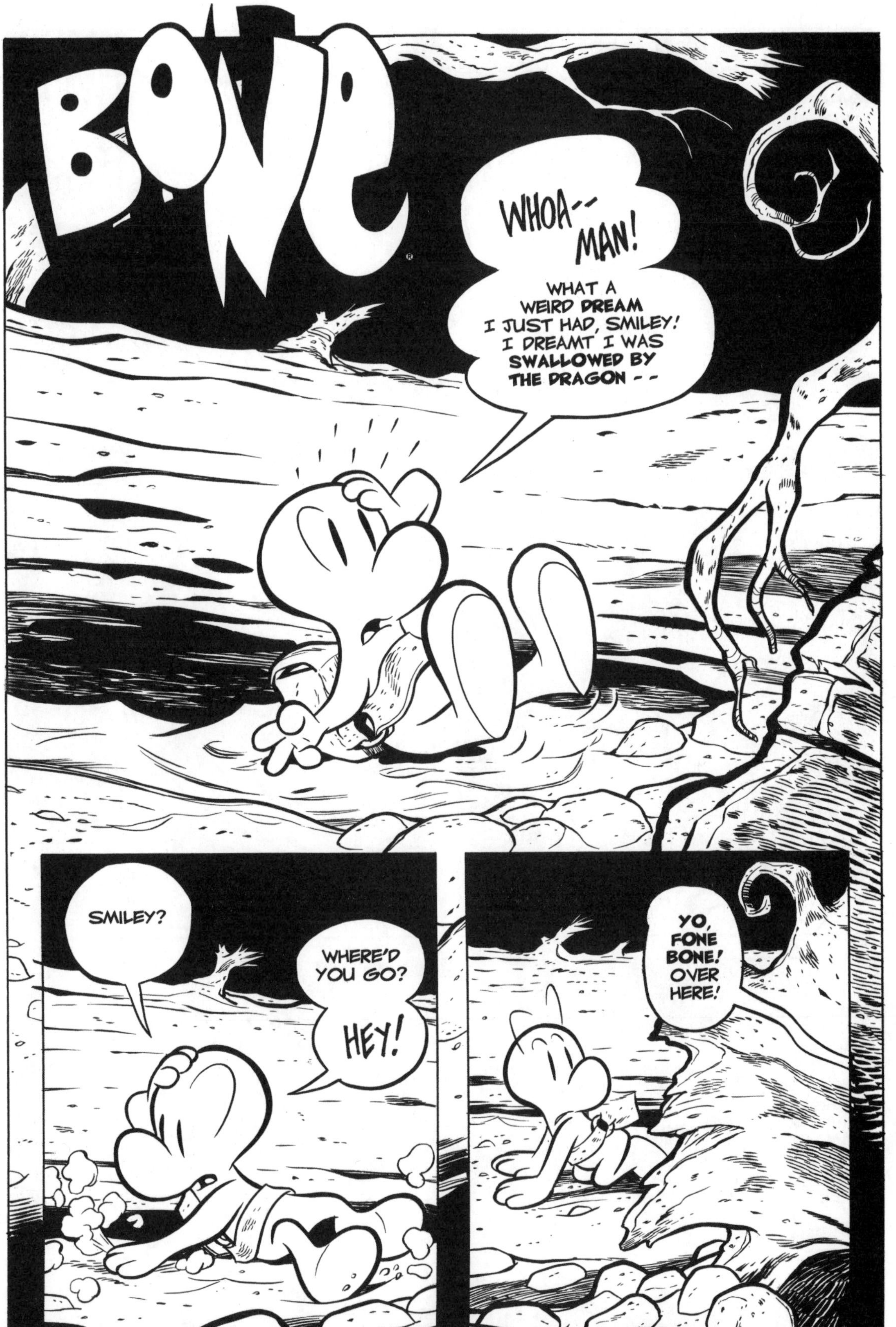
BONE®
WHOA-- MAN!
WHAT A WEIRD DREAM I JUST HAD, SMILEY! I DREAMT I WAS SWALLOWED BY THE DRAGON --
SMILEY?
WHERE'D YOU GO?
HEY!
YO, FONE BONE! OVER HERE!

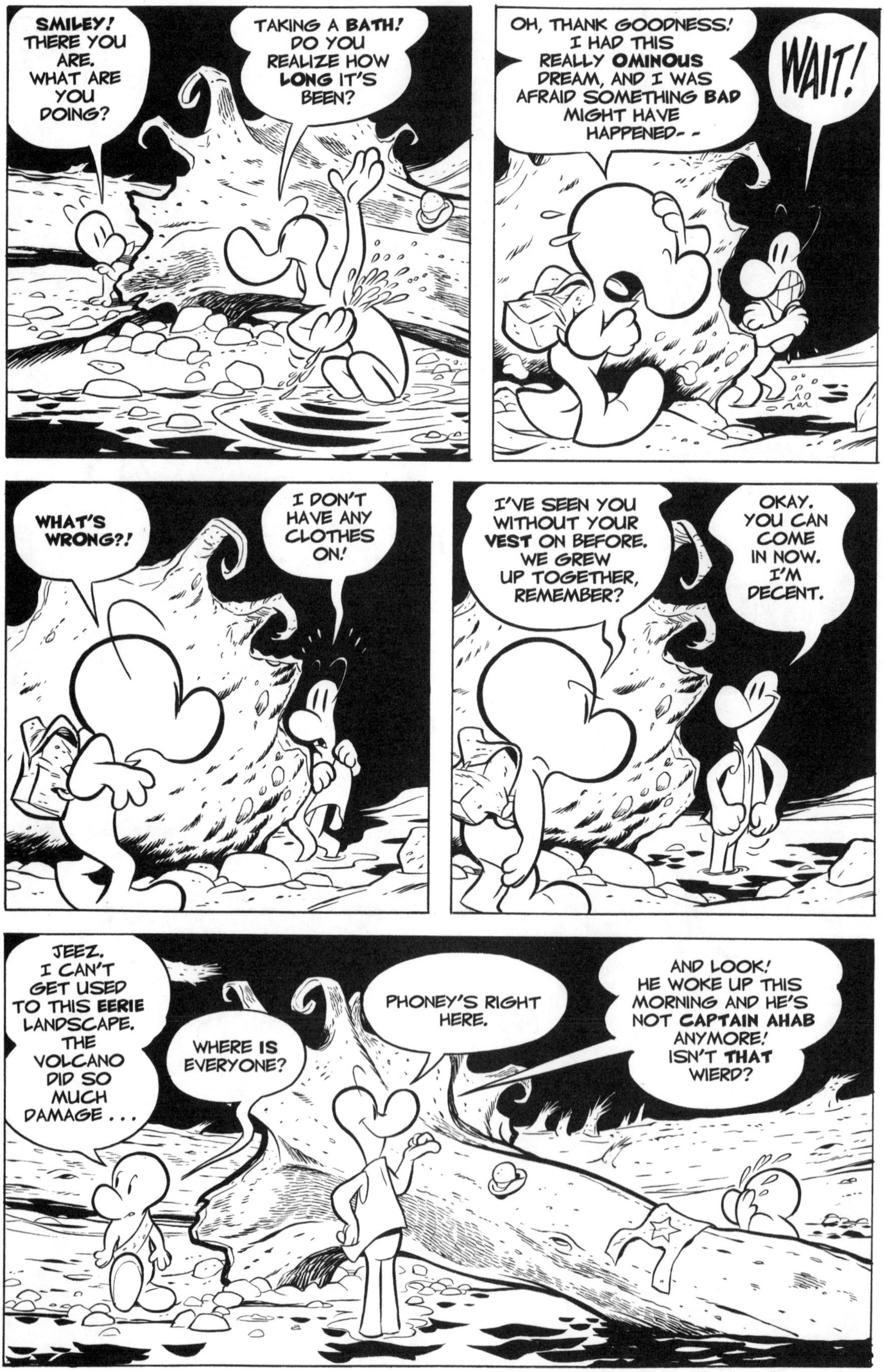
SMILEY! THERE YOU ARE. WHAT ARE YOU DOING?
TAKING A BATH! DO YOU REALIZE HOW LONG IT'S BEEN?
OH, THANK GOODNESS! I HAD THIS REALLY OMINOUS DREAM, AND I WAS AFRAID SOMETHING BAD MIGHT HAVE HAPPENED- -
WAIT!
WHAT'S WRONG?!
I DON'T HAVE ANY CLOTHES ON!
I'VE SEEN YOU WITHOUT YOUR VEST ON BEFORE. WE GREW UP TOGETHER, REMEMBER?
OKAY. YOU CAN COME IN NOW. I'M DECENT.
JEEZ. I CAN'T GET USED TO THIS EERIE LANDSCAPE. THE VOLCANO DID SO MUCH DAMAGE . . .
WHERE IS EVERYONE?
PHONEY'S RIGHT HERE.
AND LOOK! HE WOKE UP THIS MORNING AND HE'S NOT CAPTAIN AHAB ANYMORE! ISN'T THAT WIERD?

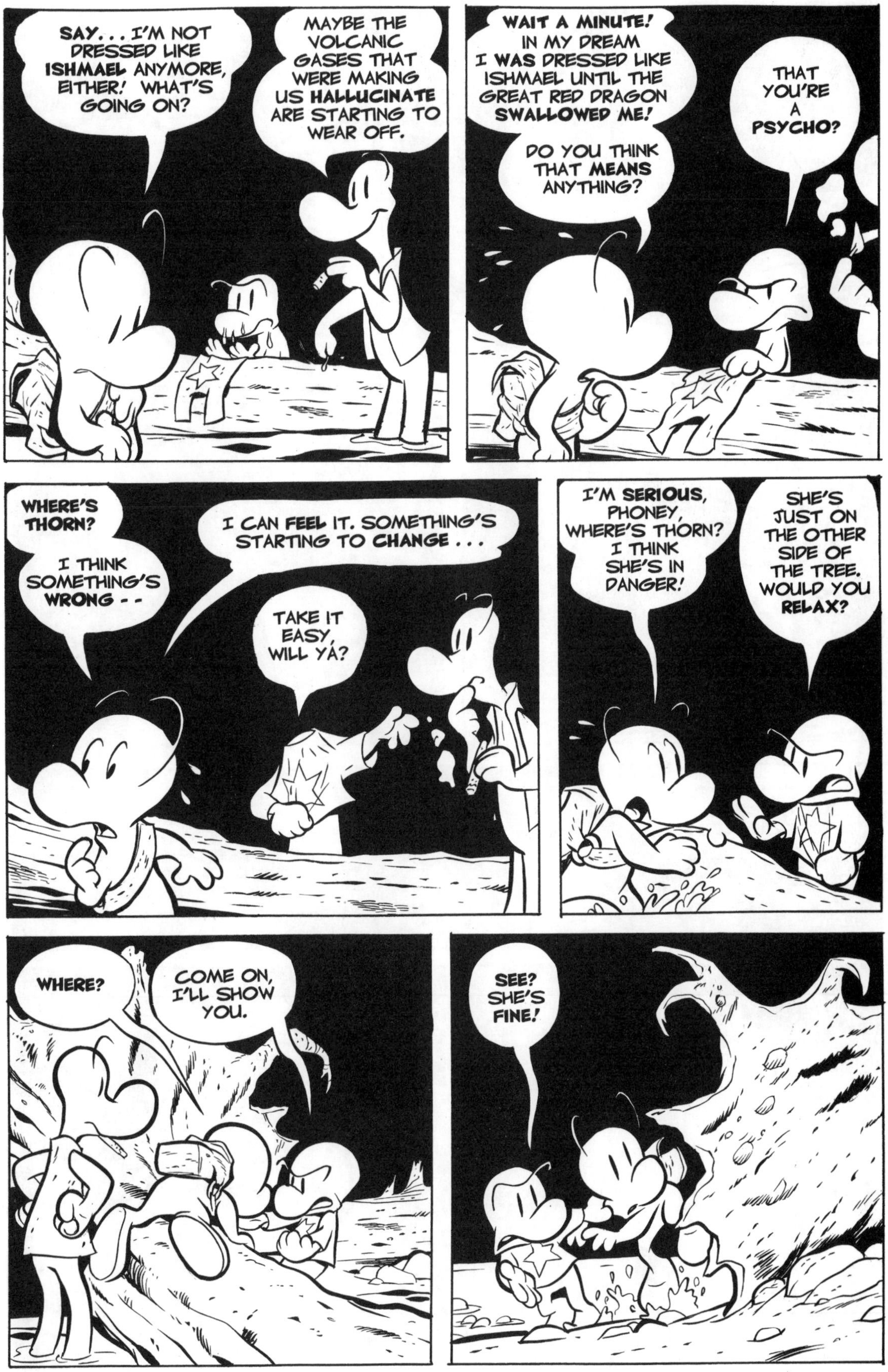
SAY... I'M NOT DRESSED LIKE ISHMAEL ANYMORE, EITHER! WHAT'S GOING ON?
MAYBE THE VOLCANIC GASES THAT WERE MAKING US HALLUCINATE ARE STARTING TO WEAR OFF.
WAIT A MINUTE! IN MY DREAM I WAS DRESSED LIKE ISHMAEL UNTIL THE GREAT RED DRAGON SWALLOWED ME!
DO YOU THINK THAT MEANS ANYTHING?
THAT YOU'RE A PSYCHO?
WHERE'S THORN?
I THINK SOMETHING'S WRONG --
I CAN FEEL IT. SOMETHING'S STARTING TO CHANGE...
TAKE IT EASY, WILL YA?
I'M SERIOUS, PHONEY, WHERE'S THORN? I THINK SHE'S IN DANGER!
SHE'S JUST ON THE OTHER SIDE OF THE TREE. WOULD YOU RELAX?
WHERE?
COME ON, I'LL SHOW YOU.
SEE? SHE'S FINE!

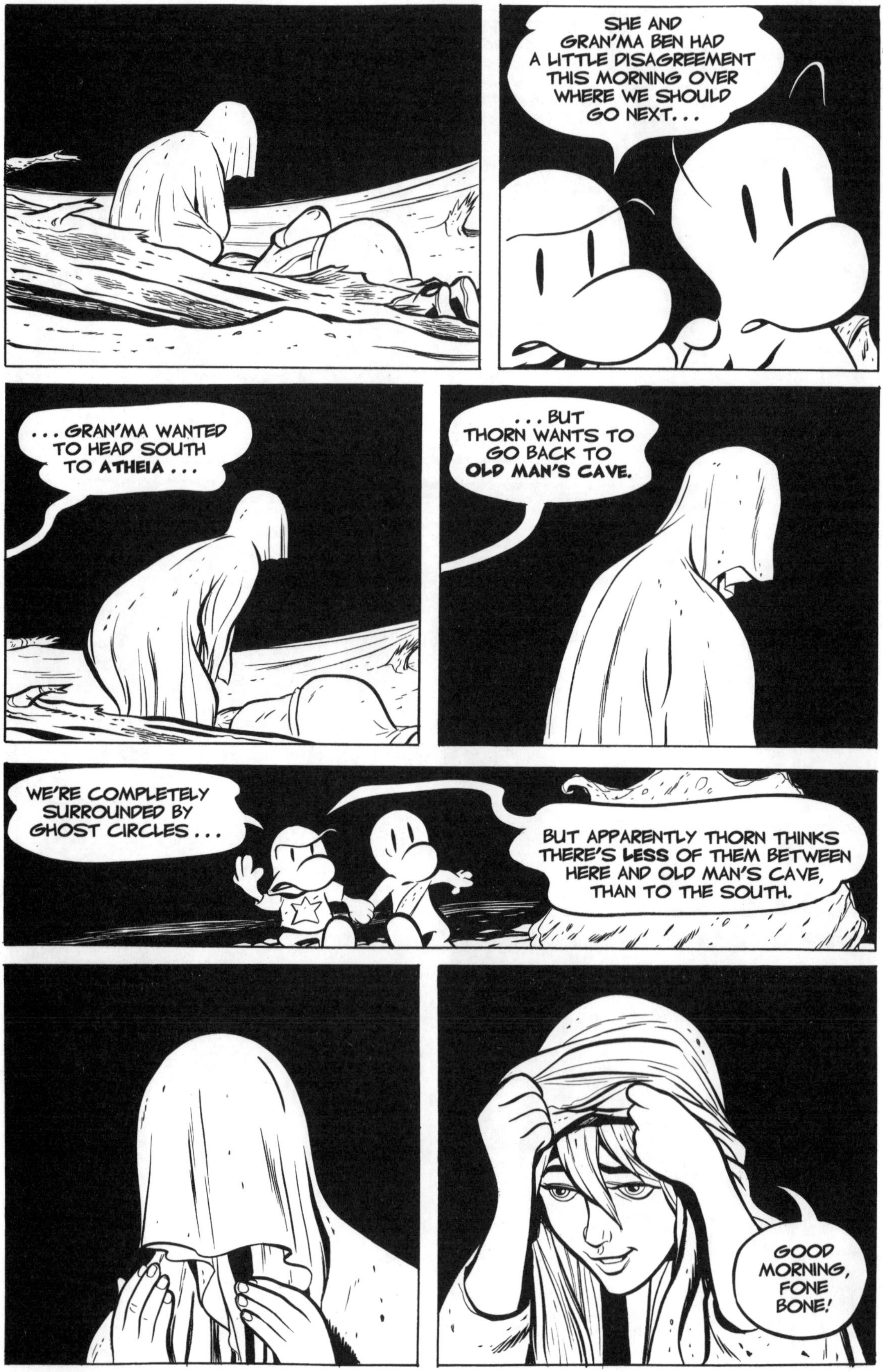
SHE AND GRAN'MA BEN HAD A LITTLE DISAGREEMENT THIS MORNING OVER WHERE WE SHOULD GO NEXT...
...GRAN'MA WANTED TO HEAD SOUTH TO ATHEIA...
...BUT THORN WANTS TO GO BACK TO OLD MAN'S CAVE.
WE'RE COMPLETELY SURROUNDED BY GHOST CIRCLES...
BUT APPARENTLY THORN THINKS THERE'S LESS OF THEM BETWEEN HERE AND OLD MAN'S CAVE, THAN TO THE SOUTH.
GOOD MORNING, FONE BONE!

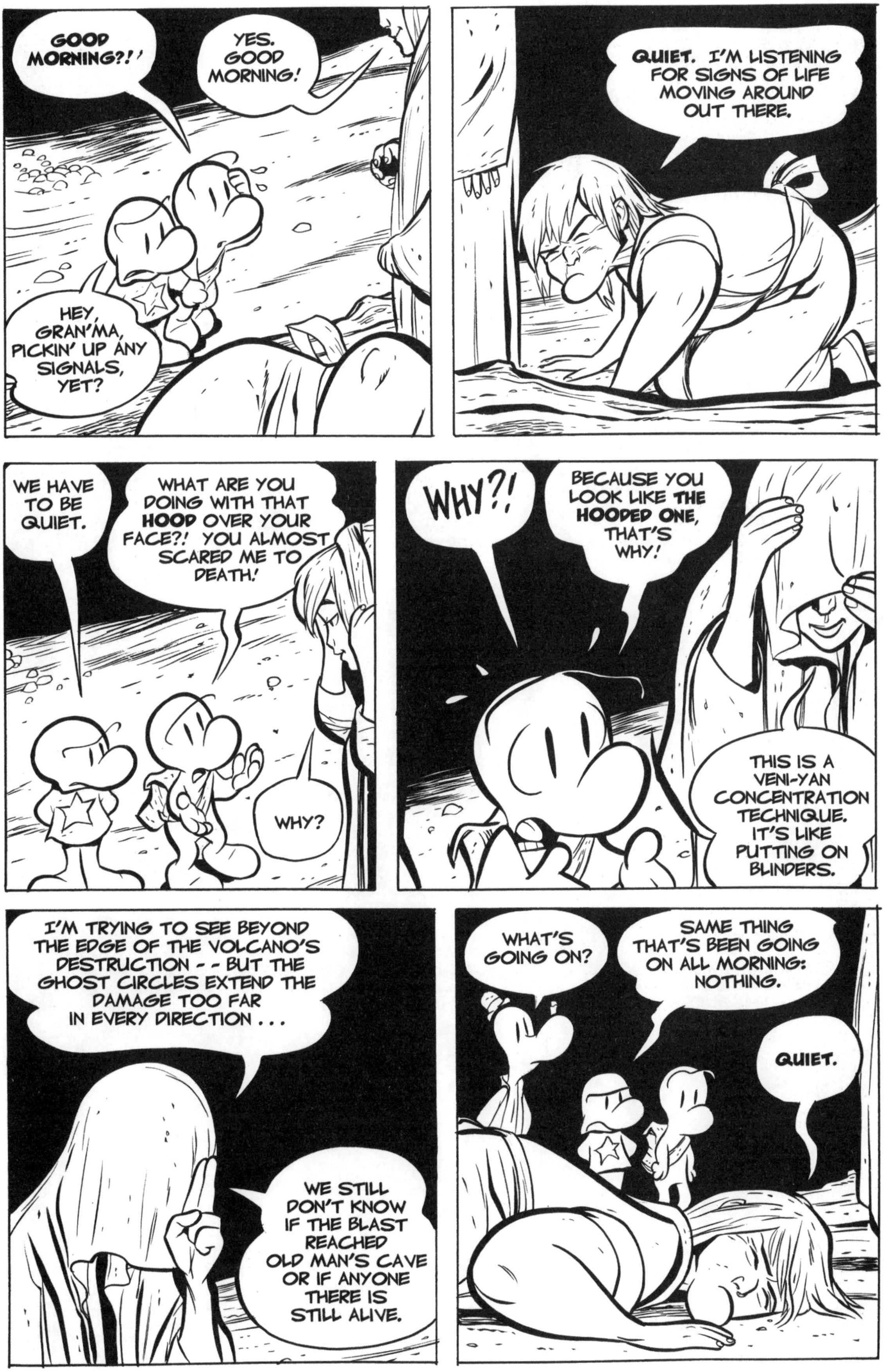
GOOD MORNING?!
YES. GOOD MORNING!
HEY, GRAN'MA, PICKIN' UP ANY SIGNALS, YET?
QUIET. I'M LISTENING FOR SIGNS OF LIFE MOVING AROUND OUT THERE.
WE HAVE TO BE QUIET.
WHAT ARE YOU DOING WITH THAT HOOD OVER YOUR FACE?! YOU ALMOST SCARED ME TO DEATH!
WHY?
WHY?!
BECAUSE YOU LOOK LIKE THE HOODED ONE, THAT'S WHY!
THIS IS A VENI-YAN CONCENTRATION TECHNIQUE. IT'S LIKE PUTTING ON BLINDERS.
I'M TRYING TO SEE BEYOND THE EDGE OF THE VOLCANO'S DESTRUCTION - - BUT THE GHOST CIRCLES EXTEND THE DAMAGE TOO FAR IN EVERY DIRECTION . . .
WE STILL DON'T KNOW IF THE BLAST REACHED OLD MAN'S CAVE OR IF ANYONE THERE IS STILL ALIVE.
WHAT'S GOING ON?
SAME THING THAT'S BEEN GOING ON ALL MORNING: NOTHING.
QUIET.

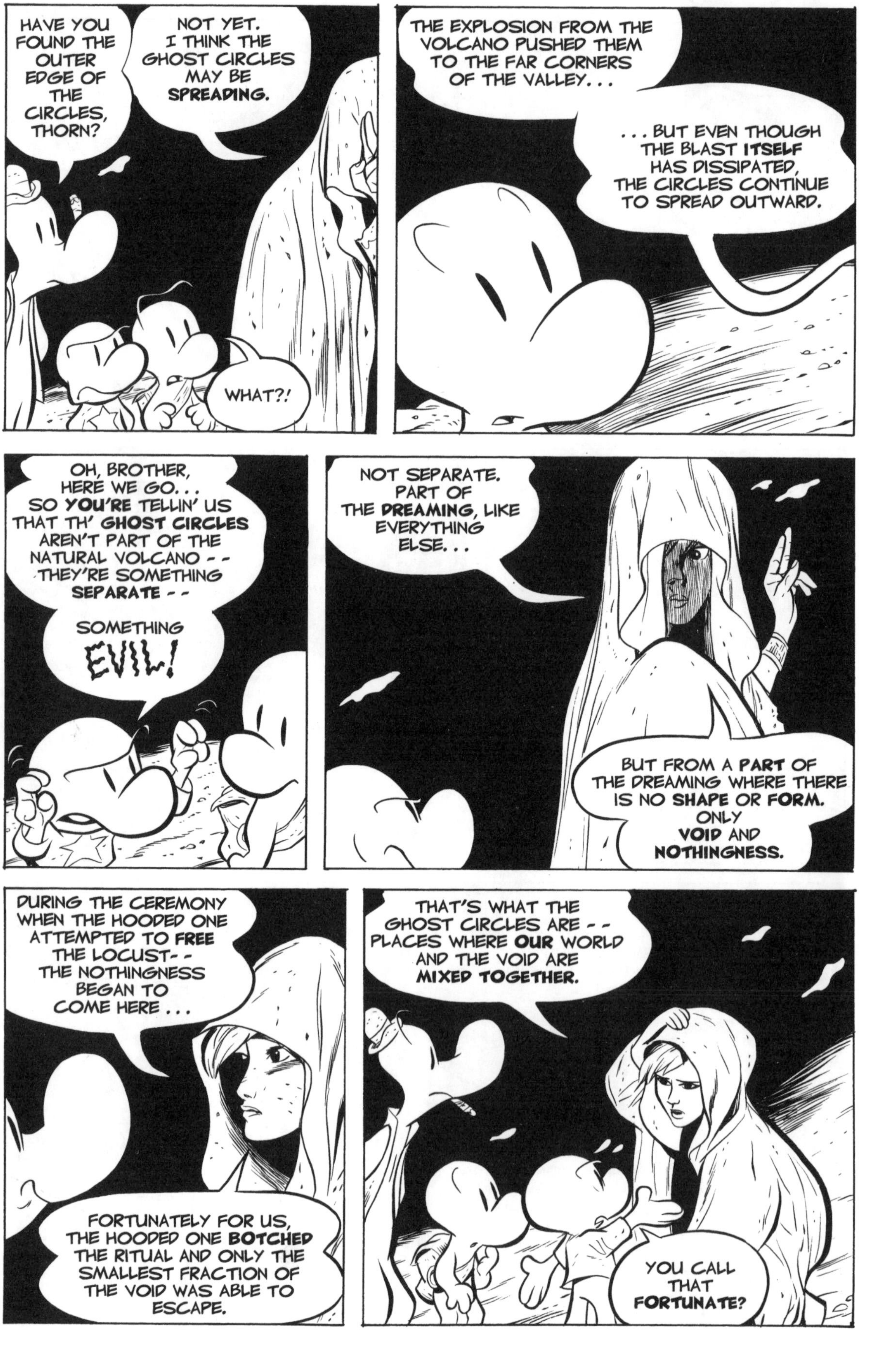
HAVE YOU FOUND THE OUTER EDGE OF THE CIRCLES, THORN?
NOT YET. I THINK THE GHOST CIRCLES MAY BE SPREADING.
WHAT?!
THE EXPLOSION FROM THE VOLCANO PUSHED THEM TO THE FAR CORNERS OF THE VALLEY...
...BUT EVEN THOUGH THE BLAST ITSELF HAS DISSIPATED, THE CIRCLES CONTINUE TO SPREAD OUTWARD.
OH, BROTHER, HERE WE GO... SO YOU'RE TELLIN' US THAT TH' GHOST CIRCLES AREN'T PART OF THE NATURAL VOLCANO -- THEY'RE SOMETHING SEPARATE --
SOMETHING EVIL!
NOT SEPARATE. PART OF THE DREAMING, LIKE EVERYTHING ELSE...
BUT FROM A PART OF THE DREAMING WHERE THERE IS NO SHAPE OR FORM. ONLY VOID AND NOTHINGNESS.
DURING THE CEREMONY WHEN THE HOODED ONE ATTEMPTED TO FREE THE LOCUST-- THE NOTHINGNESS BEGAN TO COME HERE...
FORTUNATELY FOR US, THE HOODED ONE BOTCHED THE RITUAL AND ONLY THE SMALLEST FRACTION OF THE VOID WAS ABLE TO ESCAPE.
THAT'S WHAT THE GHOST CIRCLES ARE -- PLACES WHERE OUR WORLD AND THE VOID ARE MIXED TOGETHER.
YOU CALL THAT FORTUNATE?

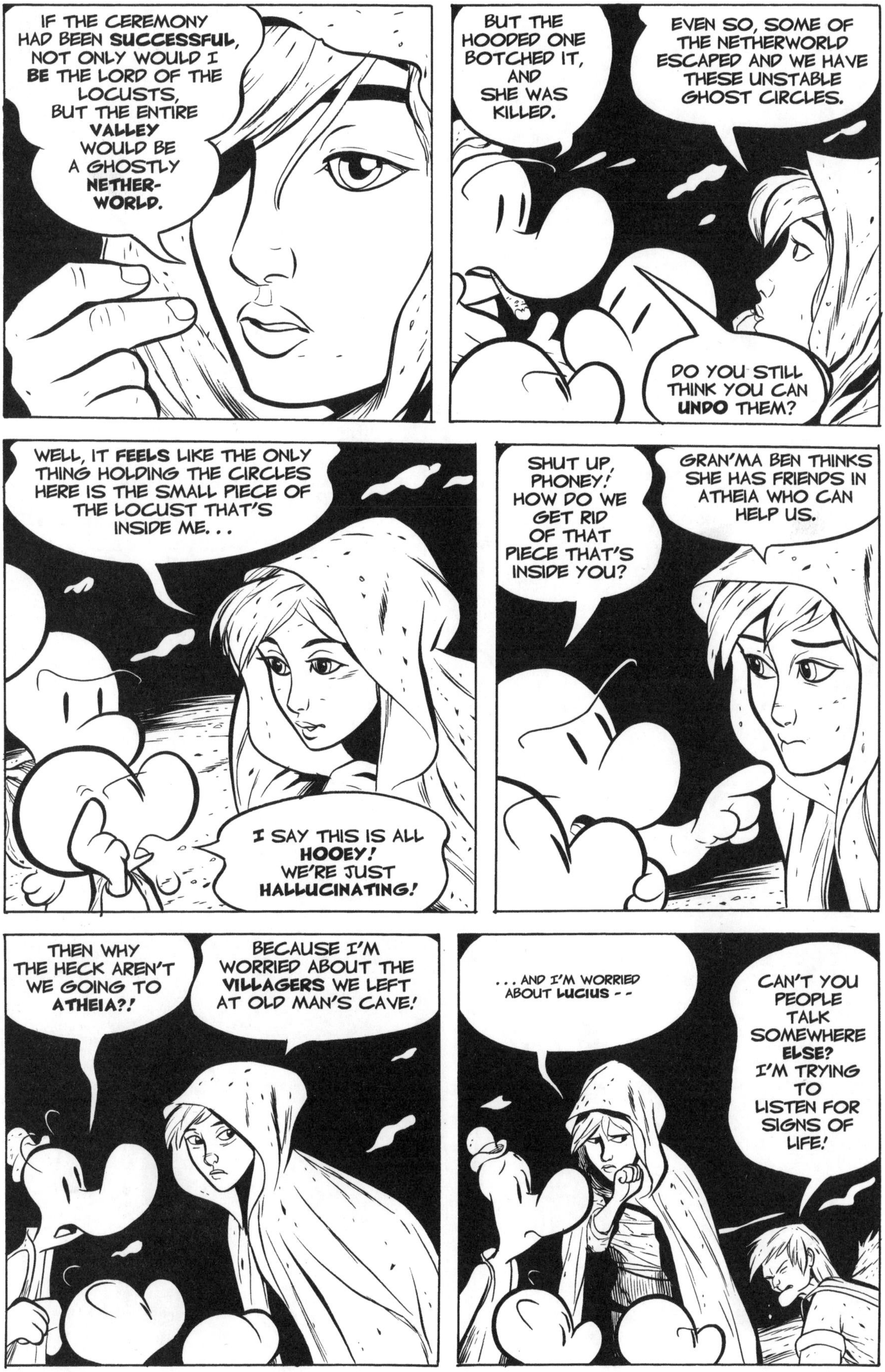
IF THE CEREMONY HAD BEEN SUCCESSFUL, NOT ONLY WOULD I BE THE LORD OF THE LOCUSTS, BUT THE ENTIRE VALLEY WOULD BE A GHOSTLY NETHER-WORLD.
BUT THE HOODED ONE BOTCHED IT, AND SHE WAS KILLED.
EVEN SO, SOME OF THE NETHERWORLD ESCAPED AND WE HAVE THESE UNSTABLE GHOST CIRCLES.
DO YOU STILL THINK YOU CAN UNDO THEM?
WELL, IT FEELS LIKE THE ONLY THING HOLDING THE CIRCLES HERE IS THE SMALL PIECE OF THE LOCUST THAT'S INSIDE ME...
I SAY THIS IS ALL HOOEY! WE'RE JUST HALLUCINATING!
SHUT UP, PHONEY! HOW DO WE GET RID OF THAT PIECE THAT'S INSIDE YOU?
GRAN'MA BEN THINKS SHE HAS FRIENDS IN ATHEIA WHO CAN HELP US.
THEN WHY THE HECK AREN'T WE GOING TO ATHEIA?!
BECAUSE I'M WORRIED ABOUT THE VILLAGERS WE LEFT AT OLD MAN'S CAVE!
...AND I'M WORRIED ABOUT LUCIUS --
CAN'T YOU PEOPLE TALK SOMEWHERE ELSE? I'M TRYING TO LISTEN FOR SIGNS OF LIFE!

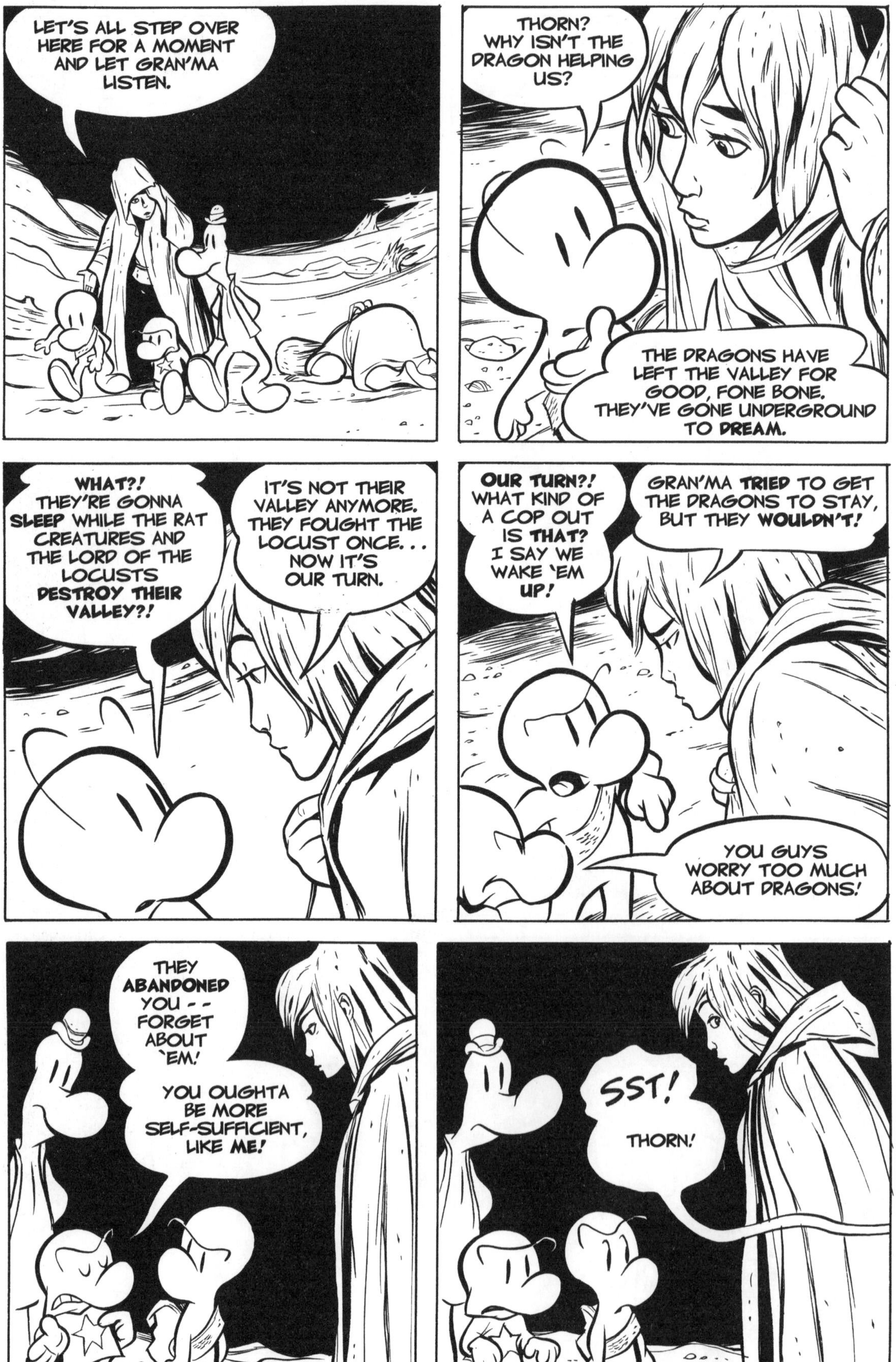
LET'S ALL STEP OVER HERE FOR A MOMENT AND LET GRAN'MA LISTEN.
THORN? WHY ISN'T THE DRAGON HELPING US?
THE DRAGONS HAVE LEFT THE VALLEY FOR GOOD, FONE BONE. THEY'VE GONE UNDERGROUND TO **DREAM.**
WHAT?! THEY'RE GONNA **SLEEP** WHILE THE RAT CREATURES AND THE LORD OF THE LOCUSTS **DESTROY THEIR VALLEY?!**
IT'S NOT THEIR VALLEY ANYMORE. THEY FOUGHT THE LOCUST ONCE. . . NOW IT'S OUR TURN.
OUR TURN?! WHAT KIND OF A COP OUT IS **THAT?** I SAY WE WAKE 'EM **UP!**
GRAN'MA **TRIED** TO GET THE DRAGONS TO STAY, BUT THEY **WOULDN'T!**
YOU GUYS WORRY TOO MUCH ABOUT DRAGONS!
THEY **ABANDONED** YOU - - FORGET ABOUT 'EM!
YOU OUGHTA BE MORE SELF-SUFFICIENT, LIKE **ME!**
SST!
THORN!

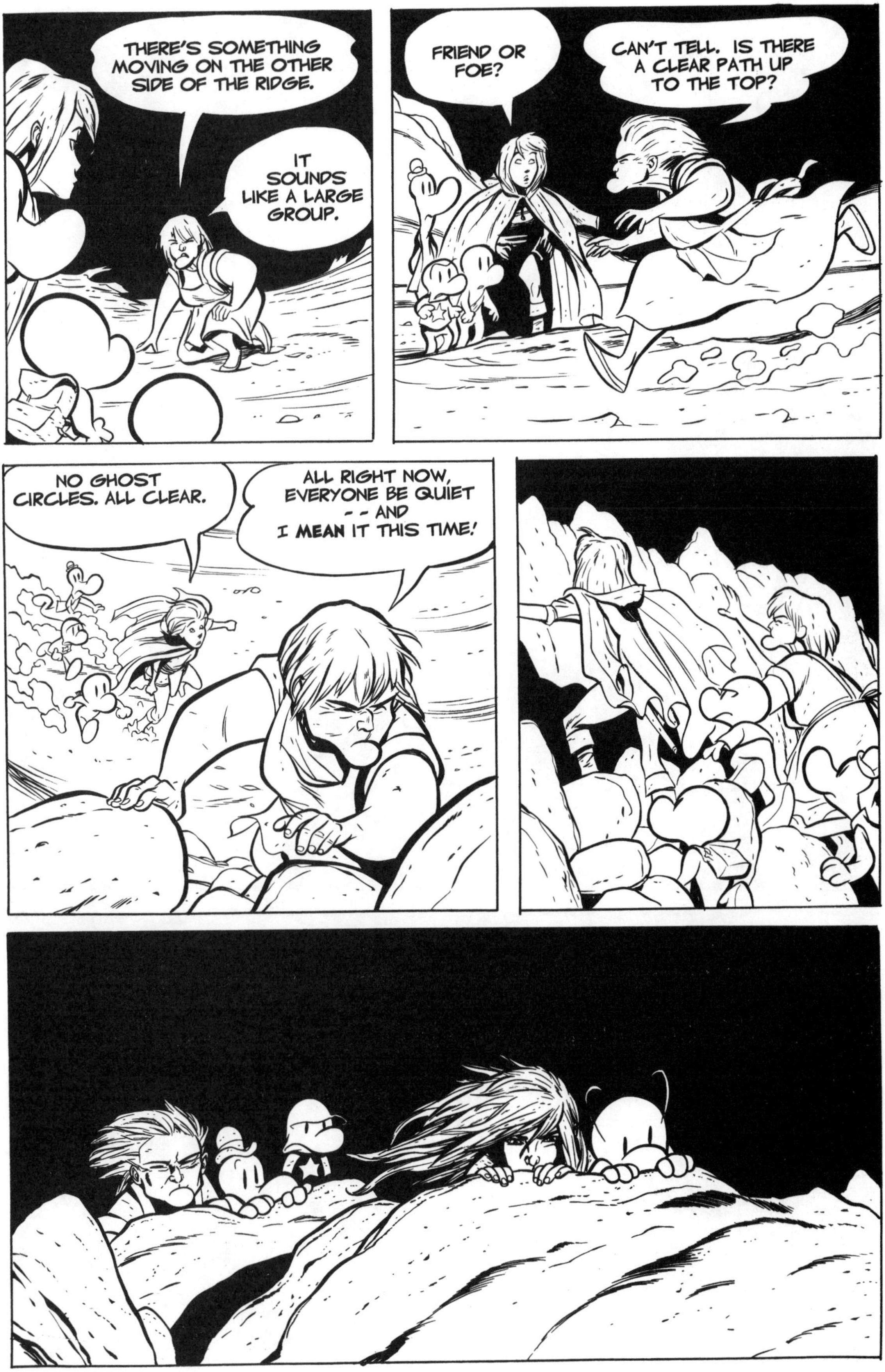
THERE'S SOMETHING MOVING ON THE OTHER SIDE OF THE RIDGE.
IT SOUNDS LIKE A LARGE GROUP.
FRIEND OR FOE?
CAN'T TELL. IS THERE A CLEAR PATH UP TO THE TOP?
NO GHOST CIRCLES. ALL CLEAR.
ALL RIGHT NOW, EVERYONE BE QUIET - - AND I MEAN IT THIS TIME!

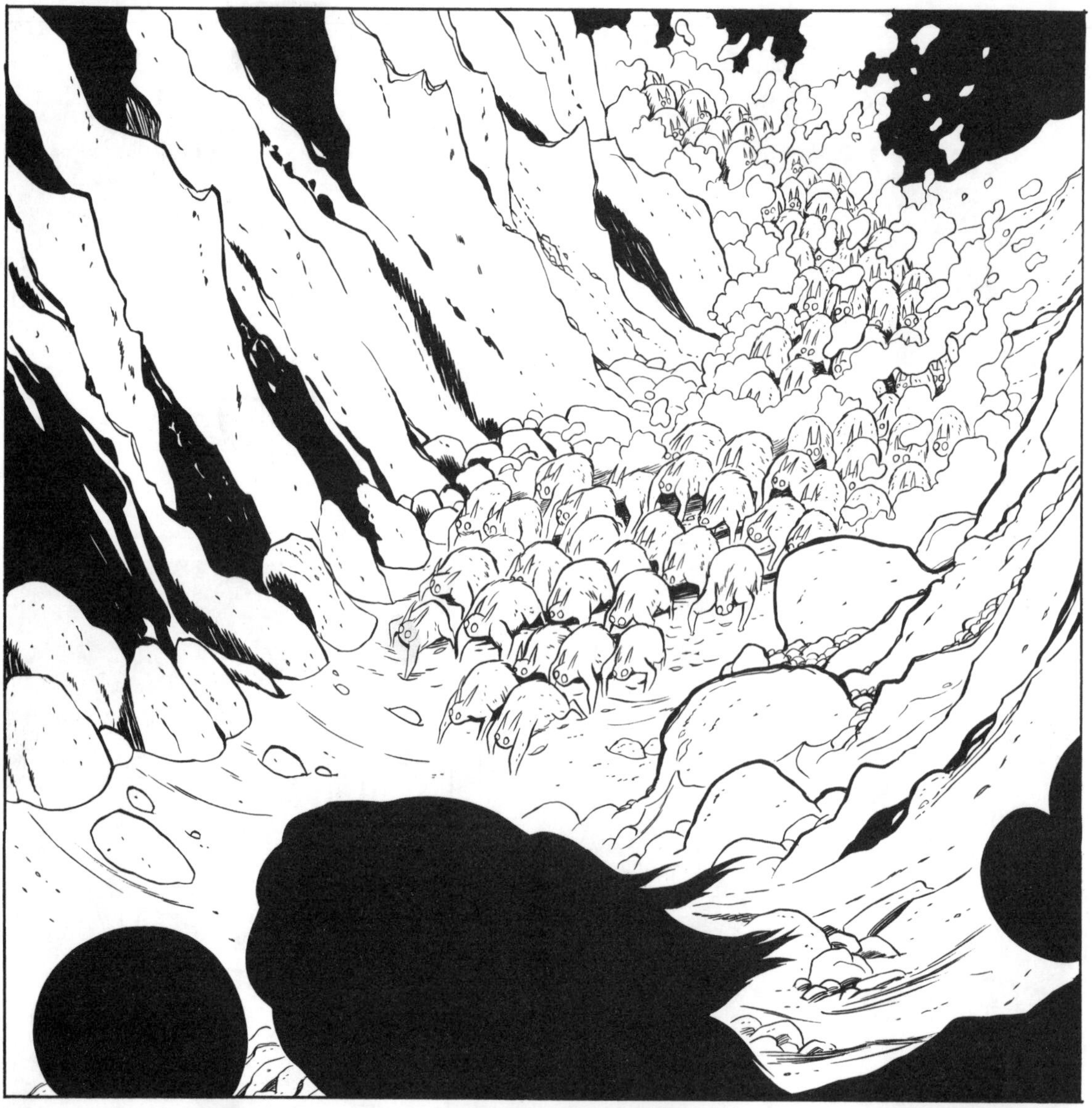

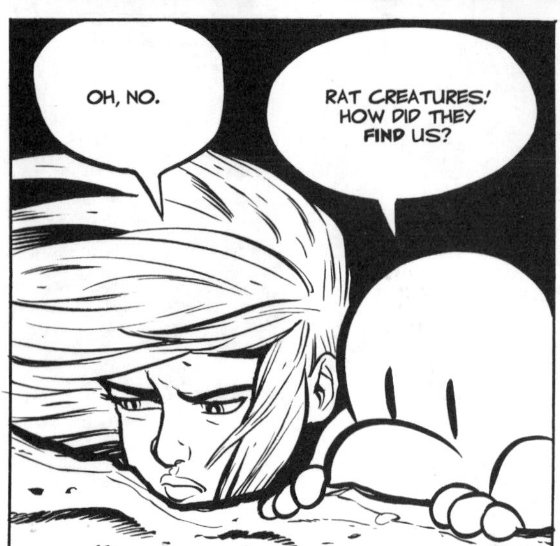
OH, NO.
RAT CREATURES! HOW DID THEY FIND US?

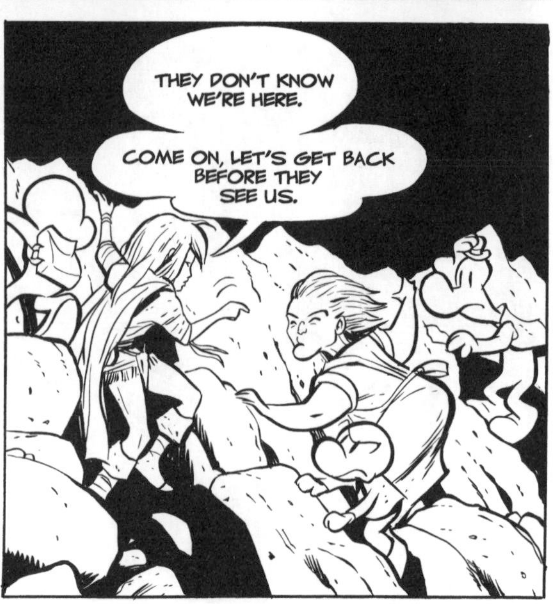
THEY DON'T KNOW WE'RE HERE.
COME ON, LET'S GET BACK BEFORE THEY SEE US.

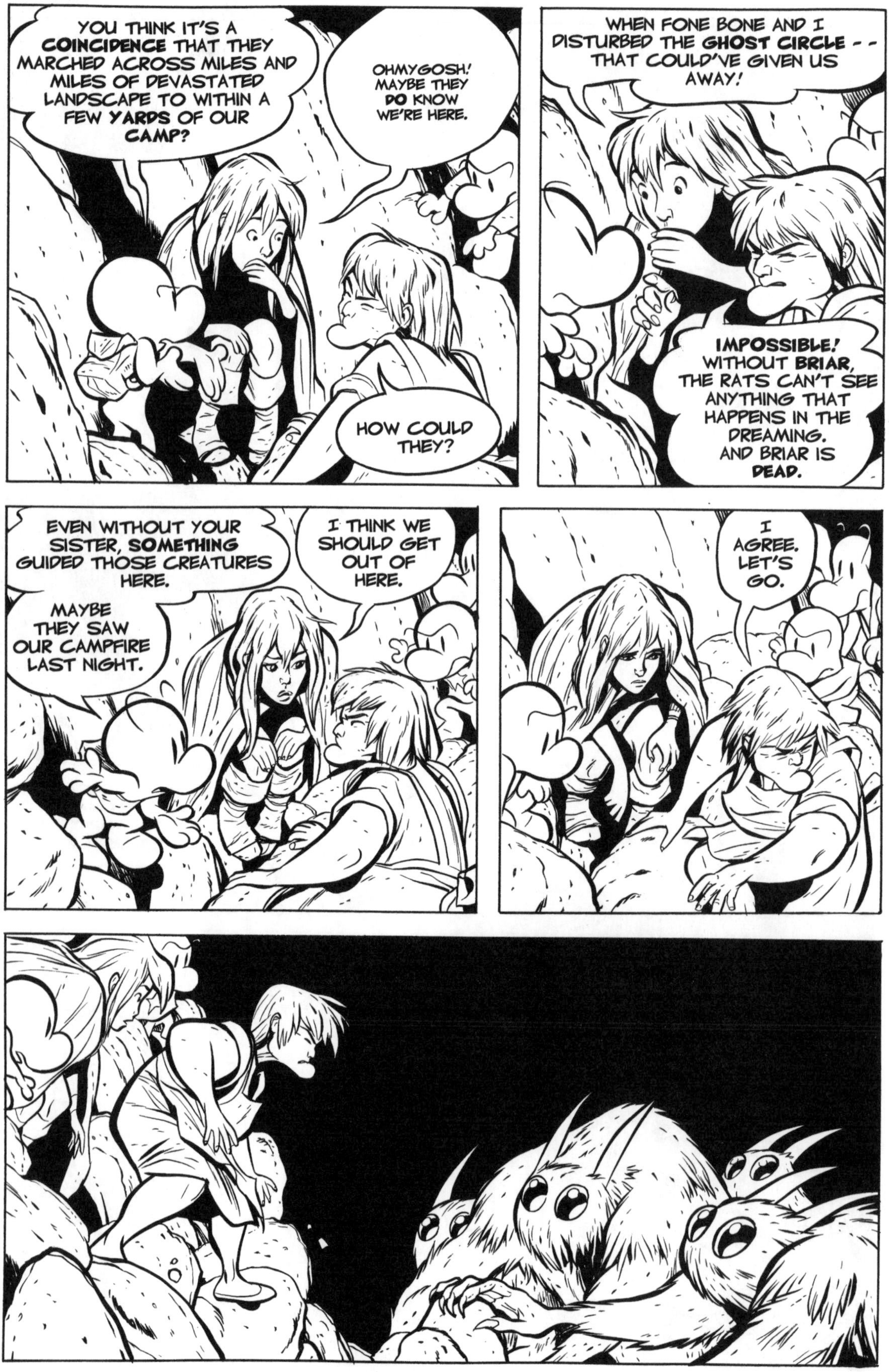
YOU THINK IT'S A COINCIDENCE THAT THEY MARCHED ACROSS MILES AND MILES OF DEVASTATED LANDSCAPE TO WITHIN A FEW YARDS OF OUR CAMP?
OHMYGOSH! MAYBE THEY DO KNOW WE'RE HERE.
HOW COULD THEY?
WHEN FONE BONE AND I DISTURBED THE GHOST CIRCLE - - THAT COULD'VE GIVEN US AWAY!
IMPOSSIBLE! WITHOUT BRIAR, THE RATS CAN'T SEE ANYTHING THAT HAPPENS IN THE DREAMING. AND BRIAR IS DEAD.
EVEN WITHOUT YOUR SISTER, SOMETHING GUIDED THOSE CREATURES HERE.
MAYBE THEY SAW OUR CAMPFIRE LAST NIGHT.
I THINK WE SHOULD GET OUT OF HERE.
I AGREE. LET'S GO.

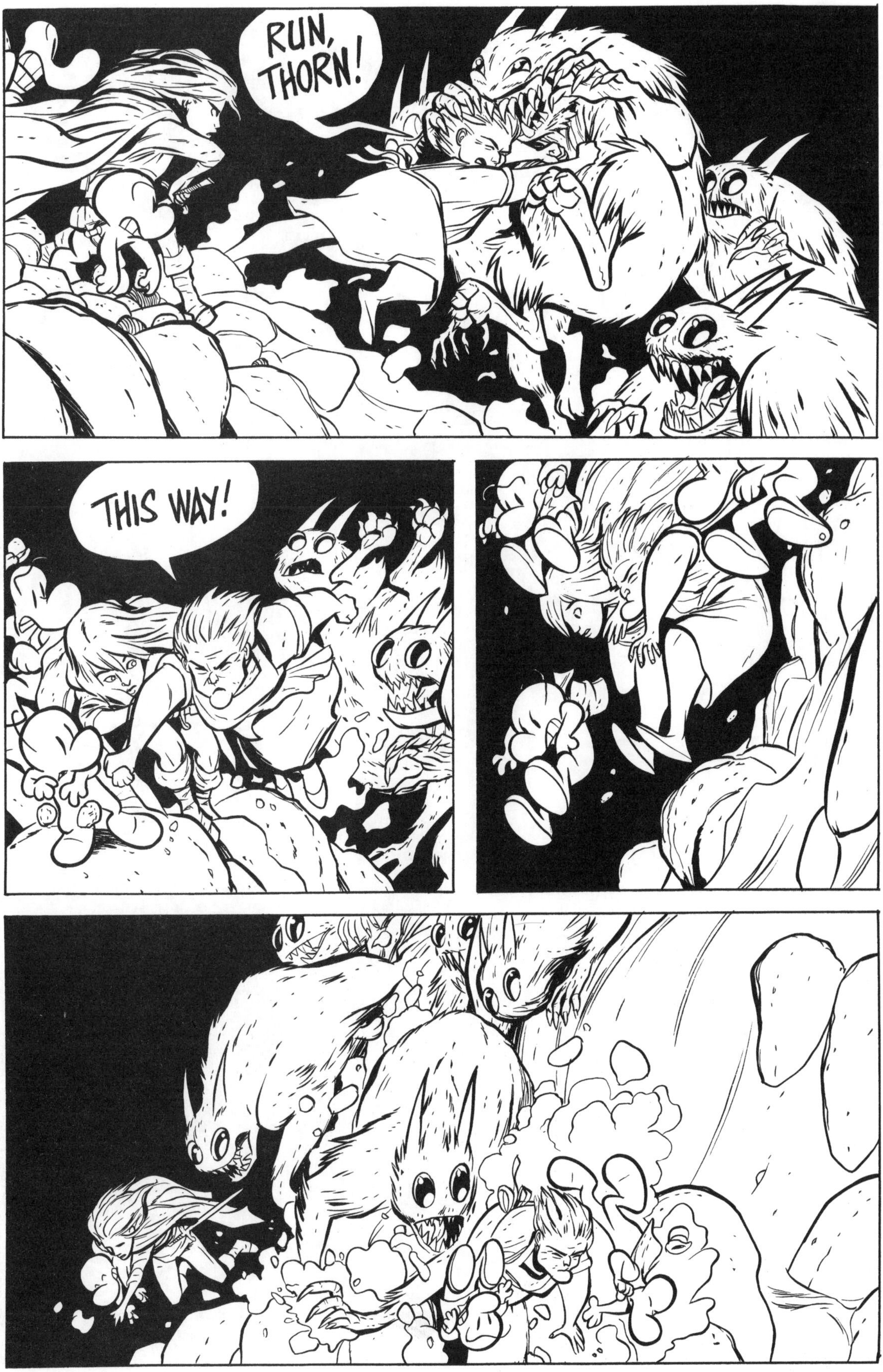
RUN, THORN!
THIS WAY!

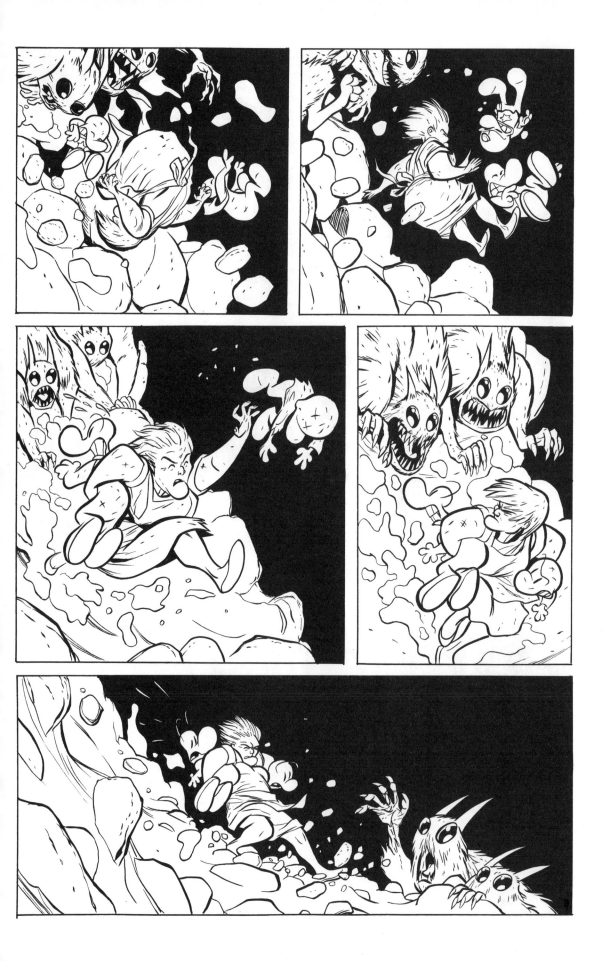

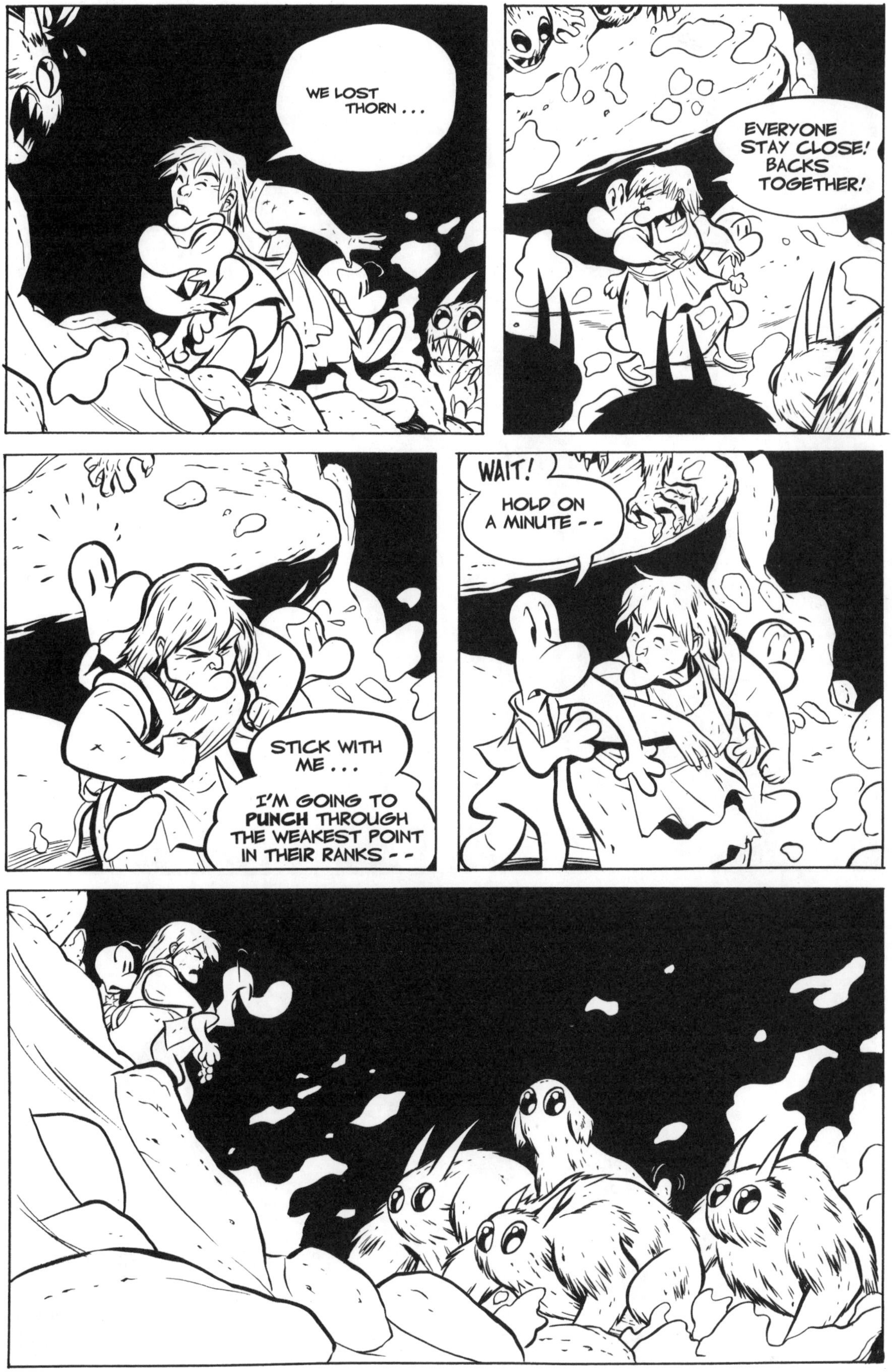
WE LOST THORN . . .
EVERYONE STAY CLOSE! BACKS TOGETHER!
STICK WITH ME . . .
I'M GOING TO **PUNCH** THROUGH THE WEAKEST POINT IN THEIR RANKS - -
WAIT!
HOLD ON A MINUTE - -

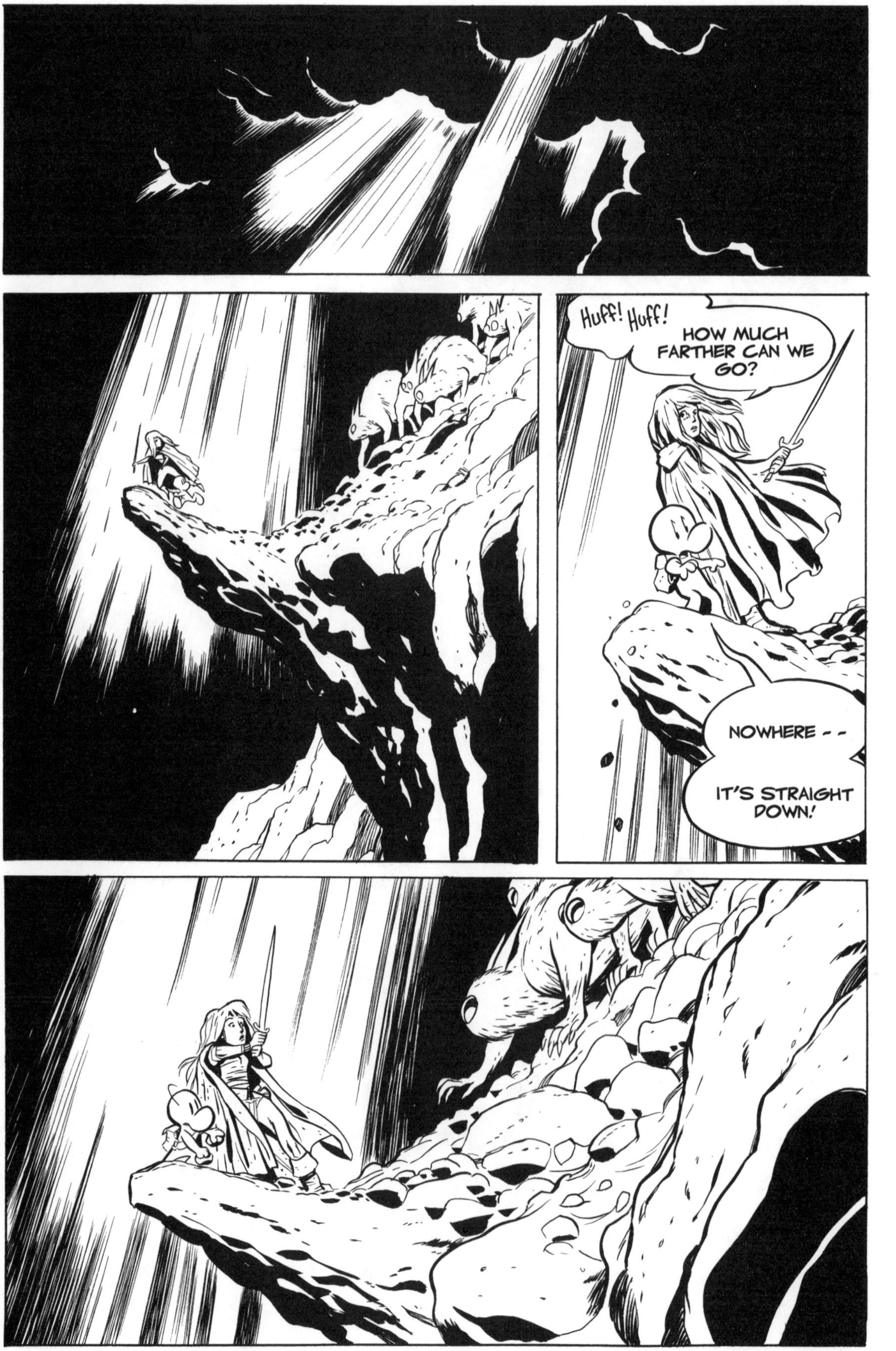
Huff! Huff!
HOW MUCH FARTHER CAN WE GO?
NOWHERE - -
IT'S STRAIGHT DOWN!

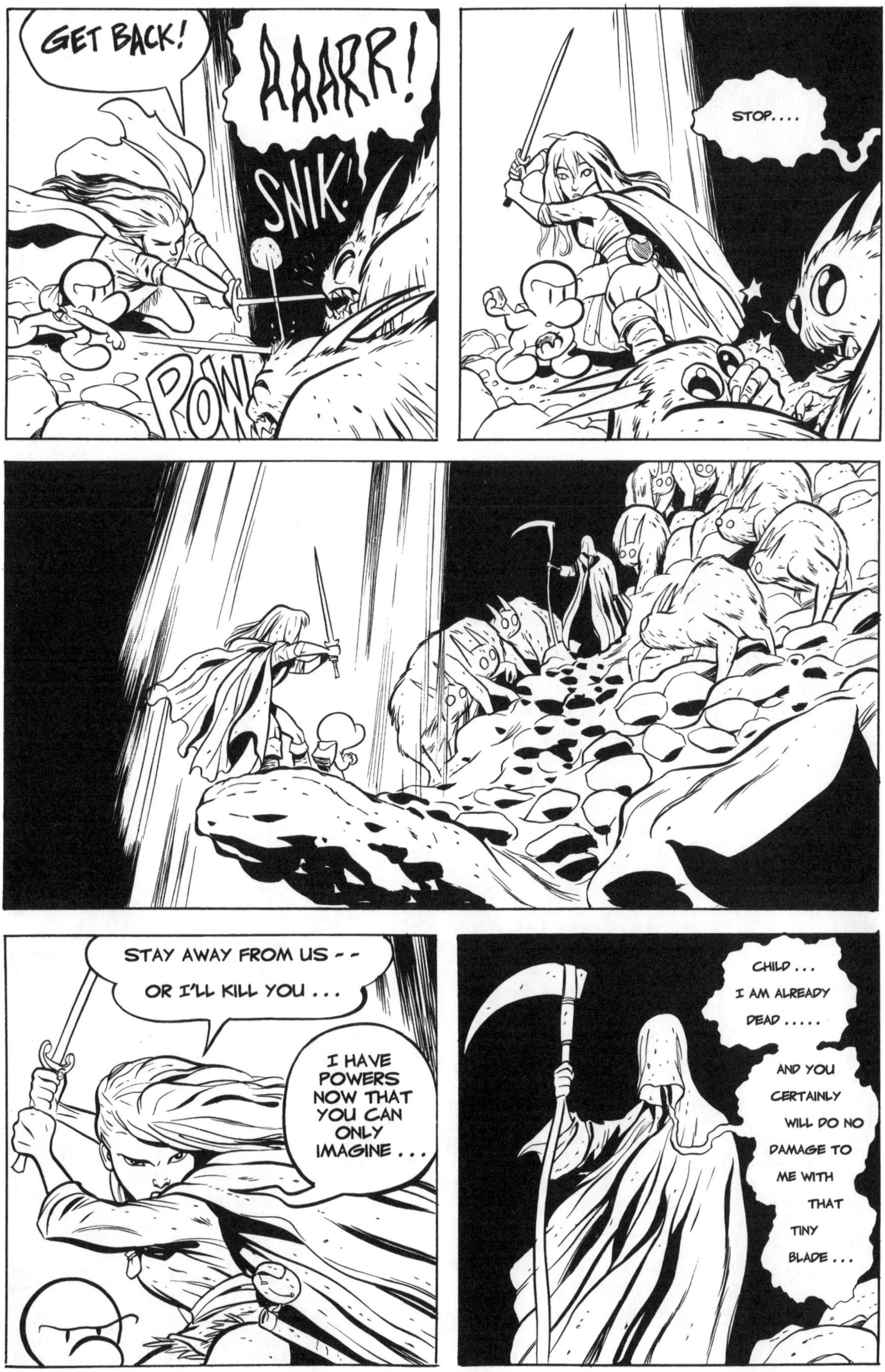
GET BACK!
AAARR!
SNIK!
POW
STOP....
STAY AWAY FROM US - - OR I'LL KILL YOU . . .
I HAVE POWERS NOW THAT YOU CAN ONLY IMAGINE . . .
CHILD . . . I AM ALREADY DEAD . . . . .
AND YOU CERTAINLY WILL DO NO DAMAGE TO ME WITH THAT TINY BLADE . . .

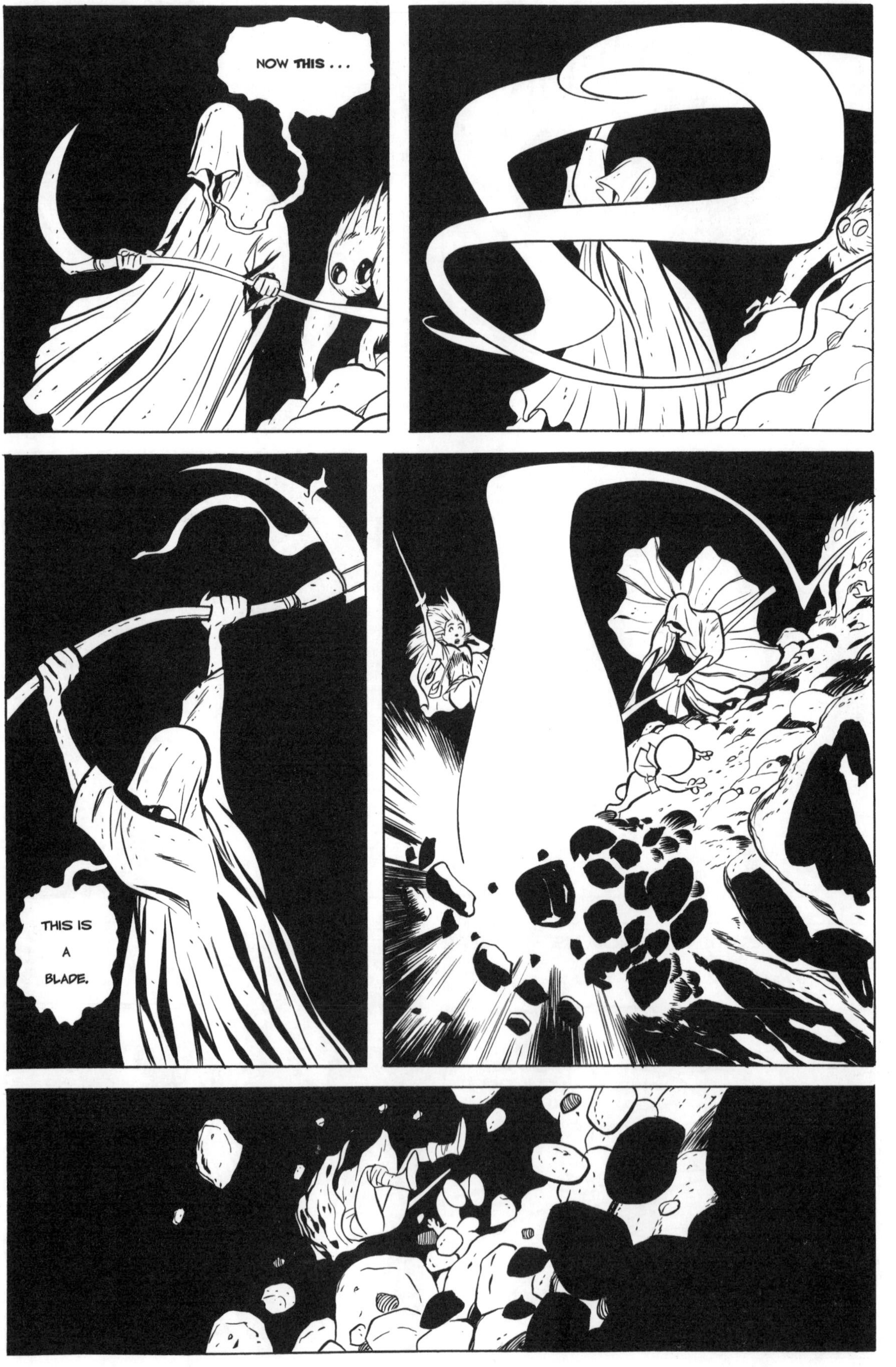
NOW THIS . . .
THIS IS A BLADE.

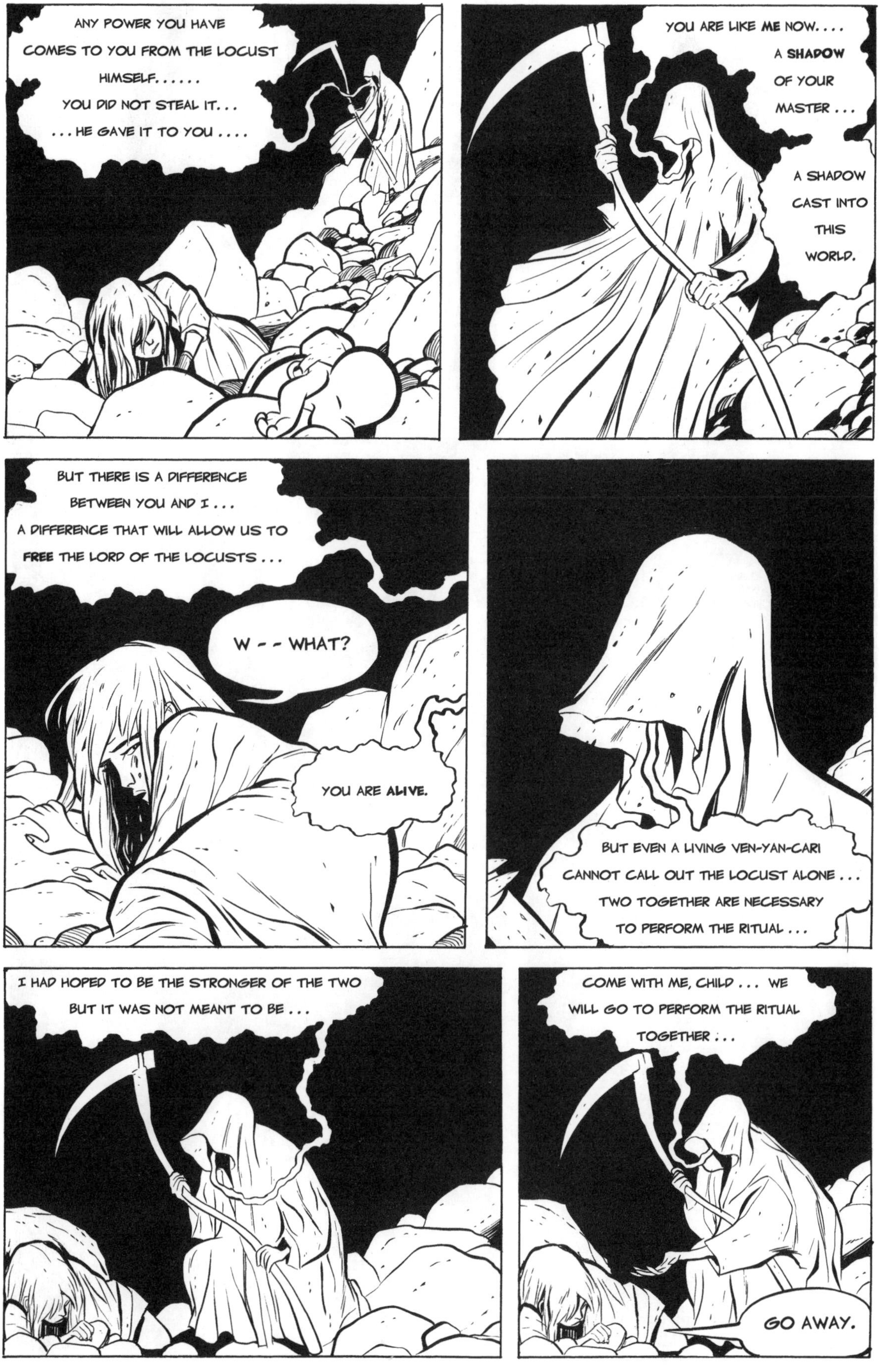
ANY POWER YOU HAVE COMES TO YOU FROM THE LOCUST HIMSELF...... YOU DID NOT STEAL IT... ...HE GAVE IT TO YOU....
YOU ARE LIKE ME NOW.... A SHADOW OF YOUR MASTER...
A SHADOW CAST INTO THIS WORLD.
BUT THERE IS A DIFFERENCE BETWEEN YOU AND I... A DIFFERENCE THAT WILL ALLOW US TO FREE THE LORD OF THE LOCUSTS...
W - - WHAT?
YOU ARE ALIVE.
BUT EVEN A LIVING VEN-YAN-CARI CANNOT CALL OUT THE LOCUST ALONE... TWO TOGETHER ARE NECESSARY TO PERFORM THE RITUAL...
I HAD HOPED TO BE THE STRONGER OF THE TWO BUT IT WAS NOT MEANT TO BE...
COME WITH ME, CHILD... WE WILL GO TO PERFORM THE RITUAL TOGETHER...
GO AWAY.

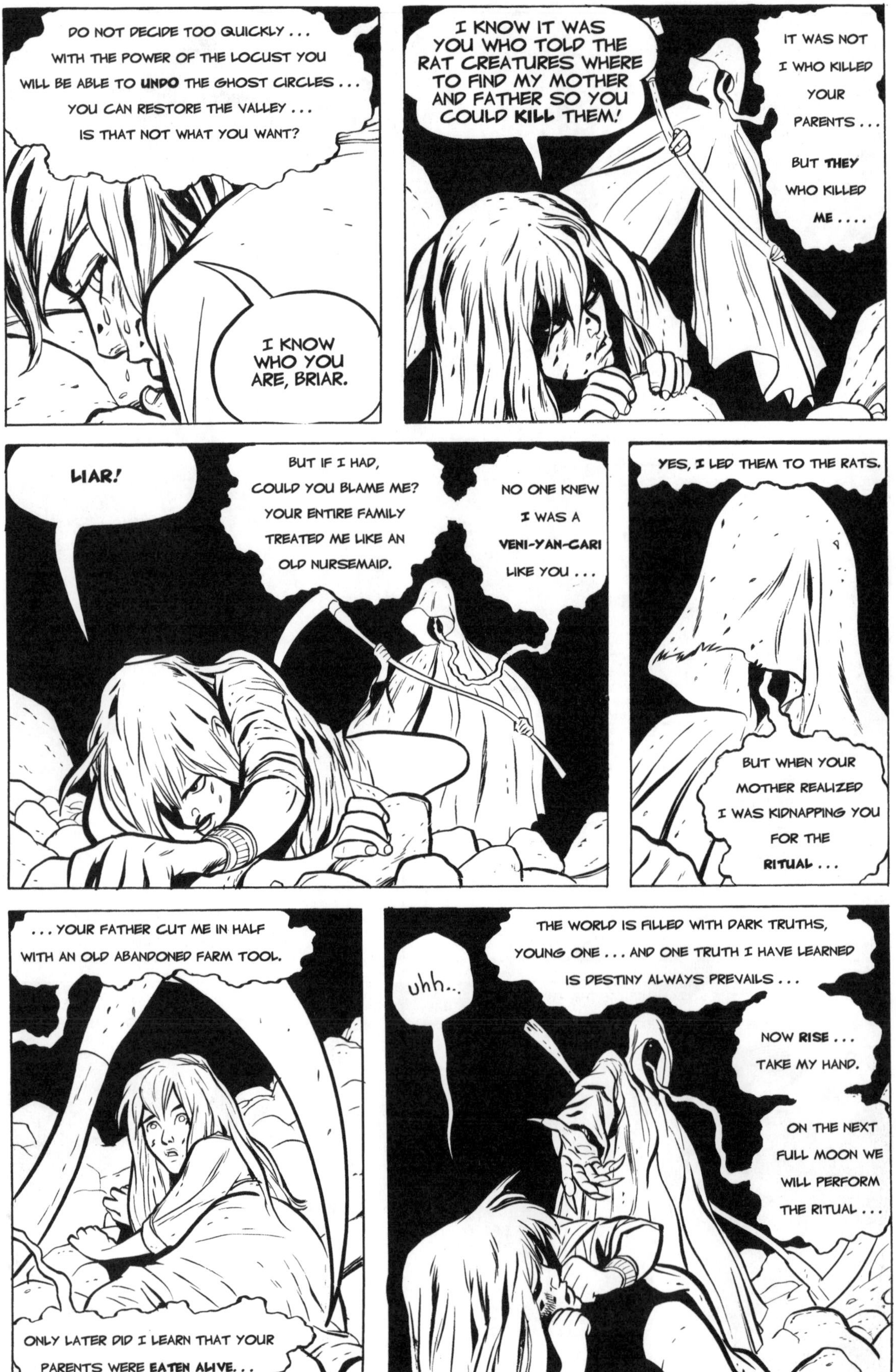
DO NOT DECIDE TOO QUICKLY . . . WITH THE POWER OF THE LOCUST YOU WILL BE ABLE TO **UNDO** THE GHOST CIRCLES . . . YOU CAN RESTORE THE VALLEY . . . IS THAT NOT WHAT YOU WANT?
I KNOW WHO YOU ARE, BRIAR.
I KNOW IT WAS YOU WHO TOLD THE RAT CREATURES WHERE TO FIND MY MOTHER AND FATHER SO YOU COULD **KILL** THEM!
IT WAS NOT I WHO KILLED YOUR PARENTS . . .
BUT **THEY** WHO KILLED **ME** . . . .
LIAR!
BUT IF I HAD, COULD YOU BLAME ME? YOUR ENTIRE FAMILY TREATED ME LIKE AN OLD NURSEMAID.
NO ONE KNEW I WAS A **VENI-YAN-CARI** LIKE YOU . . .
YES, I LED THEM TO THE RATS.
BUT WHEN YOUR MOTHER REALIZED I WAS KIDNAPPING YOU FOR THE **RITUAL** . . .
. . . YOUR FATHER CUT ME IN HALF WITH AN OLD ABANDONED FARM TOOL.
ONLY LATER DID I LEARN THAT YOUR PARENTS WERE **EATEN ALIVE** . . .
uhh...
THE WORLD IS FILLED WITH DARK TRUTHS, YOUNG ONE . . . AND ONE TRUTH I HAVE LEARNED IS DESTINY ALWAYS PREVAILS . . .
NOW **RISE** . . . TAKE MY HAND.
ON THE NEXT FULL MOON WE WILL PERFORM THE RITUAL . . .

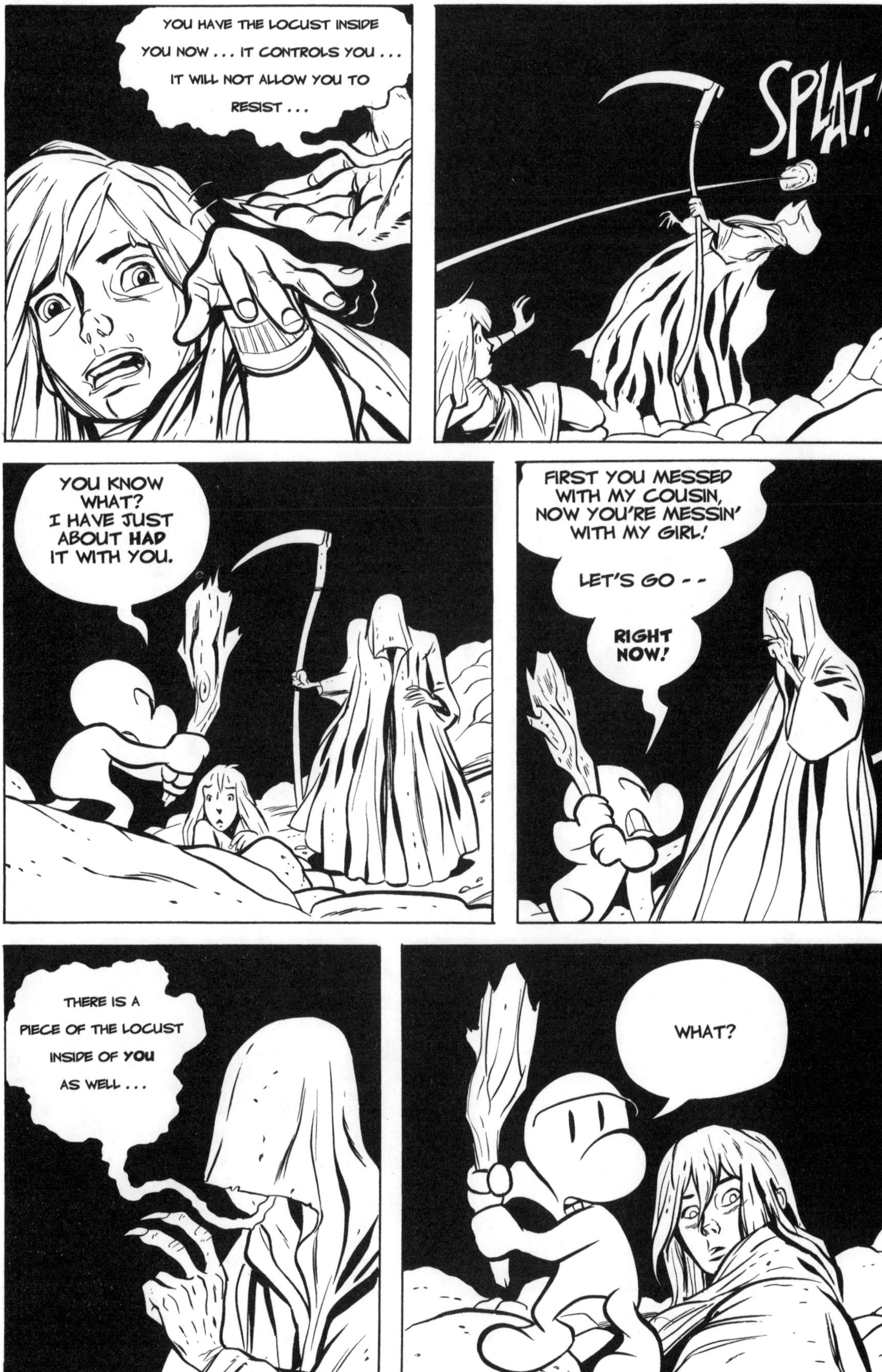
YOU HAVE THE LOCUST INSIDE YOU NOW . . . IT CONTROLS YOU . . . IT WILL NOT ALLOW YOU TO RESIST . . .
SPLAT!
YOU KNOW WHAT? I HAVE JUST ABOUT HAD IT WITH YOU.
FIRST YOU MESSED WITH MY COUSIN, NOW YOU'RE MESSIN' WITH MY GIRL!
LET'S GO - -
RIGHT NOW!
THERE IS A PIECE OF THE LOCUST INSIDE OF YOU AS WELL . . .
WHAT?

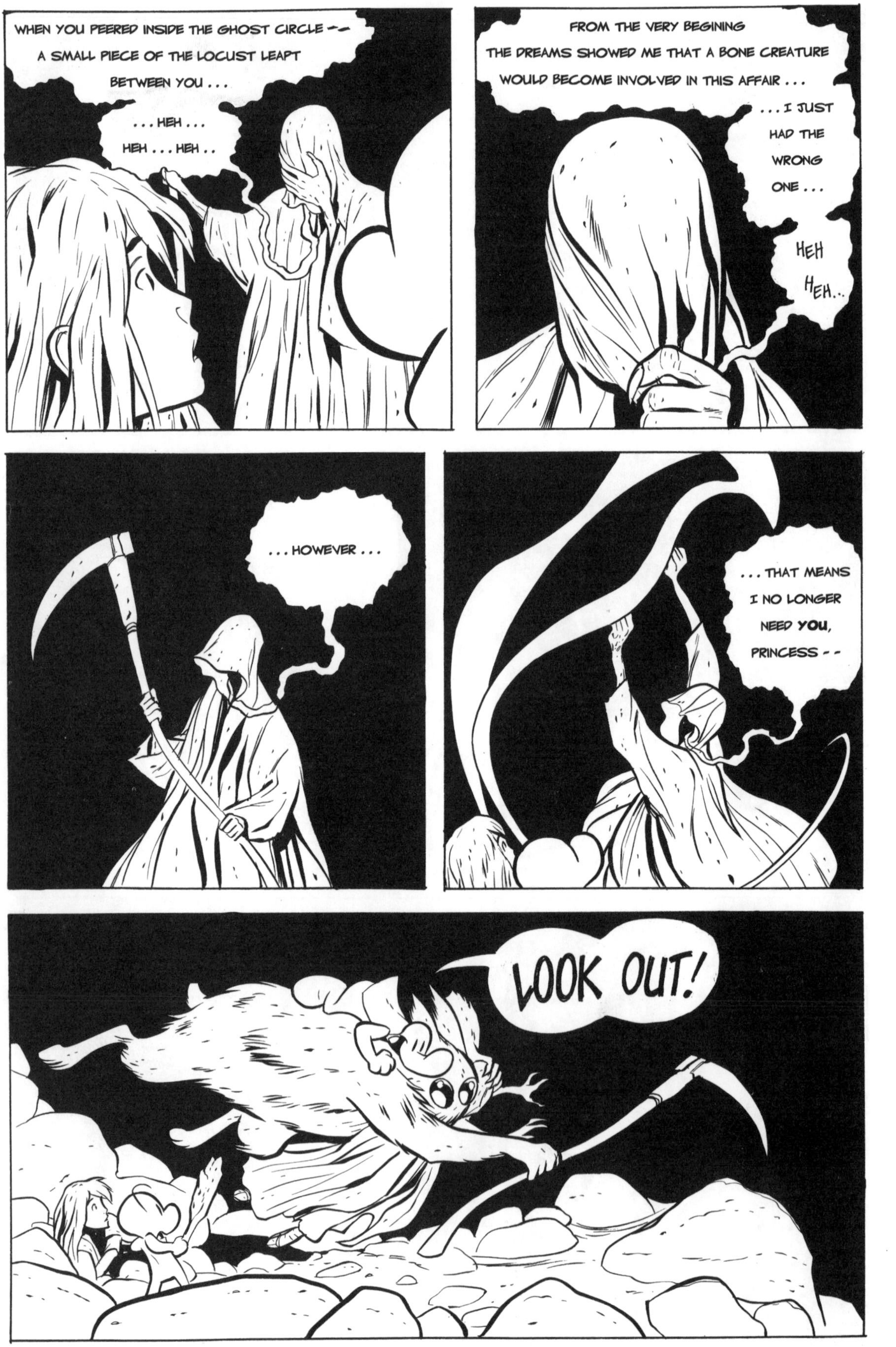
WHEN YOU PEERED INSIDE THE GHOST CIRCLE --
A SMALL PIECE OF THE LOCUST LEAPT
BETWEEN YOU . . .
. . . HEH . . .
HEH . . . HEH . .
FROM THE VERY BEGINING
THE DREAMS SHOWED ME THAT A BONE CREATURE
WOULD BECOME INVOLVED IN THIS AFFAIR . . .
. . . I JUST HAD THE WRONG ONE . . .
HEH HEH . . .
. . . HOWEVER . . .
. . . THAT MEANS I NO LONGER NEED **YOU**, PRINCESS - -
LOOK OUT!

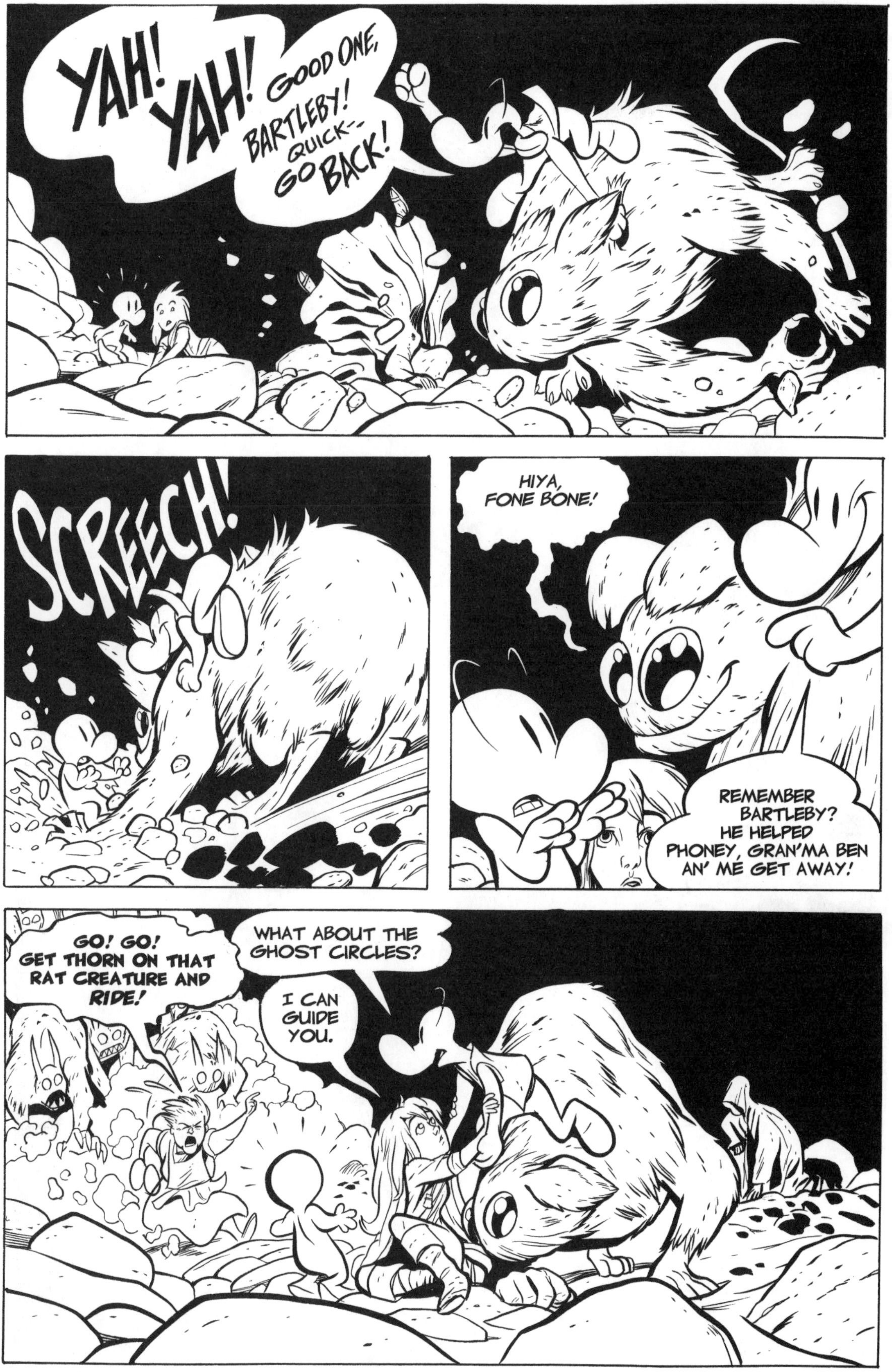
YAH! YAH! GOOD ONE, BARTLEBY! QUICK-- GO BACK!
SCREECH!
HIYA, FONE BONE!
REMEMBER BARTLEBY? HE HELPED PHONEY, GRAN'MA BEN AN' ME GET AWAY!
GO! GO! GET THORN ON THAT RAT CREATURE AND RIDE!
WHAT ABOUT THE GHOST CIRCLES?
I CAN GUIDE YOU.

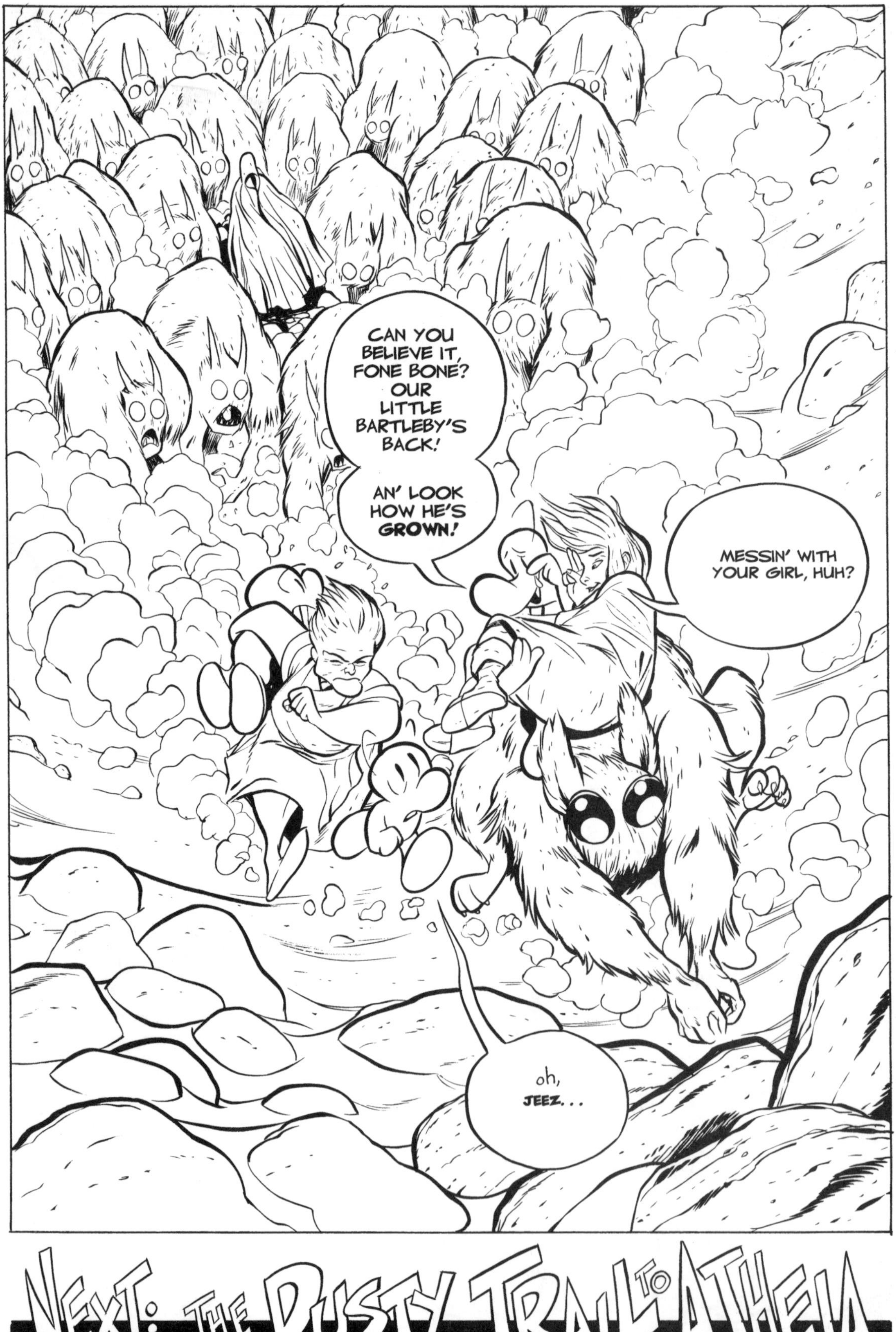
CAN YOU BELIEVE IT, FONE BONE? OUR LITTLE BARTLEBY'S BACK!
AN' LOOK HOW HE'S GROWN!
MESSIN' WITH YOUR GIRL, HUH?
oh, JEEZ...
NEXT: THE DUSTY TRAIL TO ATHEIA

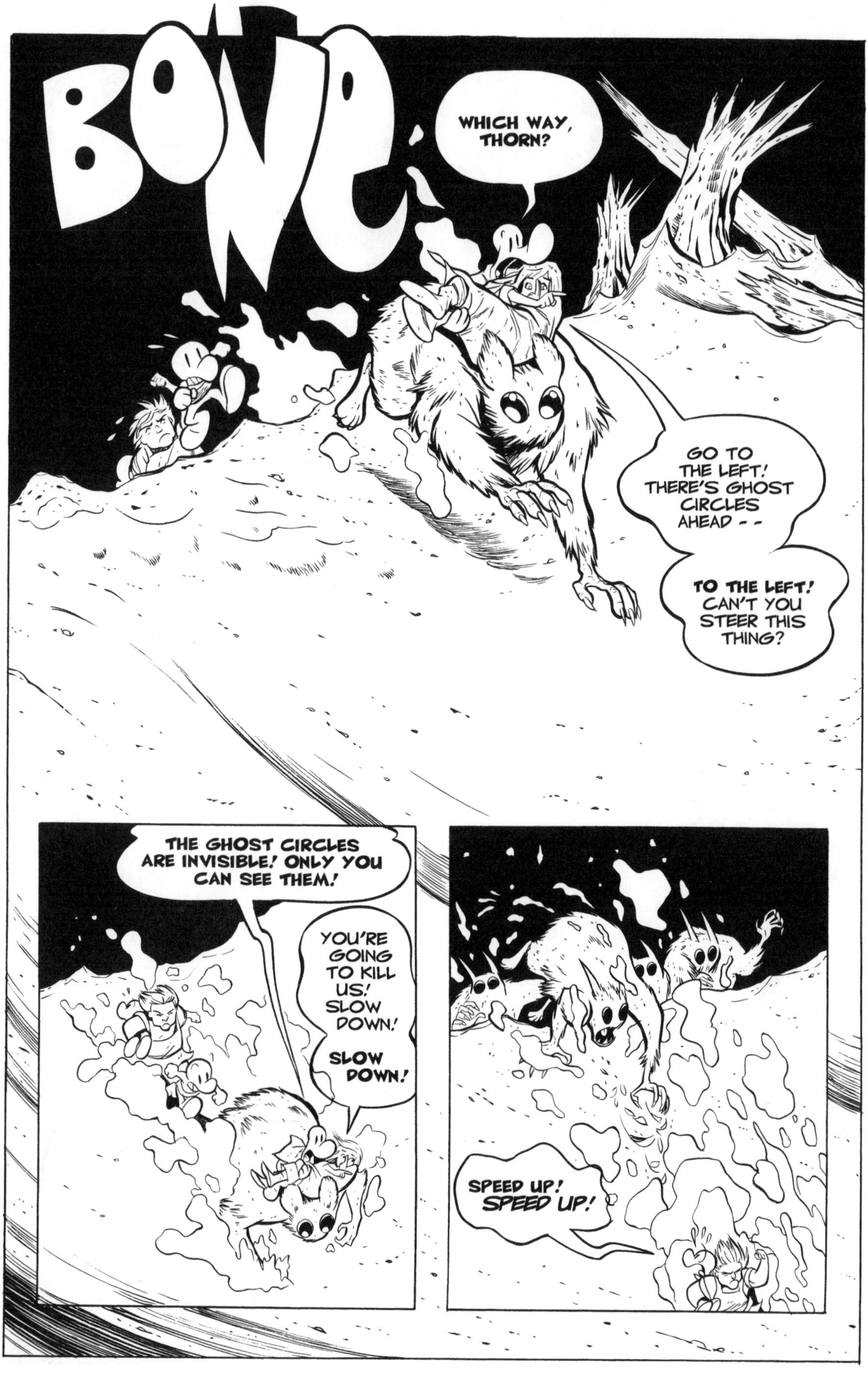
BONE
WHICH WAY, THORN?
GO TO THE LEFT! THERE'S GHOST CIRCLES AHEAD - -
TO THE LEFT! CAN'T YOU STEER THIS THING?
THE GHOST CIRCLES ARE INVISIBLE! ONLY YOU CAN SEE THEM!
YOU'RE GOING TO KILL US! SLOW DOWN!
SLOW DOWN!
SPEED UP! SPEED UP!

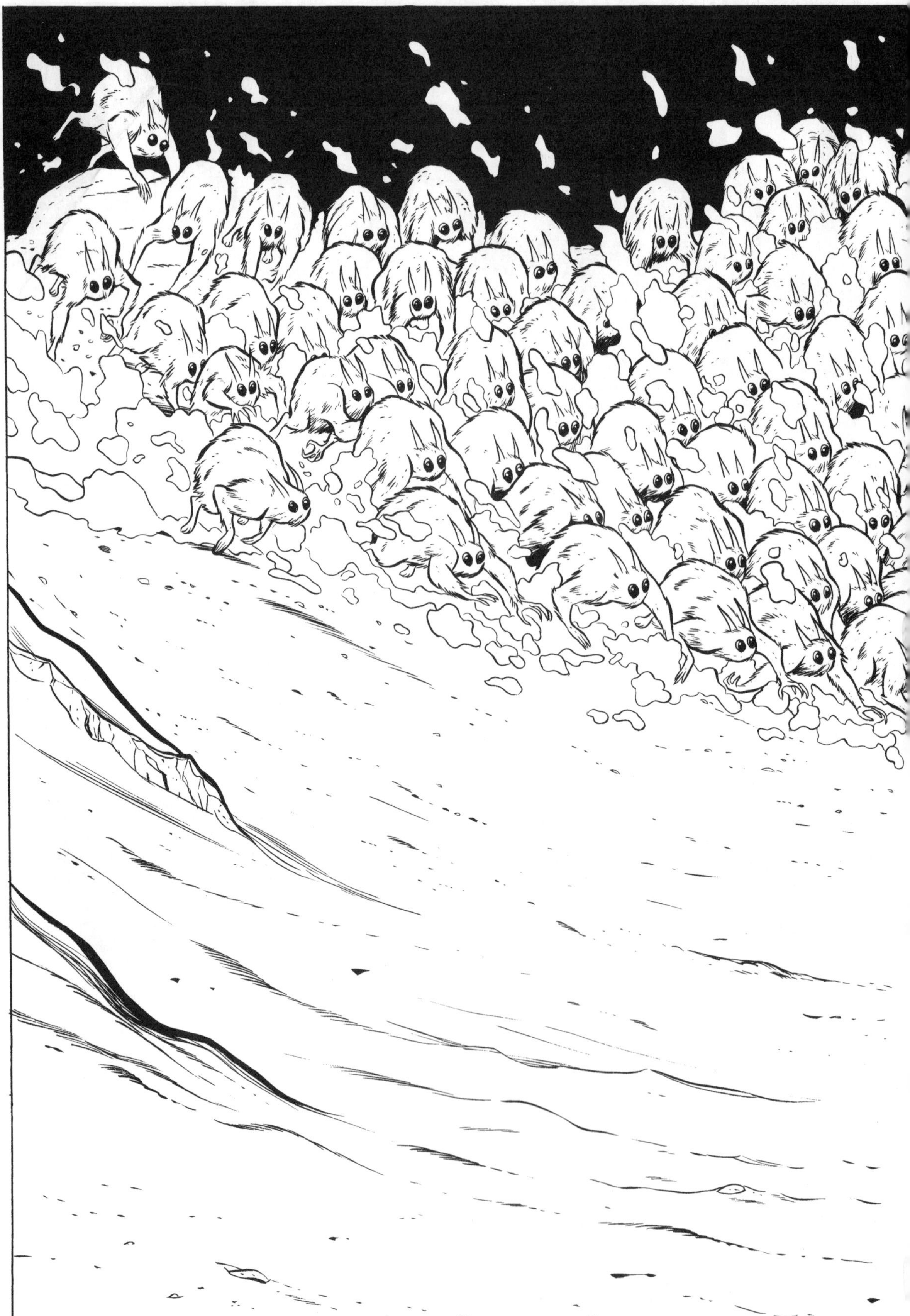

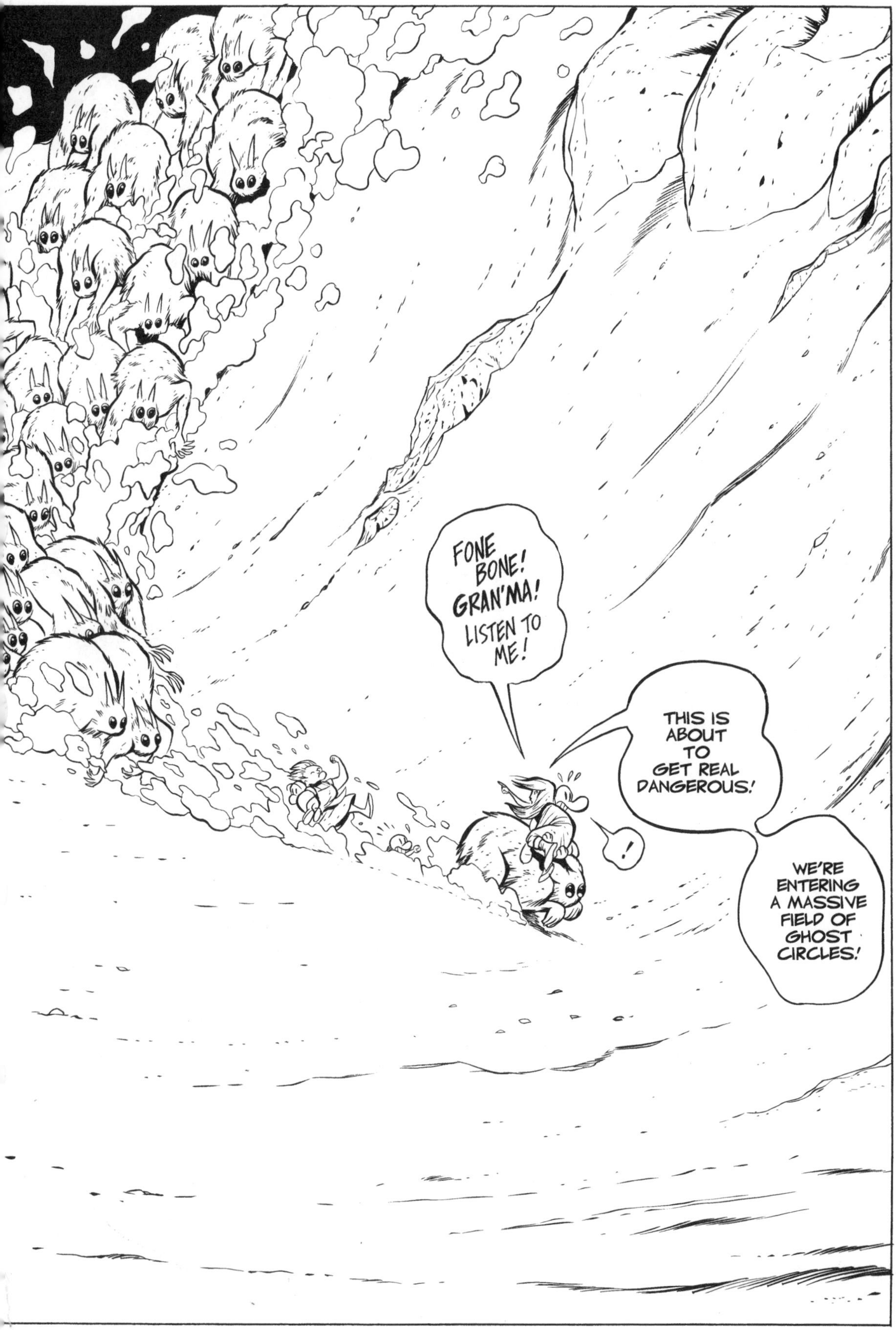
FONE BONE! GRAN'MA! LISTEN TO ME!
THIS IS ABOUT TO GET REAL DANGEROUS!
WE'RE ENTERING A MASSIVE FIELD OF GHOST CIRCLES!
!

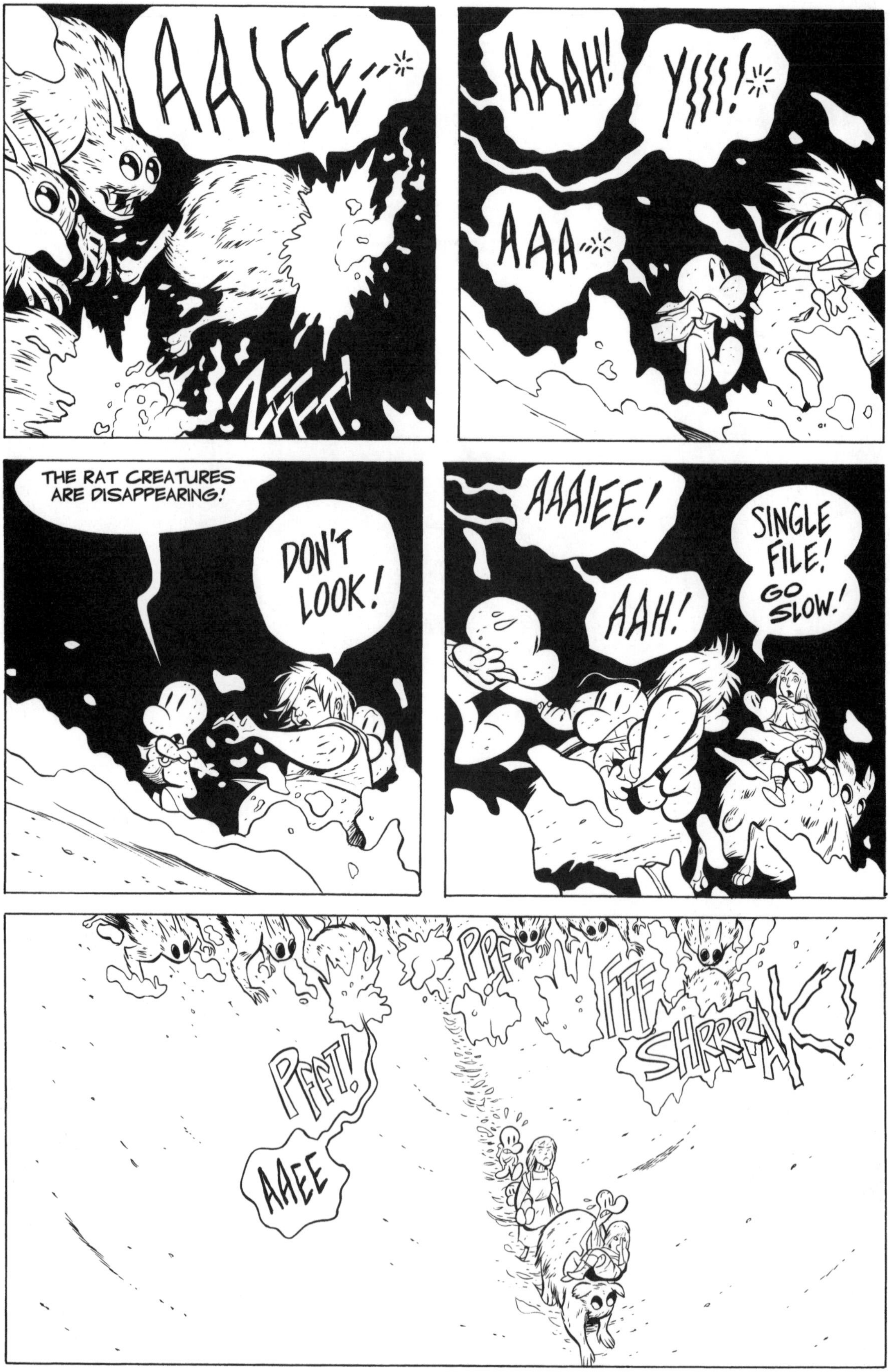
AAIEE--
ZFFT!
AAAH!
YIII!
AAA
THE RAT CREATURES ARE DISAPPEARING!
DON'T LOOK!
AAAIEE!
AAH!
SINGLE FILE! GO SLOW!
PPF
FFF
SHRRRAK!
PFFT!
AAEE

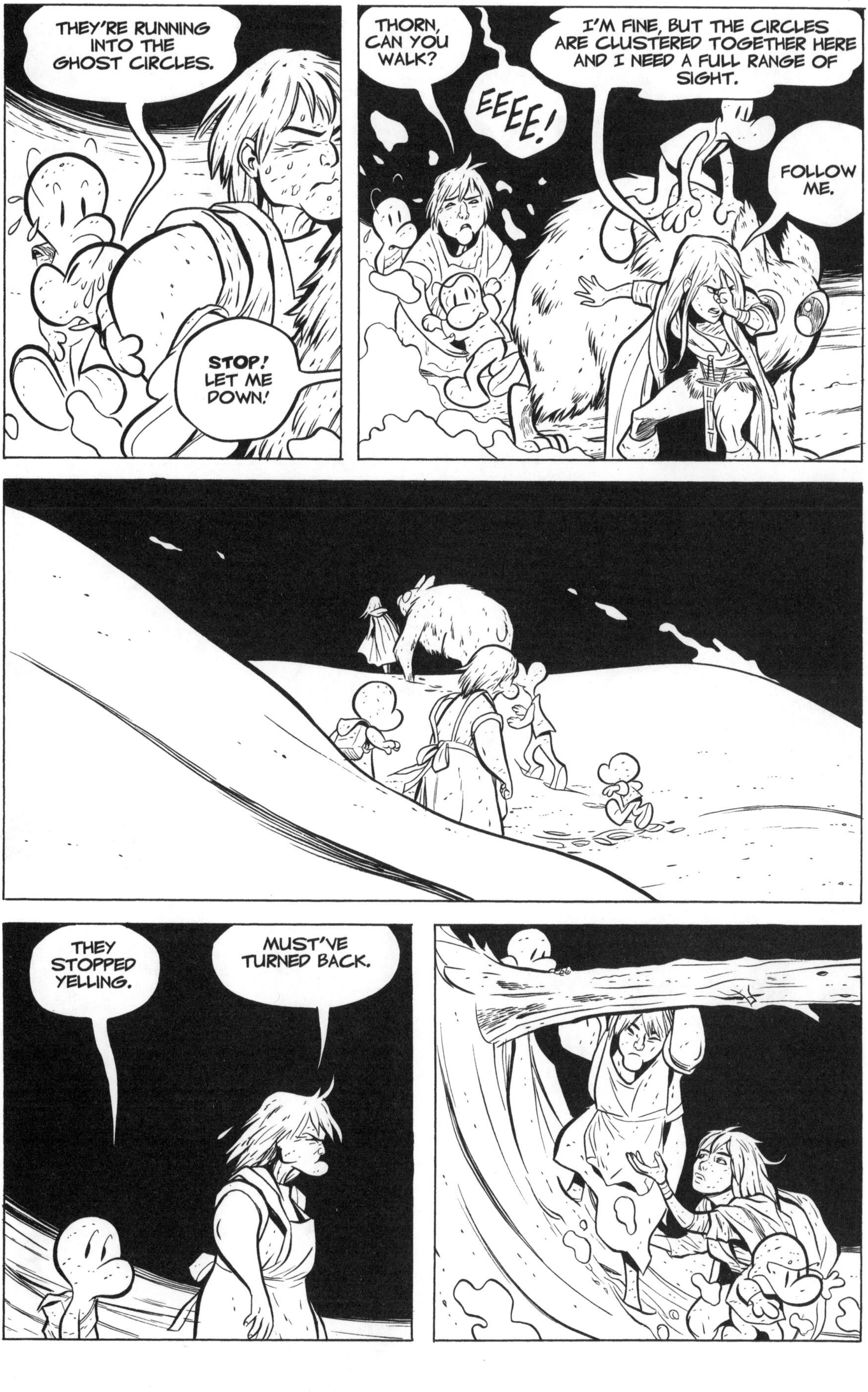
THEY'RE RUNNING INTO THE GHOST CIRCLES.
STOP! LET ME DOWN!
THORN, CAN YOU WALK?
EEEE!
I'M FINE, BUT THE CIRCLES ARE CLUSTERED TOGETHER HERE AND I NEED A FULL RANGE OF SIGHT.
FOLLOW ME.
THEY STOPPED YELLING.
MUST'VE TURNED BACK.

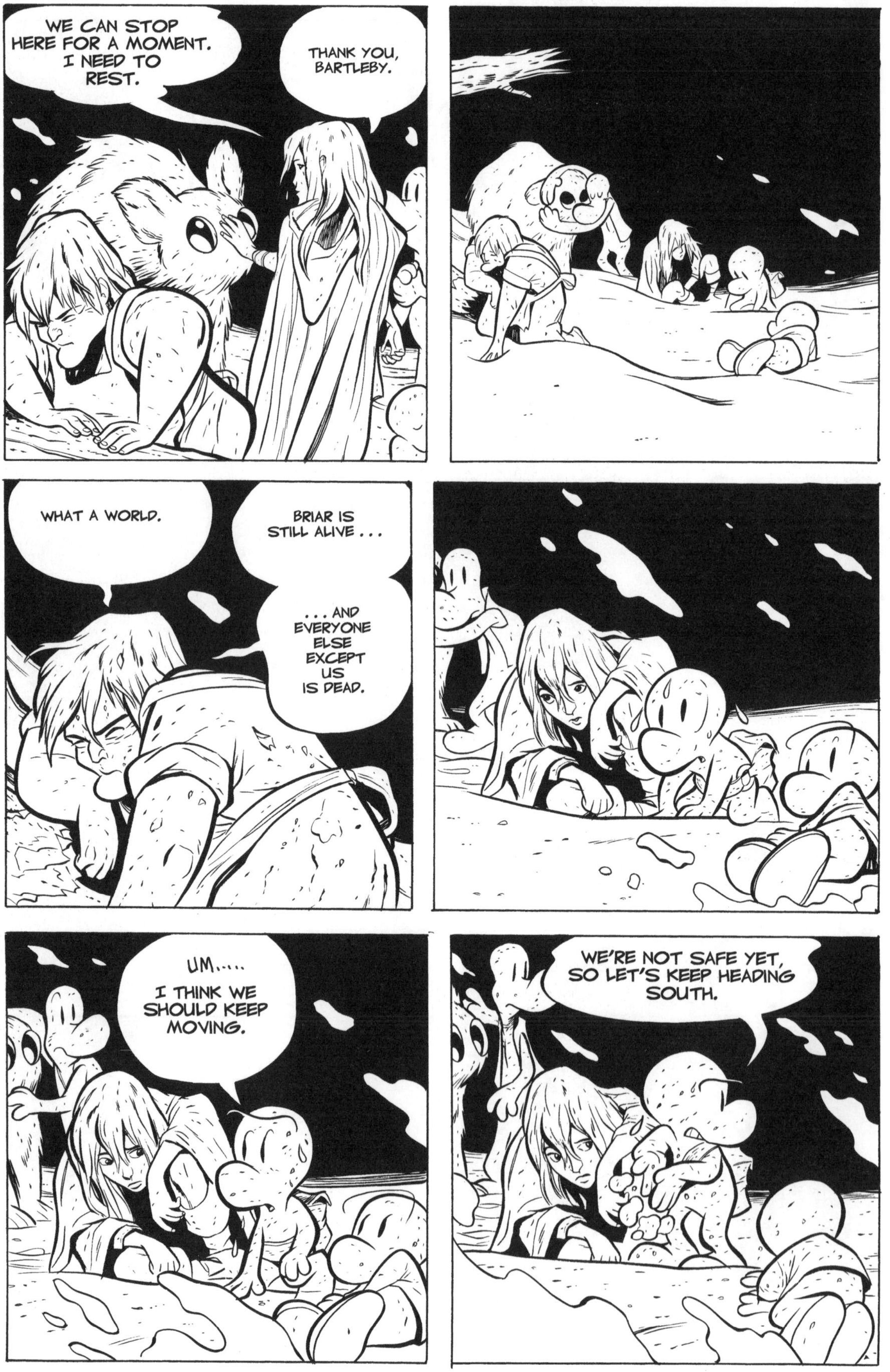
WE CAN STOP HERE FOR A MOMENT. I NEED TO REST.
THANK YOU, BARTLEBY.
WHAT A WORLD.
BRIAR IS STILL ALIVE . . .
. . . AND EVERYONE ELSE EXCEPT US IS DEAD.
UM.....
I THINK WE SHOULD KEEP MOVING.
WE'RE NOT SAFE YET, SO LET'S KEEP HEADING SOUTH.

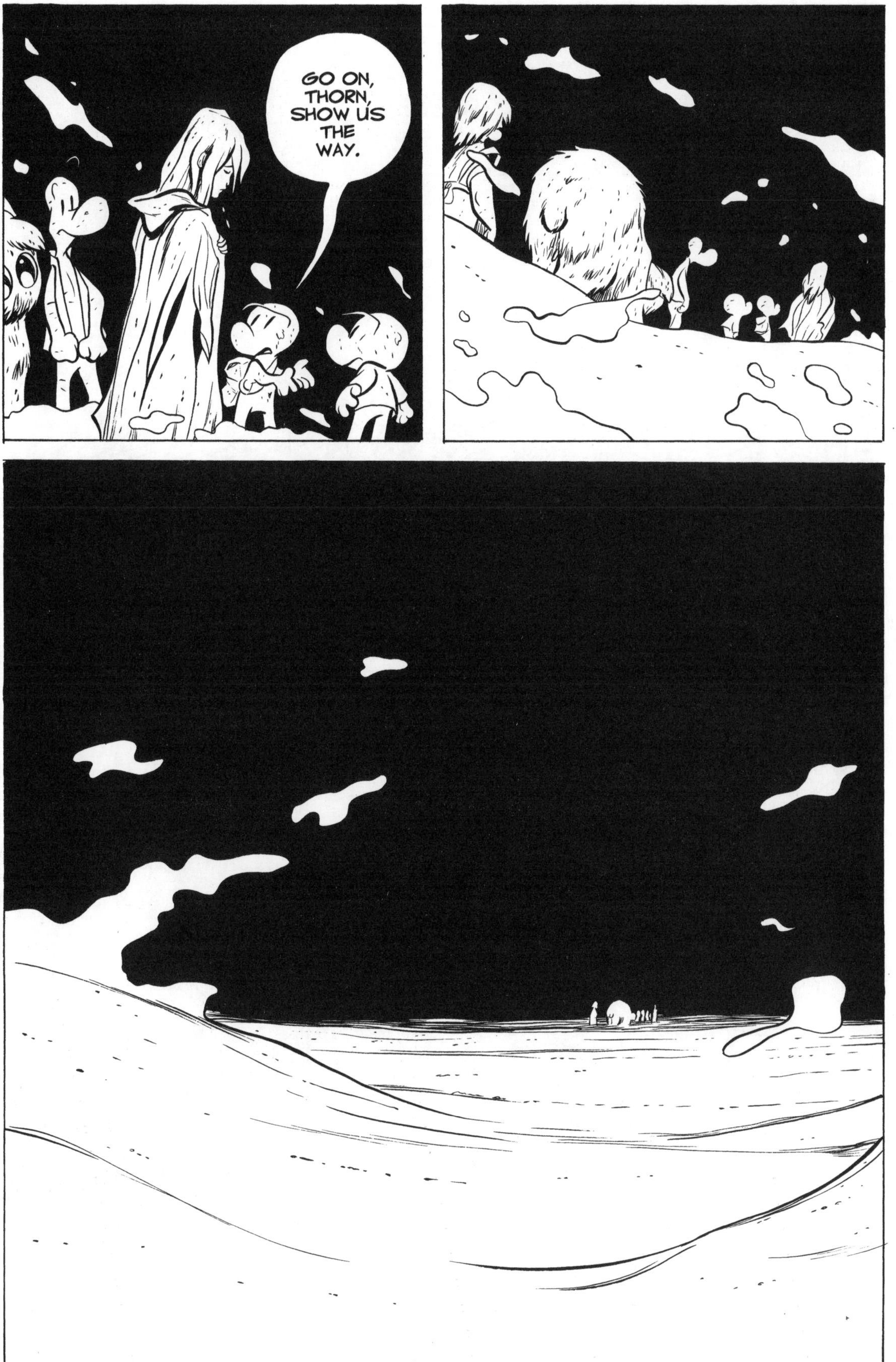
GO ON, THORN, SHOW US THE WAY.

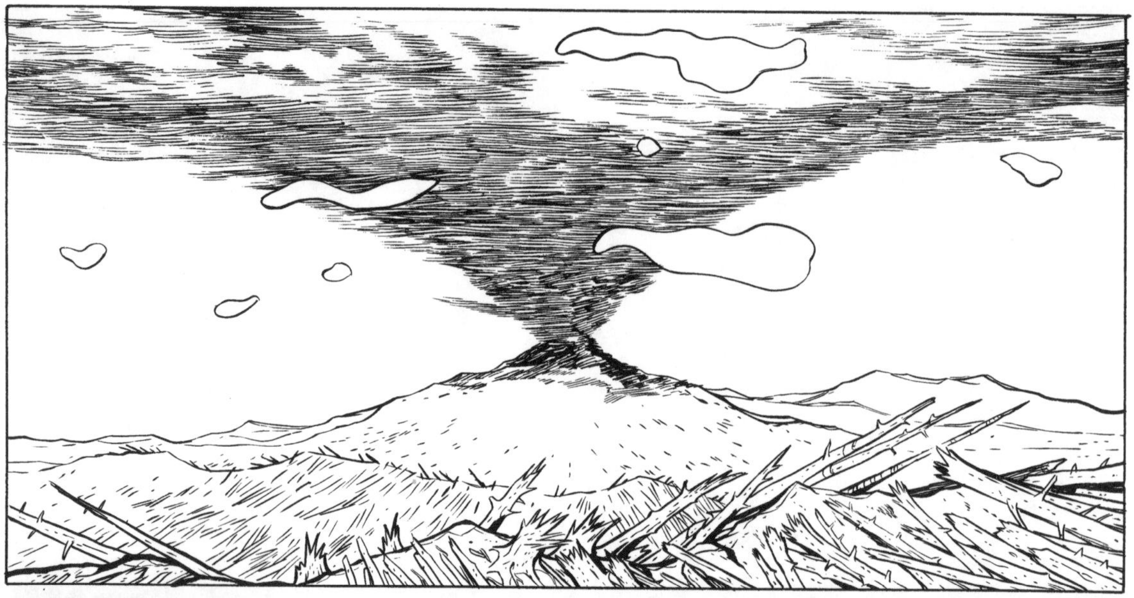

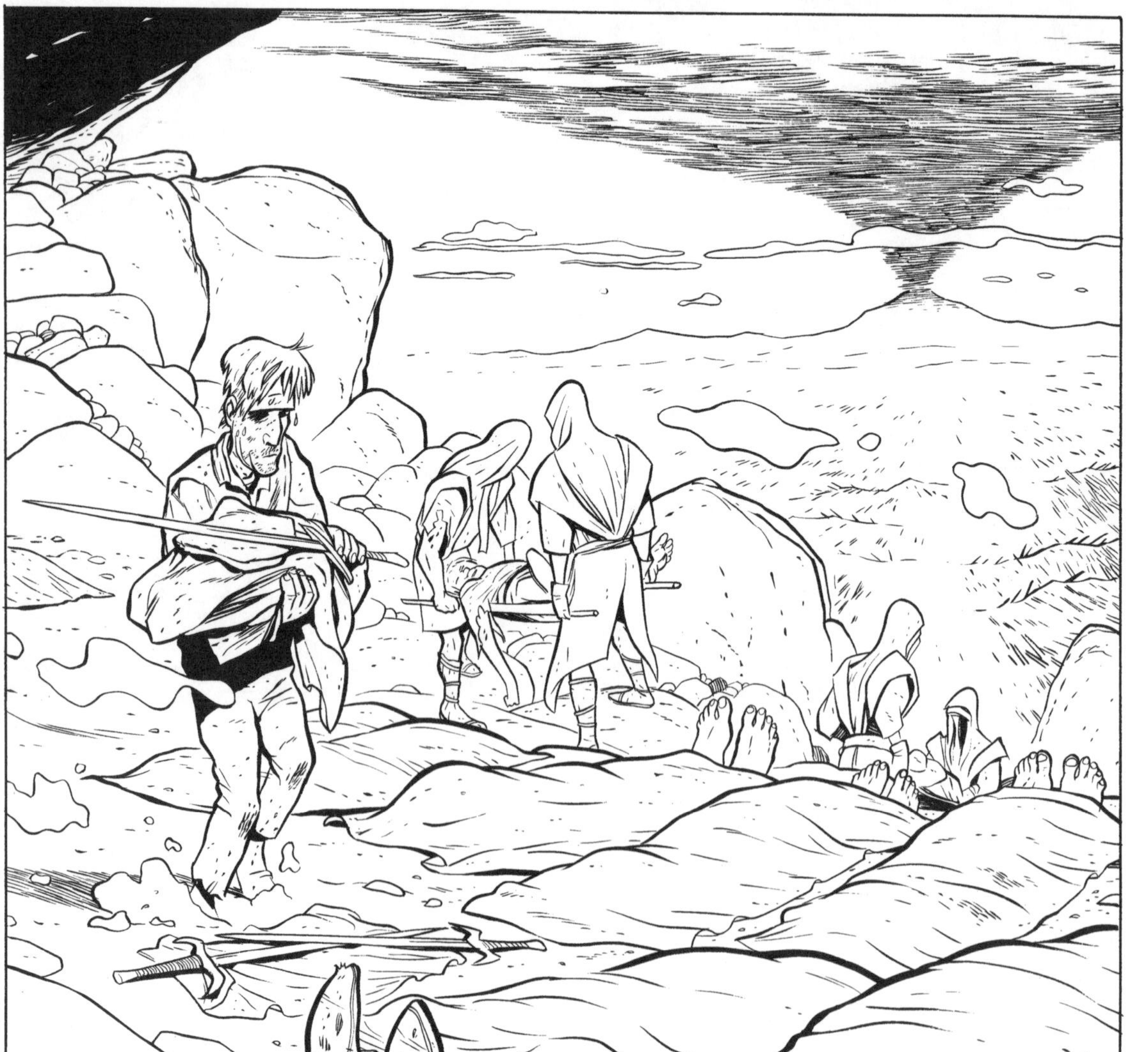

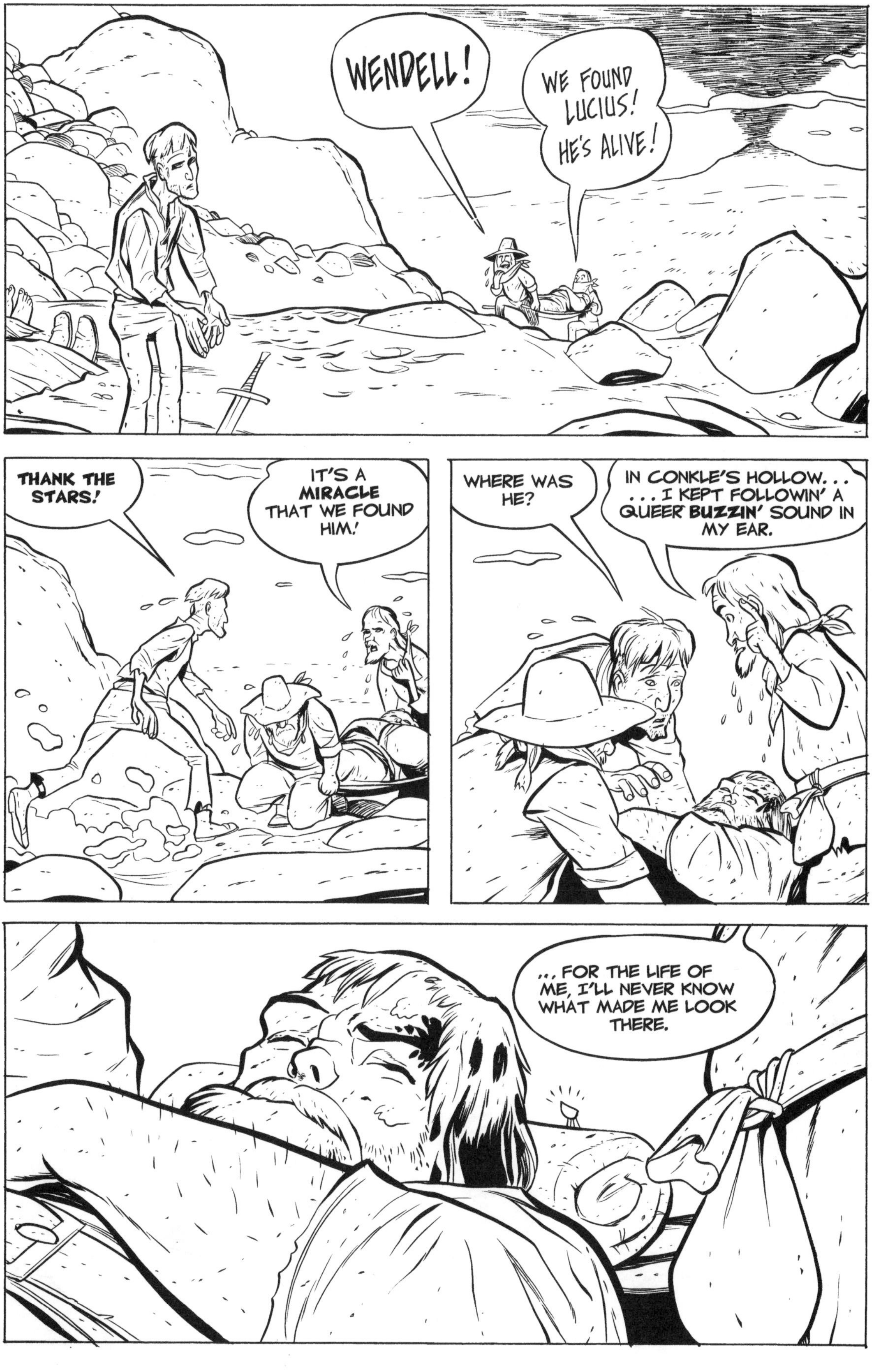
WENDELL!
WE FOUND LUCIUS! HE'S ALIVE!
THANK THE STARS!
IT'S A MIRACLE THAT WE FOUND HIM!
WHERE WAS HE?
IN CONKLE'S HOLLOW...
...I KEPT FOLLOWIN' A QUEER BUZZIN' SOUND IN MY EAR.
...FOR THE LIFE OF ME, I'LL NEVER KNOW WHAT MADE ME LOOK THERE.

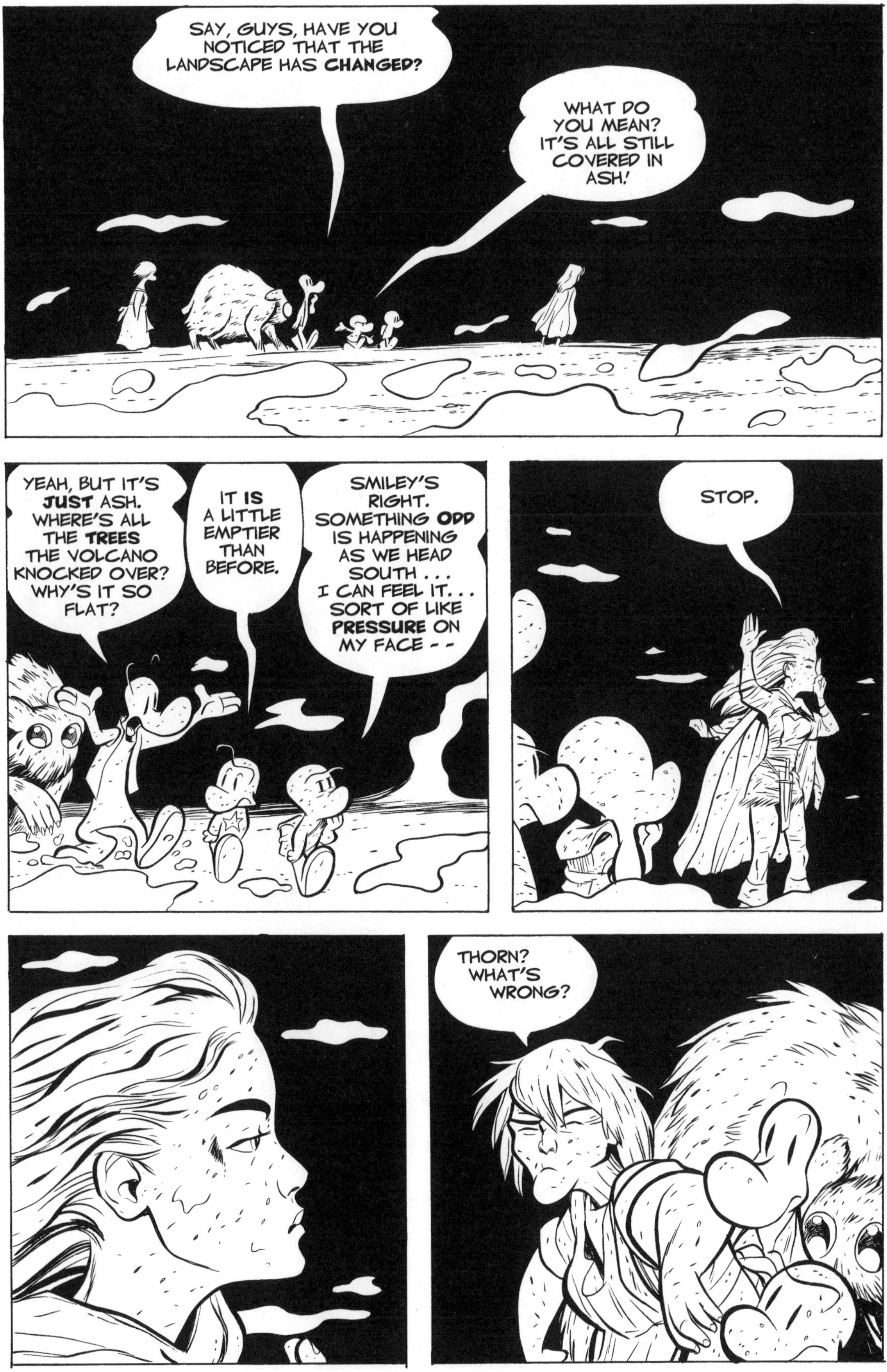
SAY, GUYS, HAVE YOU NOTICED THAT THE LANDSCAPE HAS **CHANGED?**
WHAT DO YOU MEAN? IT'S ALL STILL COVERED IN ASH!
YEAH, BUT IT'S **JUST** ASH. WHERE'S ALL THE **TREES** THE VOLCANO KNOCKED OVER? WHY'S IT SO FLAT?
IT **IS** A LITTLE EMPTIER THAN BEFORE.
SMILEY'S RIGHT. SOMETHING **ODD** IS HAPPENING AS WE HEAD SOUTH . . . I CAN FEEL IT. . . SORT OF LIKE **PRESSURE** ON MY FACE - -
STOP.
THORN? WHAT'S WRONG?

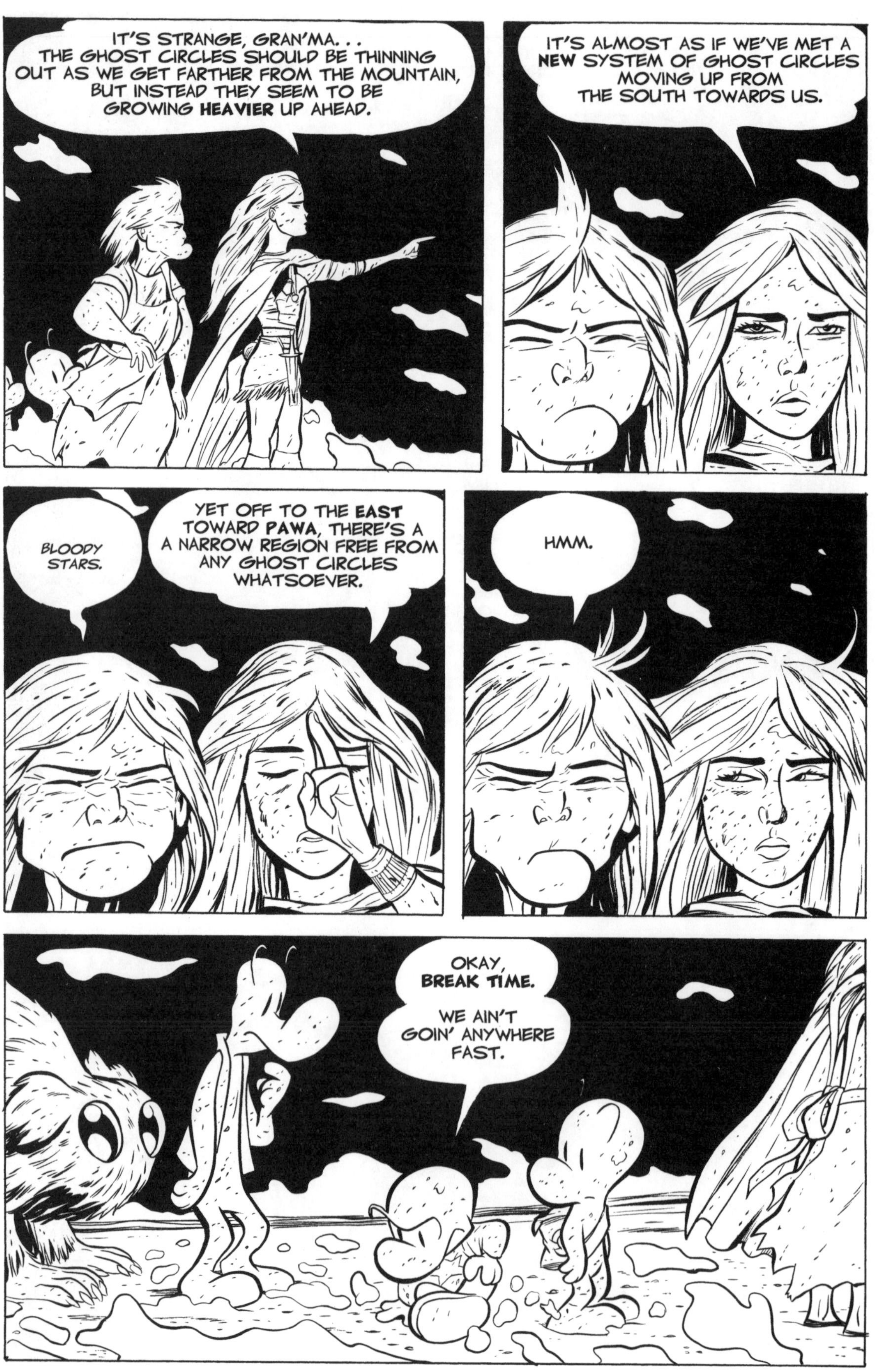
IT'S STRANGE, GRAN'MA. . . THE GHOST CIRCLES SHOULD BE THINNING OUT AS WE GET FARTHER FROM THE MOUNTAIN, BUT INSTEAD THEY SEEM TO BE GROWING **HEAVIER** UP AHEAD.
IT'S ALMOST AS IF WE'VE MET A **NEW** SYSTEM OF GHOST CIRCLES MOVING UP FROM THE SOUTH TOWARDS US.
BLOODY STARS.
YET OFF TO THE **EAST** TOWARD **PAWA**, THERE'S A A NARROW REGION FREE FROM ANY GHOST CIRCLES WHATSOEVER.
HMM.
OKAY, **BREAK TIME.**
WE AIN'T GOIN' ANYWHERE FAST.

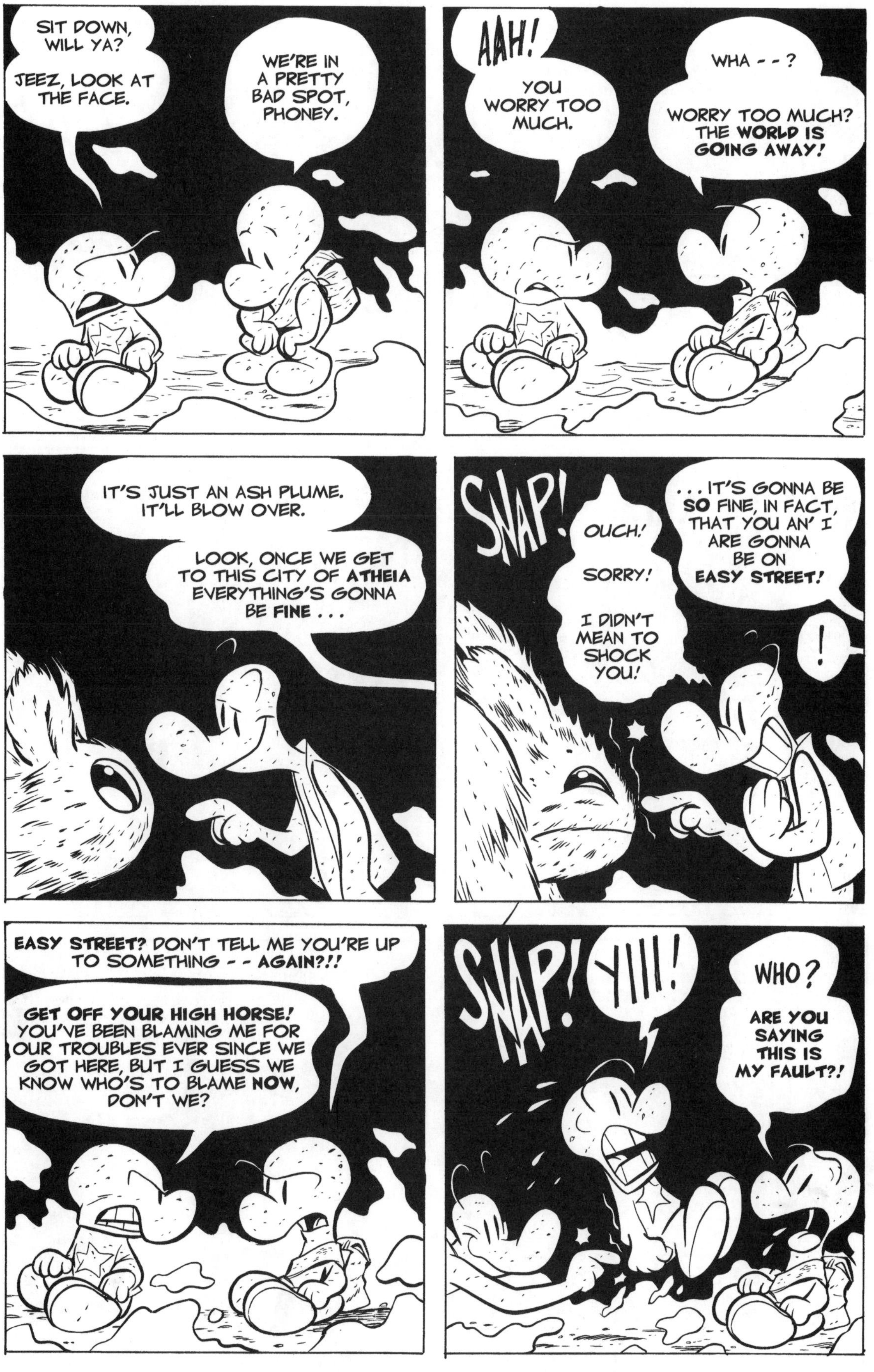

SIT DOWN, WILL YA?
JEEZ, LOOK AT THE FACE.
WE'RE IN A PRETTY BAD SPOT, PHONEY.
AAH!
YOU WORRY TOO MUCH.
WHA - - ?
WORRY TOO MUCH? THE WORLD IS GOING AWAY!
IT'S JUST AN ASH PLUME. IT'LL BLOW OVER.
LOOK, ONCE WE GET TO THIS CITY OF ATHEIA EVERYTHING'S GONNA BE FINE . . .
SNAP!
OUCH!
SORRY!
I DIDN'T MEAN TO SHOCK YOU!
. . . IT'S GONNA BE SO FINE, IN FACT, THAT YOU AN' I ARE GONNA BE ON EASY STREET!
!
EASY STREET? DON'T TELL ME YOU'RE UP TO SOMETHING - - AGAIN?!!
GET OFF YOUR HIGH HORSE! YOU'VE BEEN BLAMING ME FOR OUR TROUBLES EVER SINCE WE GOT HERE, BUT I GUESS WE KNOW WHO'S TO BLAME NOW, DON'T WE?
SNAP!
YIIII!
WHO?
ARE YOU SAYING THIS IS MY FAULT?!

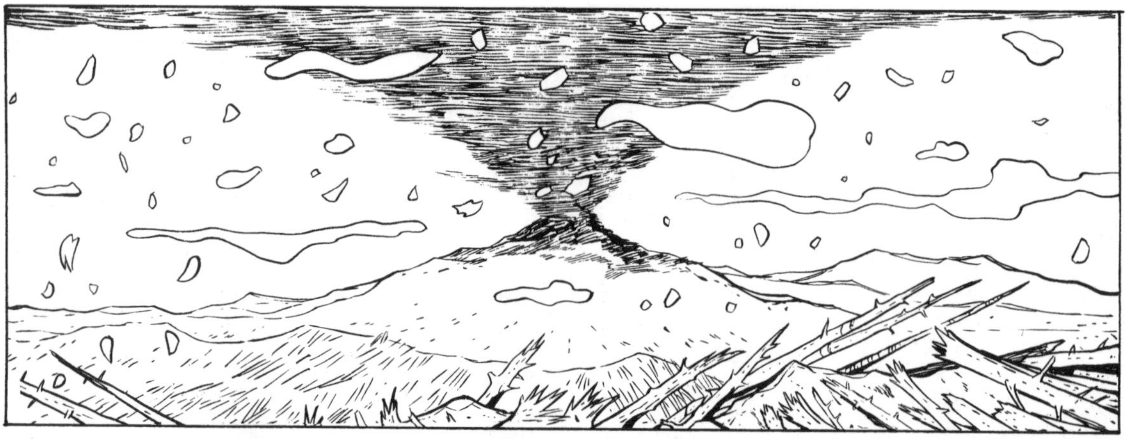

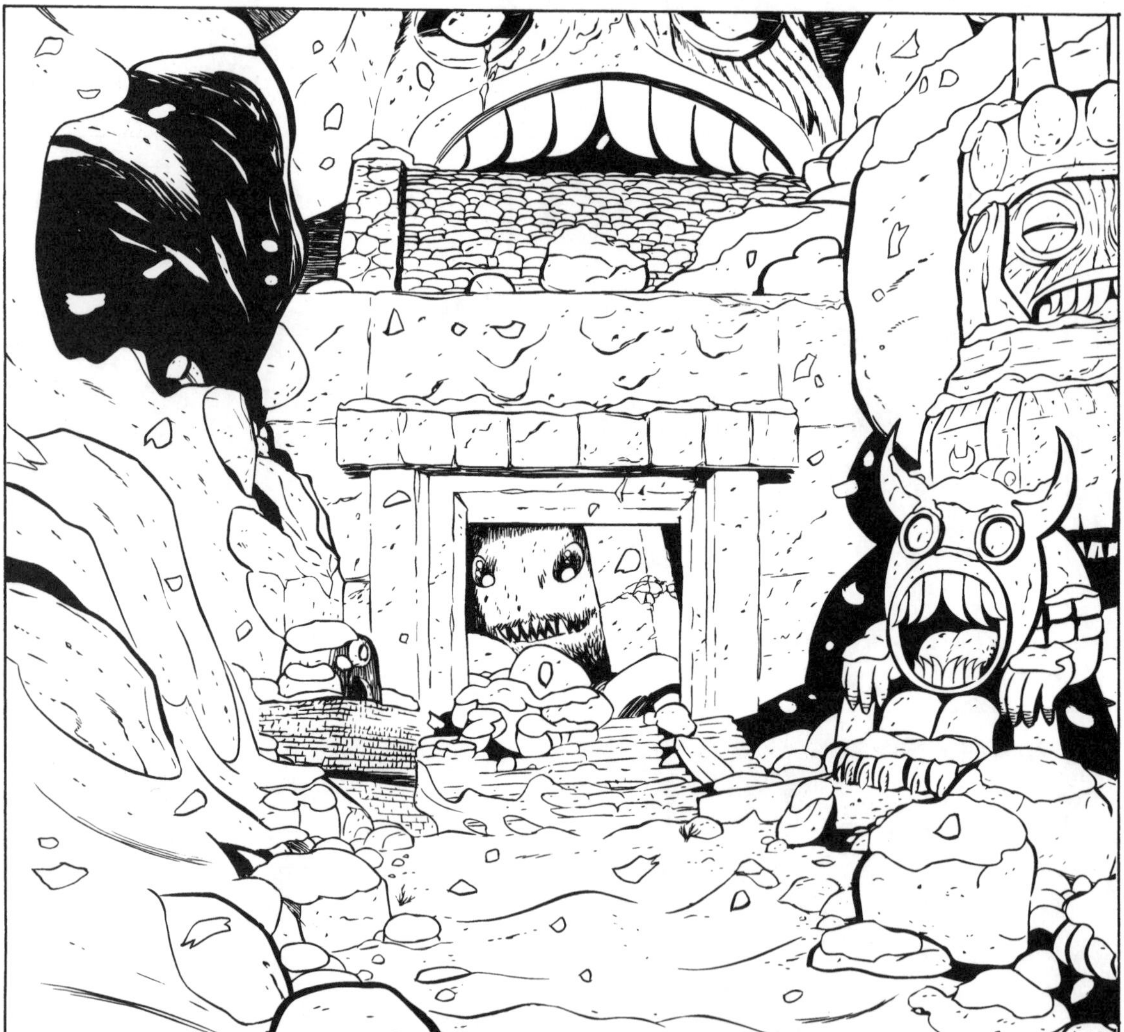

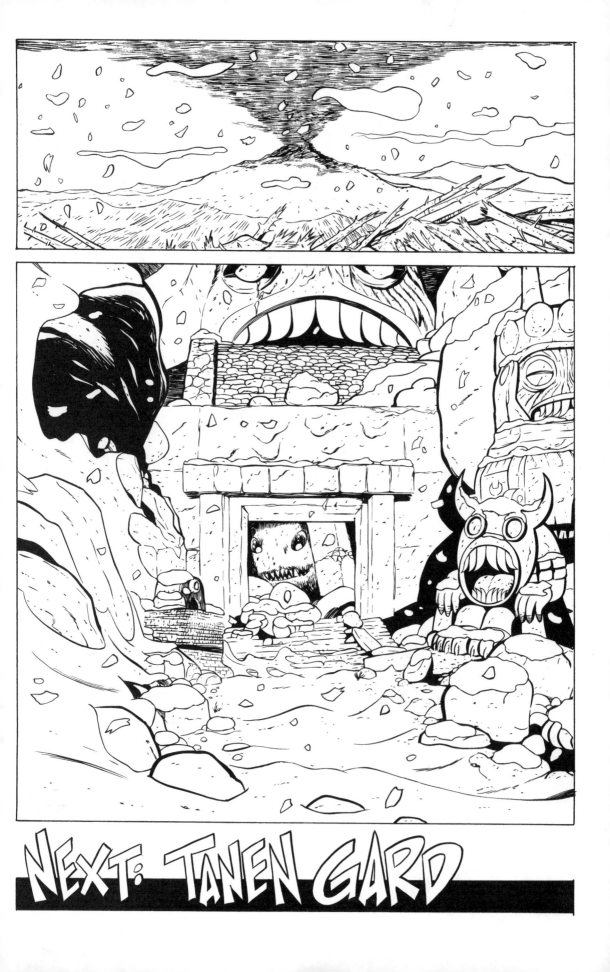

NEXT: TANEN GARD

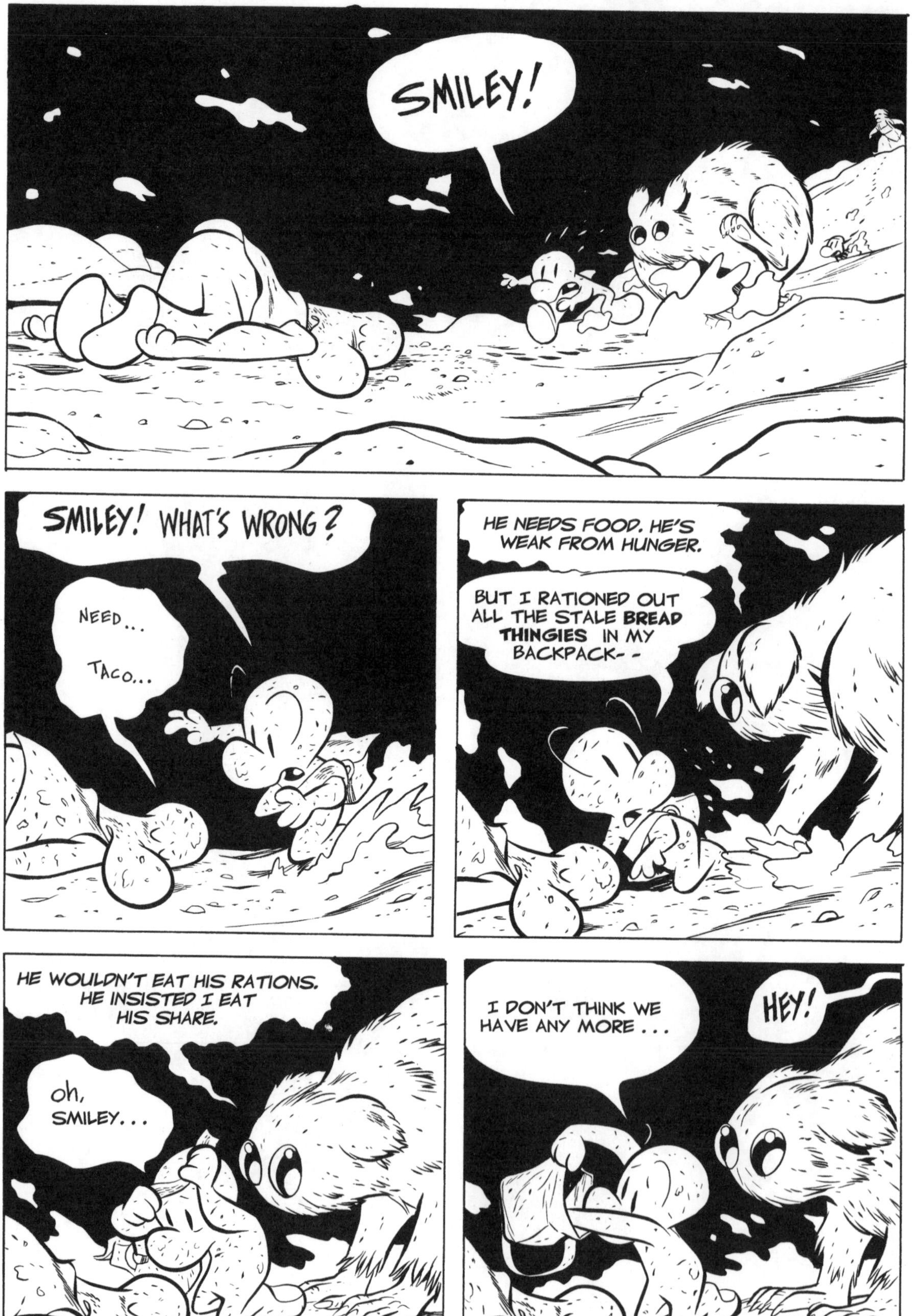
SMILEY!
SMILEY! WHAT'S WRONG?
NEED... TACO...
HE NEEDS FOOD. HE'S WEAK FROM HUNGER.
BUT I RATIONED OUT ALL THE STALE BREAD THINGIES IN MY BACKPACK--
HE WOULDN'T EAT HIS RATIONS. HE INSISTED I EAT HIS SHARE.
oh, SMILEY...
I DON'T THINK WE HAVE ANY MORE...
HEY!

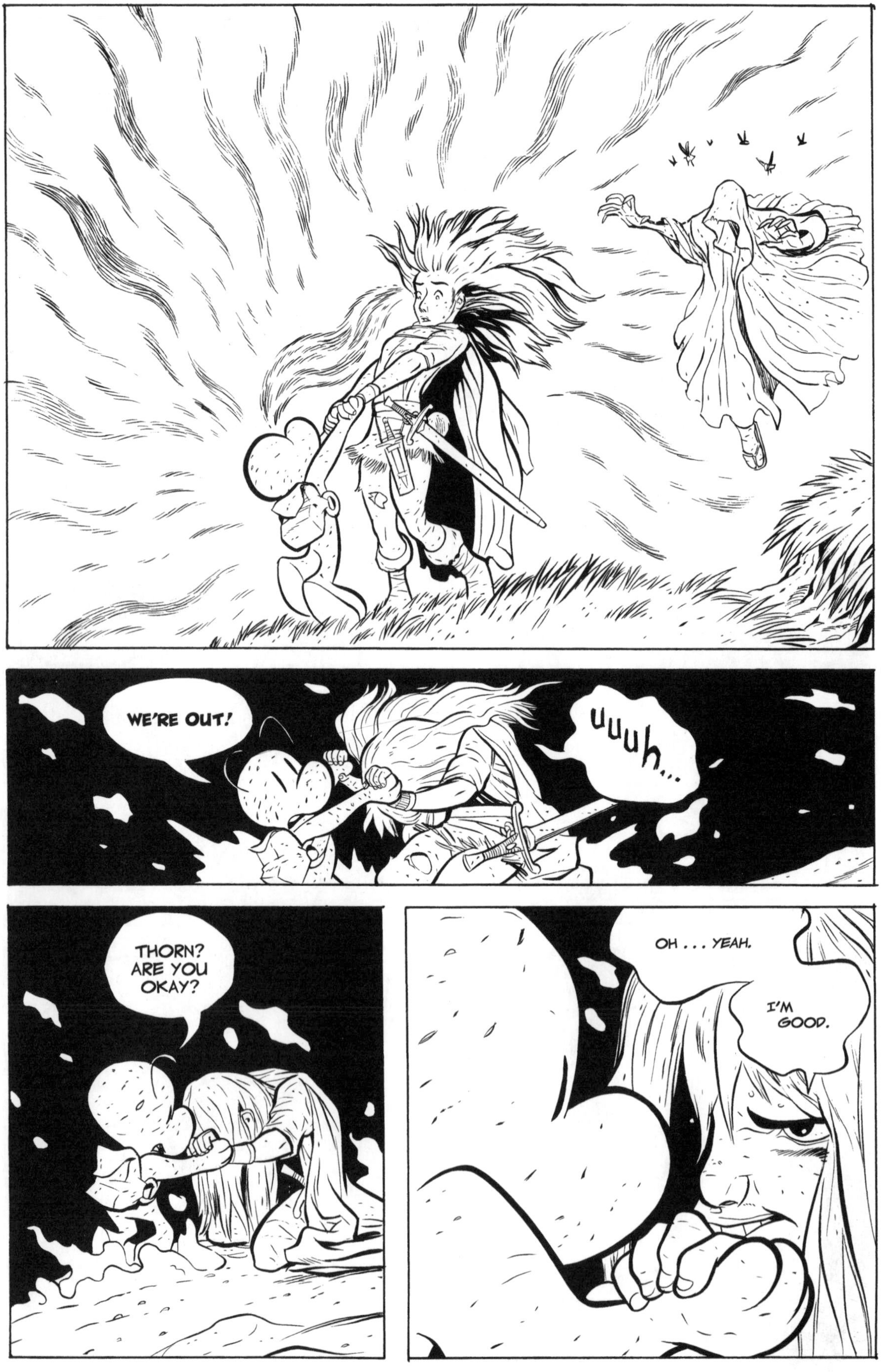
WE'RE OUT!
uuuh...
THORN? ARE YOU OKAY?
OH . . . YEAH.
I'M GOOD.

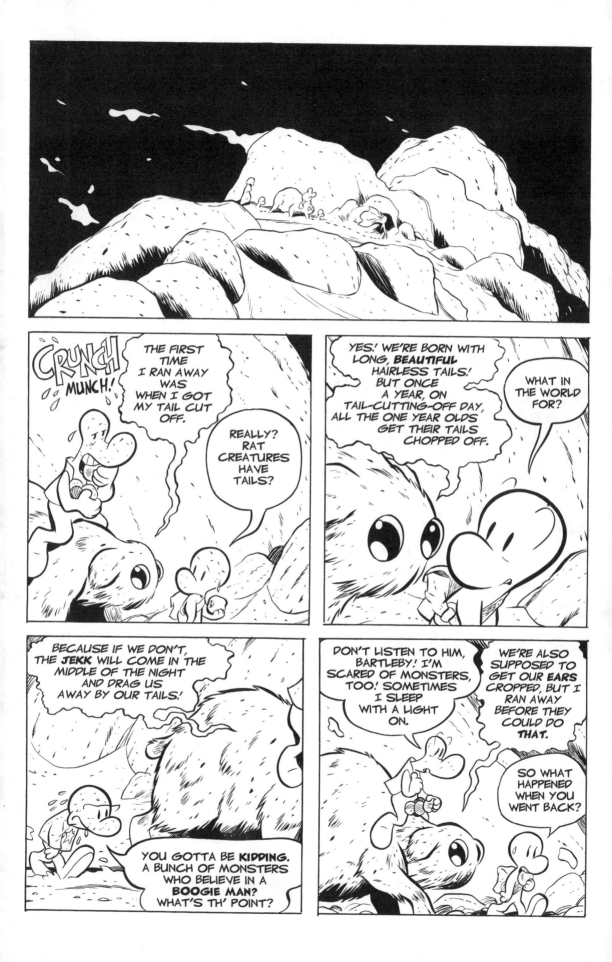

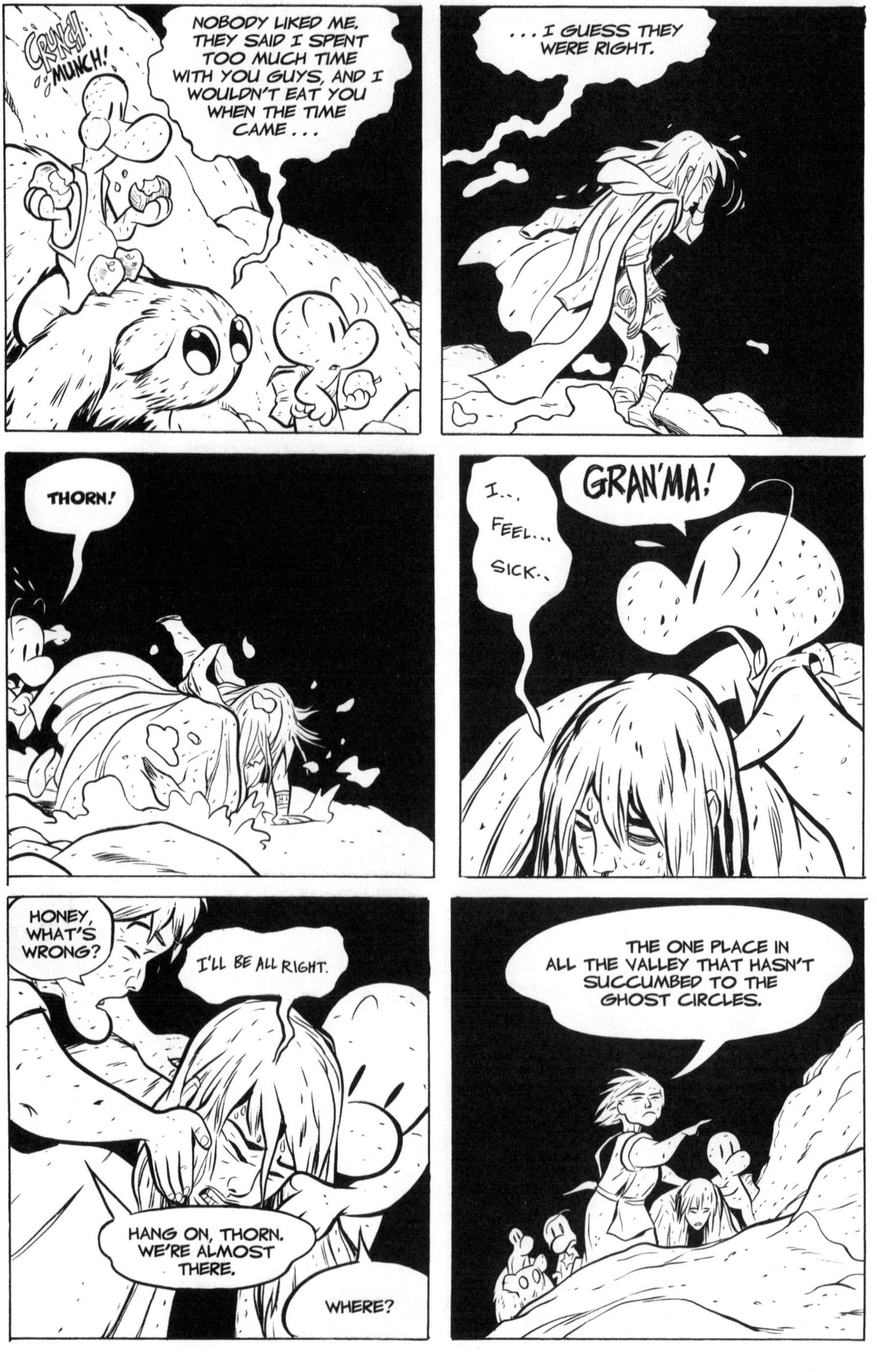
CRUNCH MUNCH!
NOBODY LIKED ME. THEY SAID I SPENT TOO MUCH TIME WITH YOU GUYS, AND I WOULDN'T EAT YOU WHEN THE TIME CAME . . .
. . . I GUESS THEY WERE RIGHT.
THORN!
I..
FEEL...
SICK..
GRAN'MA!
HONEY, WHAT'S WRONG?
I'LL BE ALL RIGHT.
HANG ON, THORN. WE'RE ALMOST THERE.
WHERE?
THE ONE PLACE IN ALL THE VALLEY THAT HASN'T SUCCUMBED TO THE GHOST CIRCLES.

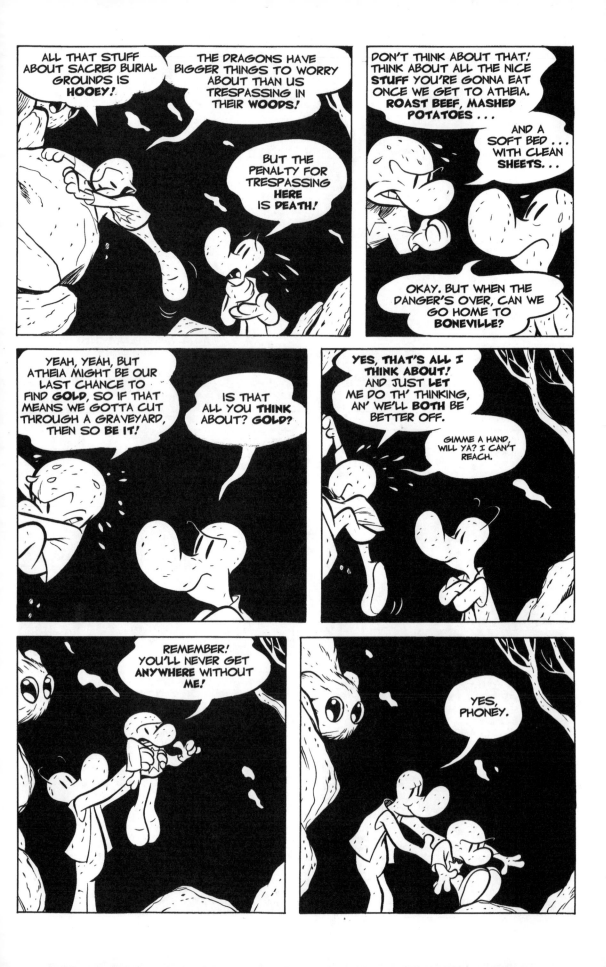

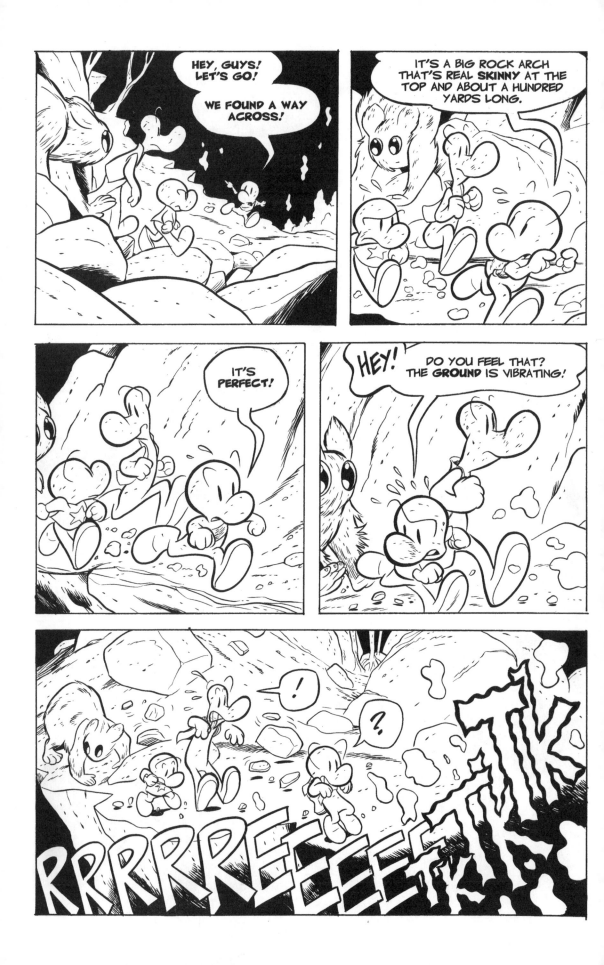

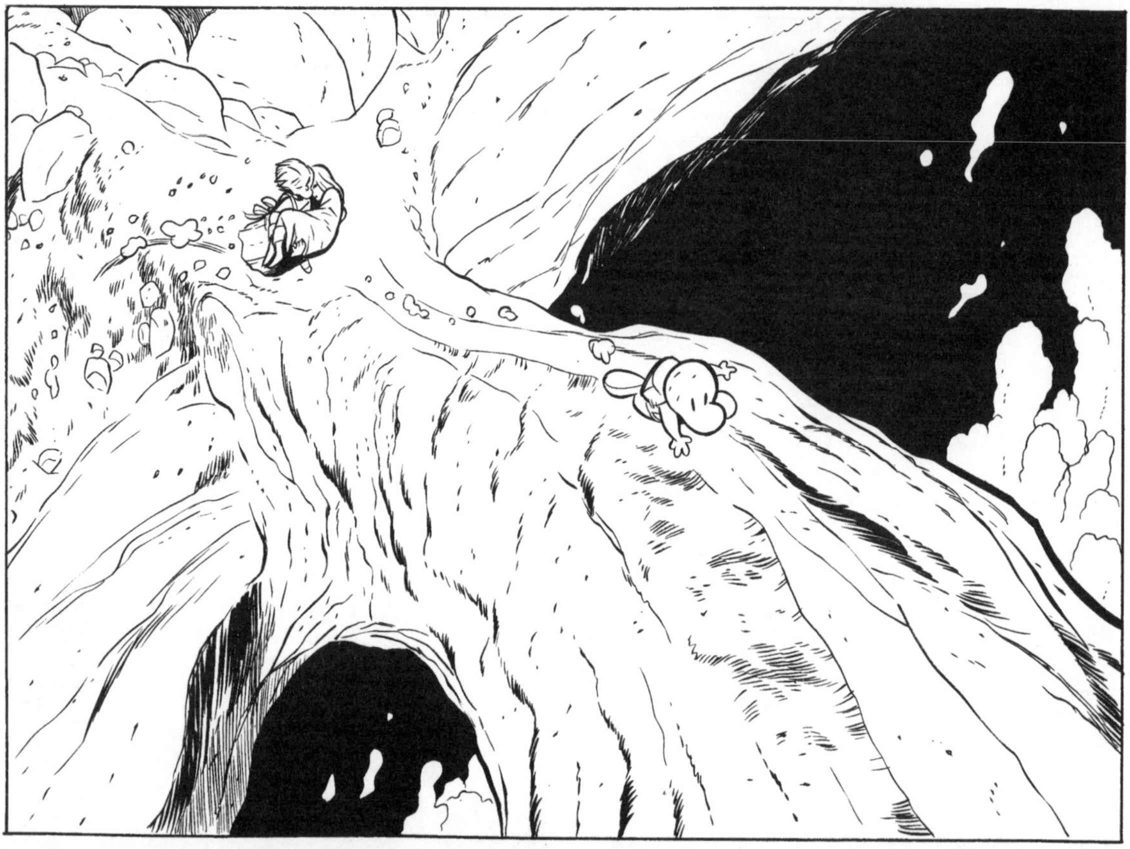

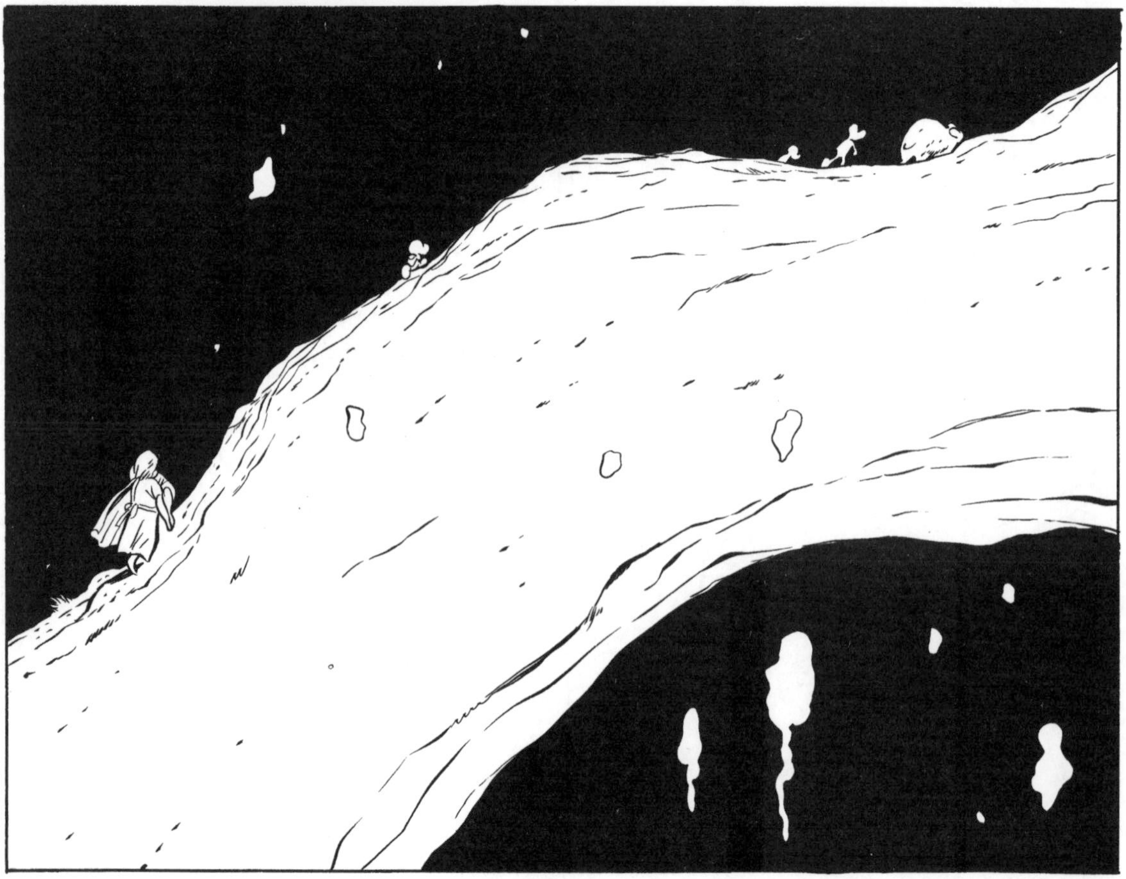

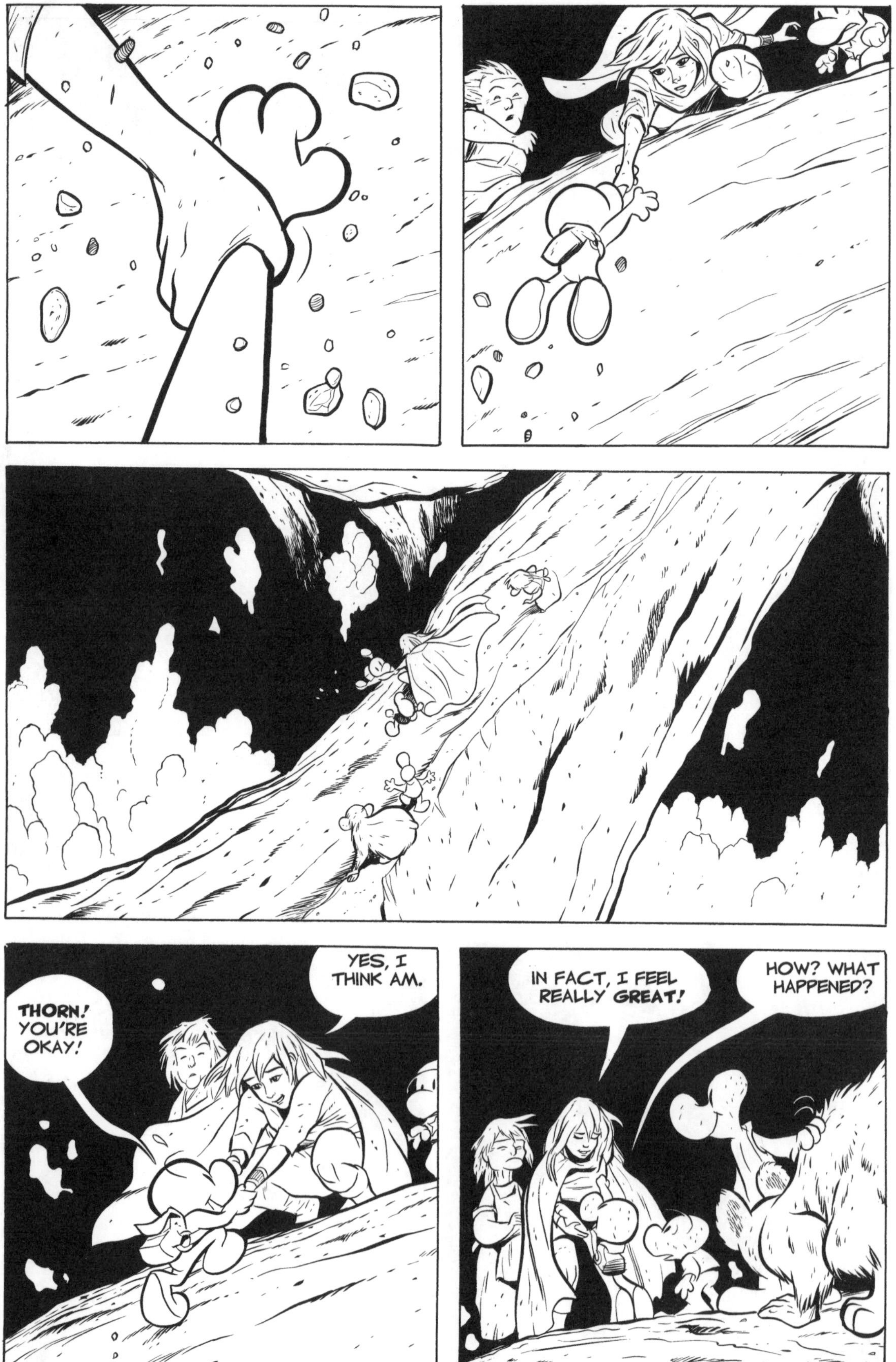
THORN! YOU'RE OKAY!
YES, I THINK AM.
IN FACT, I FEEL REALLY GREAT!
HOW? WHAT HAPPENED?

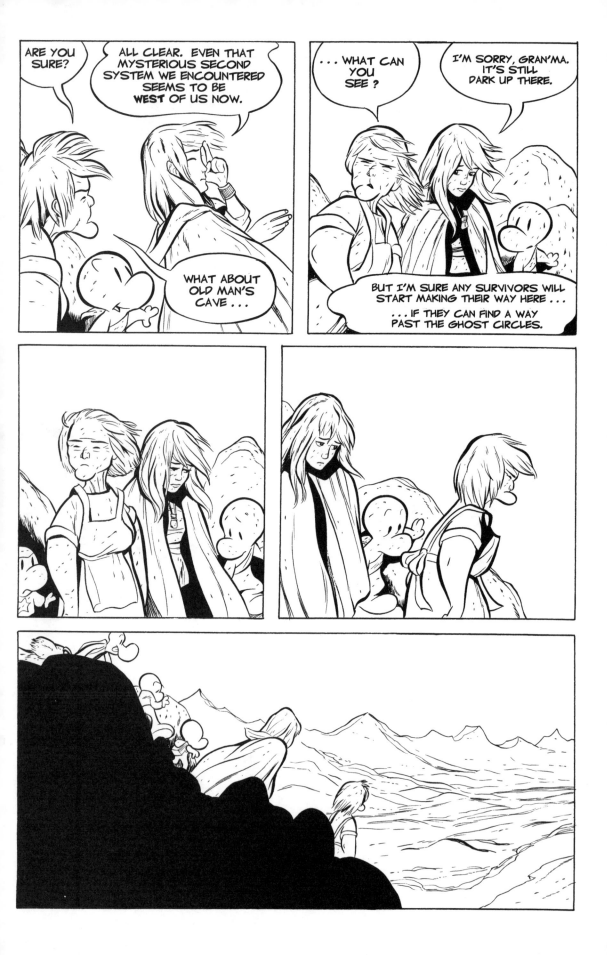

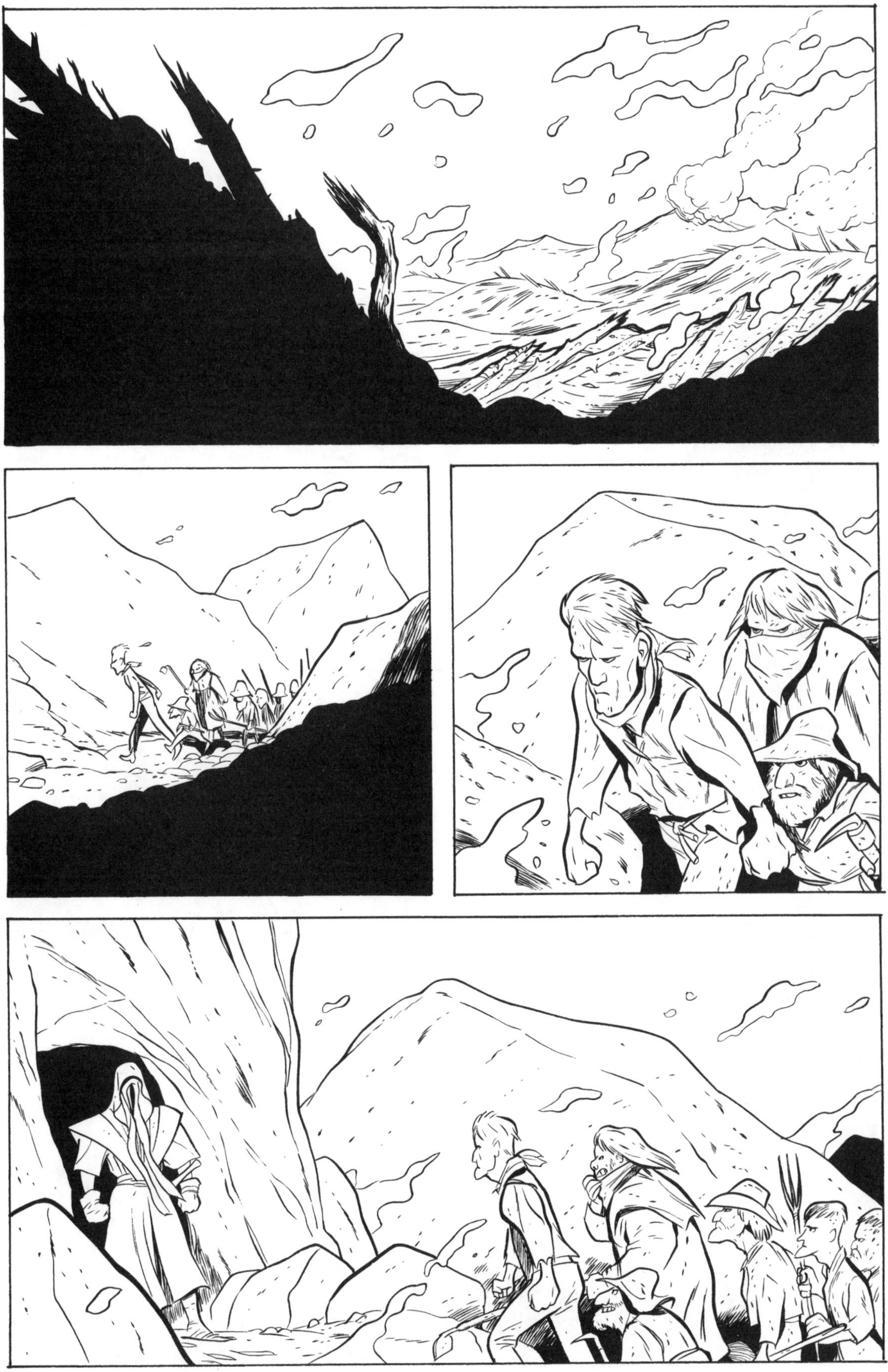

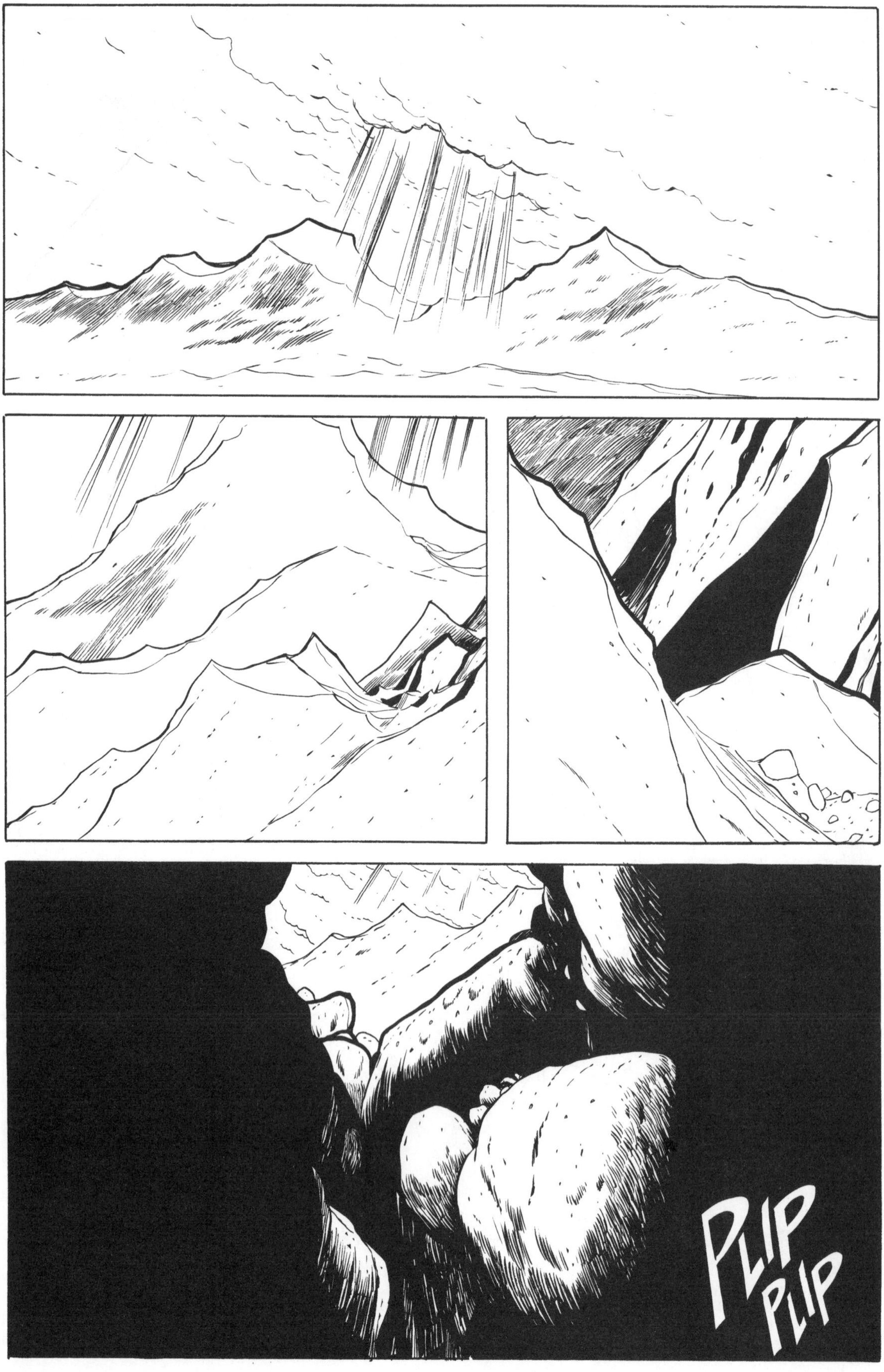
PLIP
PLIP

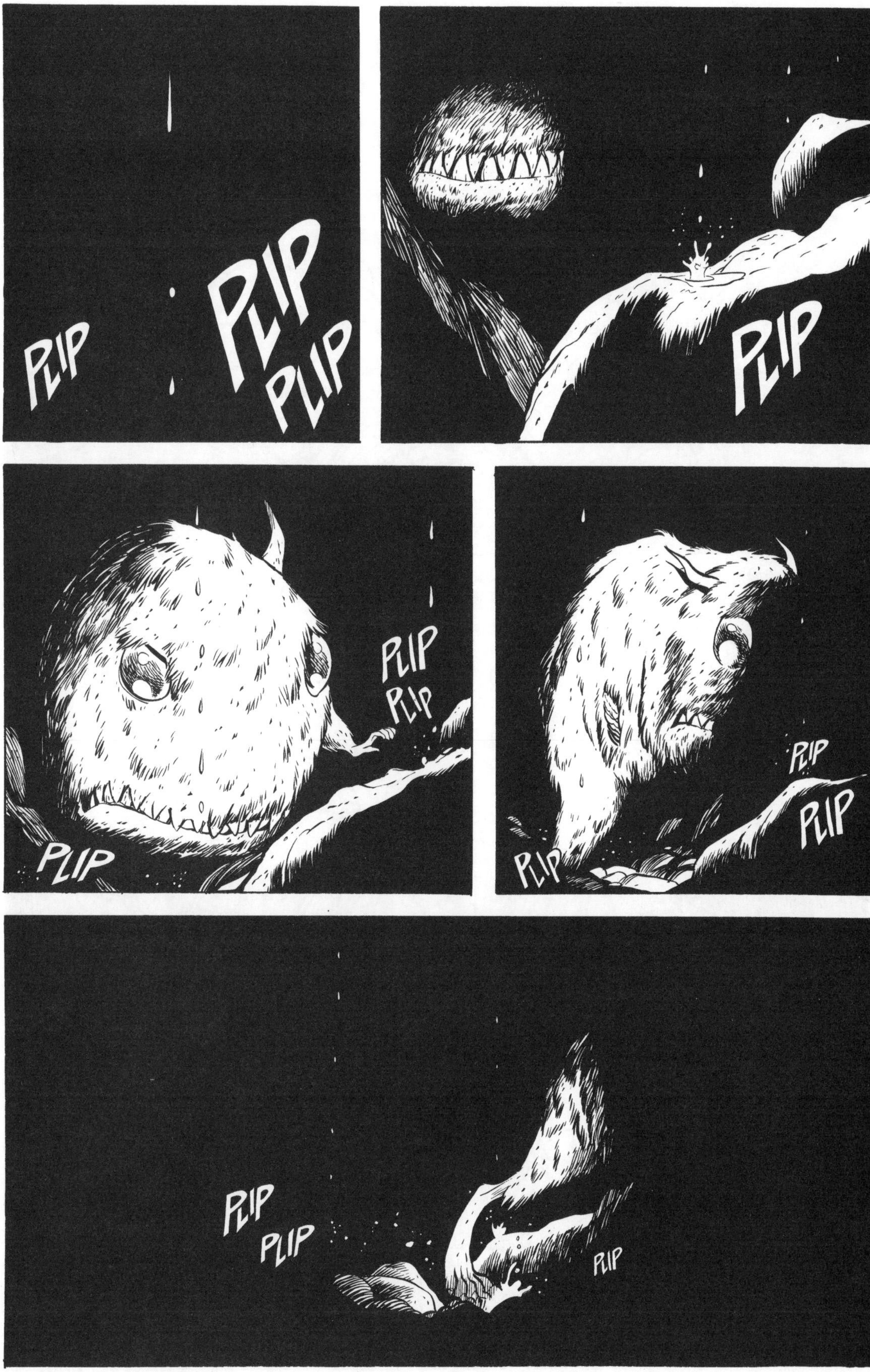
PLIP
PLIP
PLIP
PLIP
PLIP
PLIP
PLIP
PLIP
PLIP
PLIP
PLIP
PLIP
PLIP

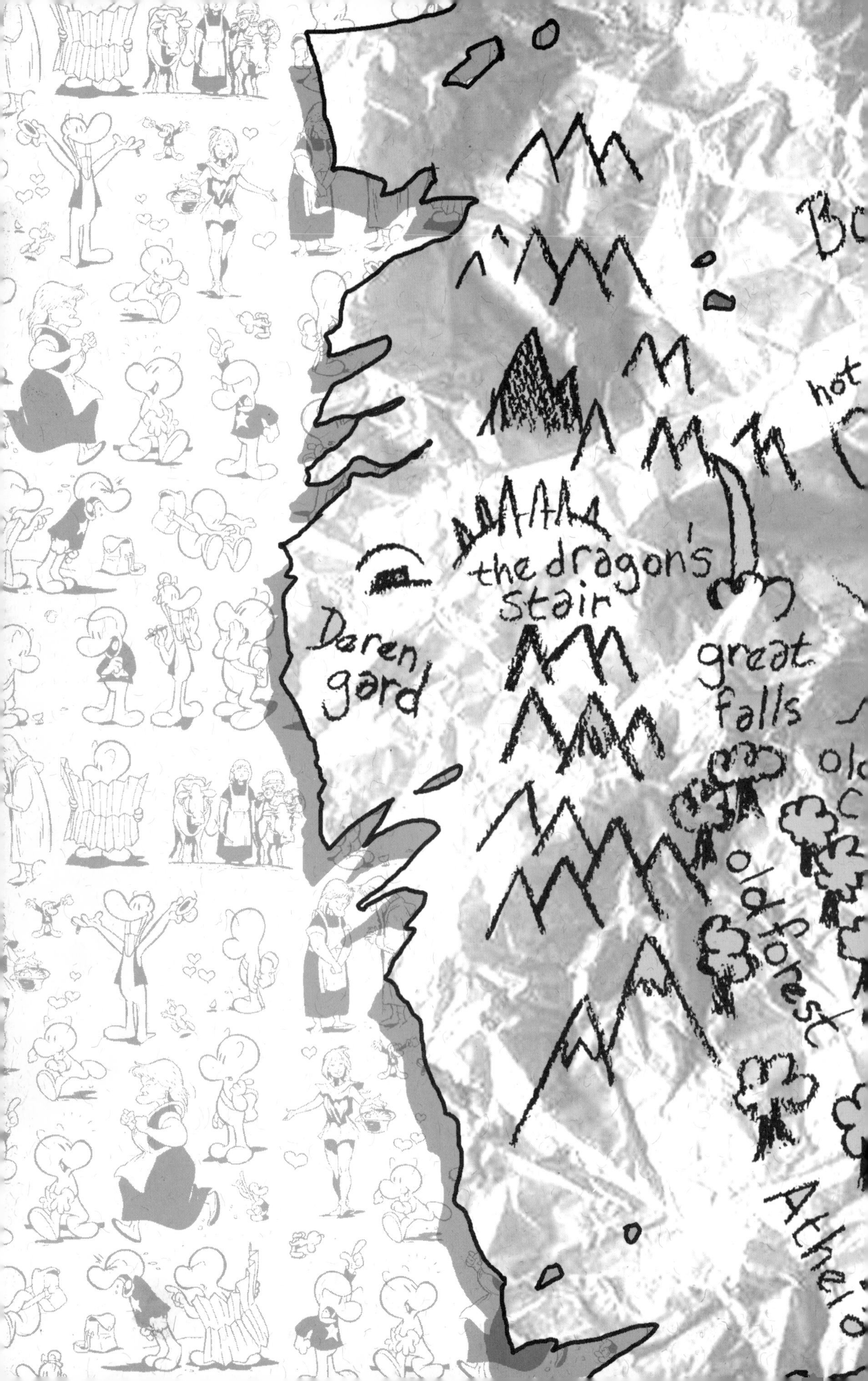
hot
the dragon's stair
Daren gard
great falls
old forest